The
ULTIMATE
CONSULTANT

The
ULTIMATE
CONSULTANT

Powerful Techniques
for the
Successful Practitioner

ALAN WEISS, Ph.D.

JOSSEY-BASS/PFEIFFER
A Wiley Company
San Francisco

The ULTIMATE
CONSULTANT
Series

Copyright © 2001 by Alan Weiss

ISBN: 0-7879-5508-6

Library of Congress Cataloging-in-Publication Data
Weiss, Alan, 1941–
    The ultimate consultant : powerful techniques for the
successful practitioner / by Alan Weiss.
        p.   cm. — (The ultimate consultant series)
Includes bibliographical references and index.
    ISBN 0-7879-55508-6 (alk. paper)
    1. Business consultants—Handbooks, manuals, etc. 2.
Consultants—Marketing—Handbooks, manuals, etc. I. Title. II.
Series.
    HD69.C6 W465 2001
001'.068—dc21
2001000189

Printed in the United States of America

Published by
JOSSEY-BASS/PFEIFFER   350 Sansome Street, 5th Floor
A Wiley Company   San Francisco, California 94104-1342
San Francisco   (415) 433-1740; Fax (415) 433-0499
                                                    (800) 274-4434; Fax (800) 569-0443

www.pfeiffer.com

Jossey-Bass/Pfeiffer is a registered trademark of Jossey-Bass Inc., A Wiley Company.

Acquiring Editor: Matthew Holt
Director of Development: Kathleen Dolan Davies
Editor: Rebecca Taff
Senior Production Editor: Dawn Kilgore
Manufacturing Supervisor: Becky Carreño
Interior Design: Gene Crofts
Illustrations: Lotus Art

Printing 10   9   8   7   6   5   4   3   2   1

 This book is printed on acid-free, recycled stock that meets or exceeds the minimum GPO and EPA requirements for recycled paper.

This is dedicated to
Danielle, the Emmy-nominated producer,
and
Jason, the stage, screen, and television actor.

Also by ALAN WEISS

Books
Getting Started in Consulting (2000)
The Unofficial Guide to Power Management (2000)
How to Market, Establish a Brand, and Sell Professional Services (2000)
Good Enough Isn't Enough (1999)
How to Write A Proposal That's Accepted Every Time (1999)
Money Talks (1998)
Million Dollar Consulting (1992; rev. ed. 1998)
Our Emperors Have No Clothes (1995)
Best Laid Plans (1991)
Managing for Peak Performance (1990)
The Innovation Formula (with Mike Robert, 1988)

Booklets
How to Maximize Fees
Raising the Bar
Leadership Every Day
Doing Well by Doing Right
Rejoicing in Diversity

Audiocassettes
Peak Performance
The Consultant's Treasury
The Odd Couple®

Videos
Stories I Could Never Tell: Alan Weiss Live and Uncensored
Alan Weiss on Marketing
Alan Weiss on Product Development

Newsletters
Balancing Act: Blending Life, Work, and Relationships (electronic)
The Consultant's Craft
What's Working in Consulting (editor)

About the Author

Alan Weiss began his own consulting firm, Summit Consulting Group, Inc., out of his home in 1985 after being fired by a boss with whom he shared a mutual antipathy. Today, he still works out of his home, having traveled to fifty-one countries and forty-nine states, published thirteen books and over four hundred articles, and consulted with some of the great organizations in the world, developing a seven-figure practice in the process.

His clients have included Merck, Hewlett-Packard, State Street Corp., Fleet Bank, Coldwell Banker, Merrill Lynch, American Press Institute, Chase, Mercedes-Benz, GE, American Institute of Architects, Arthur Andersen, Federal Reserve Bank, and over two hundred similar organizations. He delivers fifty keynote speeches a year and is one of the stars of the lecture circuit. He appears frequently in the media to discuss issues pertaining to productivity and performance and has been featured in teleconferences, video conferences, and Internet conferences.

His Ph.D. is in organizational psychology, and he has served as a visiting faculty member at Case Western Reserve, St. John's, and half a dozen other major universities. He currently holds an appointment as adjunct professor at the graduate school of business at the University of Rhode Island, where he teaches a highly popular course on advanced consulting skills. His books have been translated into German, Italian, and Chinese.

Dr. Weiss resides with his wife of thirty-two years, Maria, in East Greenwich, RI.

Contents

CHAPTER 3

Marketing and Publicity   51

Creating Gravitational Pull

CHAPTER 4

Branding and Celebrity   77

A Brand in the Hand Beats Feet on the Street

CHAPTER 8

Managing Time 163

Or How to Be at the Pool by Two in the Afternoon

CHAPTER 9

Working with Family-Owned and Smaller Businesses 185

*What to Do When You're Competing
with the Mortgage Payments*

Introduction

Have you exploited your success,
or merely avoided failure?

This is not a beginner's book. I've already written them. This is a book for sophisticated, successful consultants who want to raise their performance, results, and life styles still higher.

That's not to say that people new to the profession can't read these chapters, or that novices won't learn a great deal from them. But I have assumed when putting down the ideas contained herein that a sufficient amount of learning, experiences, and consulting work—both successful and unsuccessful—have already occurred. I'm not going to be describing what a press kit is or why a proposal is important, although I will be detailing how to use a press kit to maximum effectiveness and how to create proposals that are nearly "bulletproof."

Many very good consultants fall victim to the "success trap," in that they achieve a certain level of proficiency and reward and, consciously or unconsciously, resolve to keep doing more of what got them there. This is professional suicide. We need to grow continually, to search out and acquire new clients, and to stretch our abilities and competencies so that we are of value to higher level buyers in a wider range of organizations. I'm not touting growth for growth's sake or saying that success is dependent merely on maximizing income. But I am strongly espousing the pragmatic fact that the more prospects you attract, the more you are able to determine with whom you'll work, where you'll work, when you'll work, and for what fee you'll work. Success in this business is about controlling those dynamics.

Typically, new consultants are at the mercy of the market and the work that comes along, just as a young lion has to settle for small prey and stay on the fringes of other lions' territories. But once full-grown and well-fed, the hunting can be much more selective and the territory becomes much more secure. Experienced, successful consultants should be able to at least strongly influence— and, often, tightly control—the types of clients and the nature of business they accept.

I call this "ultimate consulting," because the ultimate professional reward in this work is to be able to choose your clients, gain immediate acceptance about fees, provide for passive income, and find the work and the interactions constantly stimulating and educational. Not that you allow yourself to be complacent at that point, either, but at least you're thoroughly enjoying the climb.

You'll find within the chapters my reports "from the trenches," which are interviews I've conducted with a diverse array of consultants around the world. My single criterion is that each had to be generating a minimum of $250,000 in annual revenues for themselves or their firms. Many of the interviewees are generating well into seven figures by themselves year in and year out. Yet their backgrounds and focus are disparate and varied. They prove that there is no "royal road," but that there are common processes and principles involved in outstanding performance.

I know, because that's where I've been. Join me in the discussions that follow, and I hope to see you at the summit.

Alan Weiss, Ph.D.
East Greenwich, RI
September 2000

Acknowledgments

At the age of 54, I've led a full and rich life, perhaps the envy of most. I've learned that such great good fortune is only partially due to talent—and is largely due to family, friends, and happenstance.

My deepest appreciation for a loving, smart, strong-willed family, who had the confidence and strength to put up with me and ensure that my head never exceeded the size of our doorways: my wife and lover, Maria; daughter and television producer, Danielle; and son and actor, Jason.

And to enduring friendships, rare and rewarding trusts, which have the capacity to make time stand still: Bill Howe, Keith Darcy, Mike Magsig, Bob and Patsy Janson.

For the hundreds of people who have participated in my mentoring program over the years, keeping me in touch with the trials and opportunities of the profession at so many differing levels, my thanks for your trust and infusion of ideas and experiences.

My thanks to Phoebe for her energy and stimulation. And as always, through a never-imagined thirteen books, my thanks and profound admiration to L.T. Weiss, who knows more about life than any of us will ever be able to understand.

CHAPTER 1

Acquiring Fortune 1000 Clients

Why Size Doesn't Matter

n 1985, after I had been on my own for a couple of months at the age of 38, a human resources director at Merck & Co. who had known me from years prior called to ask if I'd be interested in a possible project running some focus groups on values and ethics. When I told him I would (I desperately needed the work), that I'd be happy to put together a proposal (I desperately needed the work), and that I'd of course travel down to New Jersey for a meeting with someone (I desperately needed the work), he promised to "match our calendars."

On our "matched day" my contact introduced me to a senior vice president, who reviewed my proposal on the spot. The human resources director explained the organizational need, I explained the methodology and expected results, and we both answered the vice president's questions, until the final one, when the executive turned to me and said, "How much?" I had, incredibly, never cited a fee in the proposal, assuming that Merck would tell me how much they'd give me.

I began to see shooting lights and to perspire heavily, which I took to be the onset of a heart attack and the recognition that I was not cut out for the consulting business. My internist later told me that I was probably holding my breath for about two minutes and depriving myself of oxygen.

After what I thought was forty minutes, but in reality was an inadvertently dignified and confident pause of about nine seconds, I said, "Fourteen." (Why did I say, "fourteen"? Because I remembered that was the amount I owed at the time on my credit cards.)

"Okay," replied the senior vice president, "let's do it." We all shook hands; I had landed my first consulting assignment and, not incidentally, my first Fortune 1000 client. When I arrived home that evening and had a chance to catch my breath—and begin worrying now not whether I would get the business but whether I could really deliver it—I realized that I had learned several important lessons:

1. My good friend in human resources, with whom I'm still friendly today, fifteen years later and well into his retirement, could introduce me to an array of managers and executives with needs for my services, but he could not purchase my services himself. His key function for me was matchmaking, and if he were my only contact without those matches, I'd have a good friend but no business.

2. The senior vice president had a budget from which he could purchase discretionary services without anyone else's approval. He was the only person I needed to meet, and if I could develop a relationship with people like him I didn't even need an introduction. He wasn't my friend, but he was my buyer.

3. The project price should have been $35,000. Both of the other people in the room were interested in the results of the project and what it would do for the organization. *Neither was interested in the fee until the buyer was actually ready to proceed in any case.* It was never a consideration until the benefits and outcomes were understood. If they were insufficient, the fee was academic in any case. In other words, low fees wouldn't guarantee business, but high value could guarantee not only business but also high fees for that business.

Merck remained a client for twelve consecutive years, during which I conducted about forty projects, large and small, across every division, domestically and internationally, from the CEO to the salespeople visiting physicians. During that tenure I had relationships with a dozen buyers whose business generated about $2 million in revenues. My friend introduced me to some, and I introduced myself to others.

I've employed those three principles—find true buyers, develop relationships with them, and establish high value outcomes that can justify high fees—since that first fortunate meeting and revelation with every major organization in my sights. They have been the basis for my development of a seven-figure practice and a host of Fortune 1000 clients. It is that easy.

ESTABLISHING RELATIONSHIPS WITH MAJOR BUYERS: RAINMAKING

Consulting is a relationship business. The old saw is that it's as difficult to sell a $10,000 piece of business as a $100,000 piece of business, so we might as well sell the latter, because the sweat equity is the same. Well, establishing relationships is a process, so why not become adept at it with significant, true buyers with large budgets, rather than with gatekeepers, intermediaries, or buyers with small budgets?

A friend of mine who is a fly fisherman—a sport I cannot begin to comprehend and would engage in only if I could not watch paint dry—confided that the intricate and bizarre lures that are at the heart of the activity really appeal to the people fishing, not to the fish. Lures are created for people, just as dog toys are created for people, not dogs, and tony private schools are oriented toward the parents' egos not necessarily the kids' preferences.

In the Fortune 1000 marketplace, which I had stumbled into but never left, you and I sell to people. We don't sell to monoliths, such as Mercedes, or Hewlett-Packard, or GE, and we don't sell to business units, such as sales, finance, or operations. We sell to people in those companies and divisions and, once you appreciate that and become good at it, no organization is too large or too complex, because the relationship building process is always the same.

Evolve so that you develop relationships with more and more powerful buyers. This power is not always a function of hierarchical position. A director of sales sometimes has a larger budget and higher value needs than an executive vice president of human resources. Find important organizational contributors who control large budgets.

Relationship building with key buyers can be called "rainmaking." In a solo practice, the consultant had better be a rainmaker. In a small practice, the principal had better be the rainmaker. In a large firm the individual practices need rainmakers, although they may not necessarily be the practice managers.

Let's deal with two aspects of rainmaking: Finding the buyer and developing a relationship with the buyer.

Finding the Buyer

To find the key buyers for you—given your type of practice, your competencies, your passions, your business goals—you must be keenly attuned to the responses to three questions:

1. What is the added value that I bring to a client?
2. Who, specifically, can write a check for that value?
3. How do I reach those people?

The problem here is that most consultants rush to question three, often prompted by the misdirected urgings of marketing gurus to "work the phones," "send out mail," and "it's a numbers game." But arbitrarily reaching out to people without knowing and acting on the answers to the first two questions is somewhat like leaving the landing lights on for Amelia Earhart: While it's a nice thought, it's simply a waste of energy.

Richard Gerson, Ph.D., CMC, is the president of Gerson Goodson Performance Management. His firm provides assistance in talent management, employee retention, performance improvement, and training. He's been on his own full-time since 1988.

Q. Why are you successful?

A. The reason for my success is the high level of service I provide to my clients, along with achieving the results that we establish at the initial engagement meeting.

Q. What would you do differently if you started over again?

A. Work a few hours longer (as I usually end my office day by mid-afternoon because of my children) and hire a salesperson from the beginning.

Q. What's your major unaccomplished achievement?

A. The major achievement I have yet to accomplish is to have so many speaking and training engagements that I have to contract out my consulting.

Question #1: What Is Your Added Value?

The value-added (or value proposition) that you bring to a client has to be expressed in client outcomes. No matter how good you are and how many former clients you can claim, the fact that you do strategy retreats, employee surveys, 360° assessments, value-chain analysis, merger and acquisition valuation, or any other tasks is of little value. A lot of firms do those things, which simply make them a commodity. Yet if you review most consulting firms' literature and visit their websites, you'll find these "billboard" advertisements for their methodology.

Value propositions must be in terms of *client outcomes*: increased sales, decreased attrition, improved communications, alleviated stress, better teamwork, higher market share, greater retention, and so forth. What you do for clients must be expressed in the client's improved condition, whether in your literature, on your website, in your conversation, or as part of your word of mouth.

While the value may well differ in kind or in degree from client to client, you must zealously present it always as the business results the client can expect.[1] You have to be clear on what your range of results typically are, given your competencies and methodology, so that you can answer question number two.

Question #2: Who Can Write a Check for That Value?

If you're enhancing sales results, then it's probably someone in the sales hierarchy. If you're developing new strategies and business initiatives, it's probably someone in the executive offices or heading up small business units. If you're providing for enhanced productivity through outsourcing, then it's any executive who can make the typical outsourcing decisions—usually in finance, information systems, human resources, and so on.

In large organizations, those specific buyers are seldom the CEO or COO, and they often reside in obscure areas and down remote hallways. In other words, they may be hard to identify in some cases and stick out like disco dancers in a country and western club in others, but they are generally accessible. And that leads us to point number three.

Question #3: How Do You Reach Those Buyers You've Identified?
- What do they read?
- To whom do they listen?
- Where do they hang out?
- To what organizations do they belong?
- What is their passion?

---

1. And this applies for non-profits, education, and government agencies as well. Profit isn't the only business outcome that's vital. Health, safety, repute and a raft of other qualitative considerations are legitimate client outcomes.

The answers to these questions will enable you to develop a relationship with your key buyers. Because relationship building is time-intensive, you want to be absolutely sure who your buyers are and what appeals to them. Most consultants I've worked with have made the mistake of building terrific relationships with people who are not their buyers.

RULE

The best way to "infiltrate" a large organization is by targeting a specific buyer. Don't get tangled up in committees, resource centers, or "auditions." Ironically, you have to be clear first on what you can accomplish for the organization and then find the buyer who has a commensurate need.

The following text is written in response to the bullet points above.

What Do They Read?   Publish in publications that they read. Elicit interviews in the newsletters, newspapers, magazines, and trade publications that gain their attention. It's not beyond the pale to provide an article for their organization's own house organ.[2]

To Whom Do They Listen?   This is where my friend at Merck came in. Are there key recommenders who are readily accessible and who can grease the skids leading to the buyer's office? Are there peers with whom you've worked who can provide an introduction or reference?

---

2. I've done this any number of times, with both articles and interviews. House organs are notorious for needing decent copy, and as long as you provide value and are not self-promotional, it's quite feasible to gain this "in house" publicity.

Where Do They Hang Out?   Are you likely to be introduced to them in certain meetings or in the company gym?[3] Can you arrange through other contacts at the company to be introduced informally?

To What Organizations Do They Belong?   Arrange to speak in front of trade association conventions that they attend. Serve on a pro bono board, task force, or committee to which they also donate time. Try to take a highly visible role in organizations that they frequent.

What Is Their Passion?   You don't have to take up sky diving to meet a buyer, but you may want to volunteer for the local soccer league if the buyer is a coach or official. If you meet the prospect and find out that baroque music is a passion, you might want to send a catalog or a website that specializes in it.

Through a logical progression of determining your own value proposition, determining who's likely (and able) to write a check for such outcomes, and establishing tactics to reach them, you're now in a position to develop the relationship that leads to the sale.

Developing a Relationship with the Buyer

Relationships are built on intellectual breadth. That's right, you heard it here. You must be able to talk to the buyer on a wide array of topics, including business and non-business issues. One of the primary reasons that consultants fail to penetrate large organizations is that they get all tangled up in their methodology, technology, and approaches, which instantly relegates them to lower-level buyers or, worse, gatekeepers and committees.

Once you've been successful in finding a true buyer for your services, don't throw the opportunity away by harping on about your approaches, bor-

---

3. I try to always eat in the client's cafeteria and work out in the company gym. I always say hello to everyone, and others assume they should know you. This leads to, "I've seen you around, haven't I?" Of course, at times I'm exchanging hopeful glances with other consultants, who are apparently almost as smart as I am.

While running role plays for the consulting arm of a Hewlett-Packard division, I found a disturbing habit among the consultants. In certain role plays I would be an actual buyer for HP's services, and the team meeting with me (while their colleagues observed and analyzed their effectiveness) would suddenly find this out. Moreover, I volunteered that I thought the team's approach made a great deal of sense and that I wanted to know how HP wanted to proceed, because I was certainly interested.

The teams invariably responded that they wanted to explain their approaches to me in detail, or wanted to do a needs analysis, or wanted to conduct some interviews around my organization. I always responded that this was fine, told them to make arrangements with my secretary who would line up the right people, and then told the observers that this was the last time the team would ever be able to speak to me.

These consultants were so focused on their technology and so unaccustomed to developing a relationship with a buyer based on more of a business and intellectual approach, that they inadvertently surrendered the hard-won relationship with an interested buyer. They actually relegated themselves to more comfortable, lower level people.

Finding that out in role plays was a revelation. Doing something about those ingrained bad habits was a revolution.

ing the buyer to death, and causing the buyer to relegate you to a subordinate whom the buyer doesn't care about boring to death.

Relationships are built on trust, candor, and peer-level considerations. That is, you and the buyer are colleagues who are jointly considering whether to move ahead in a collaborative effort. Both you and the buyer must decide the situation is right, and either of you may consider that it is wrong for any variety of reasons. You are not a vendor, a seller, a supplicant, or a "taker" who is desperate for the client's business. Sophisticated buyers see through this instantly and either take advantage of the desperation or decide that there is no basis for a trusting relationship (most buyers have a sufficient number of "yes men" around them, so paying to have another one around is not an attractive option.

RULE 3

This may sound counter-intuitive, but you will build relationships faster by confronting a buyer and questioning basic premises than you will by doing a "soft shoe" and trying to be innocuous. Low-level people are easily threatened; high-level people are readily challenged and *enjoy the joust. Get on your horse and charge.*

TEN TECHNIQUES TO BUILD HIGH-LEVEL BUYER RELATIONSHIPS: MAKING RAIN

Here are some of the best ways to build relationships with significant buyers:

1. Do Your Homework.   Find out about the company, division, or unit and prepare some provocative questions. If it is publicly traded, get the stock price that morning from the Internet or *The Wall Street Journal.* Be on the lookout for articles about the industry and/or organization in the trade press. If you use a clipping service or Internet search source, alert them to add the organization to your list.

2. Make Onsite Observations to Foster Intimate Discussions.   I arrived at an insurance company and casually asked the receptionist how the company was doing. She replied that the loss ratio was better than the plan, so people were pretty optimistic about bonuses. I remarked to my prospect, the general manager of claims, that it was pretty unusual and impressive for a receptionist to make such an observation, which said something about an inclusive culture. He then waxed eloquent about how proud he was of that for the next forty minutes.

3. Practice Non-One-Upsmanship.   This is a real ego challenge for many, but it means this difference: If the buyer says, "Sorry my desk is such a mess, but I've just returned from a week at Aspen," don't respond, "I've been to Aspen many times! Do you ski the black double diamonds?" Instead, ask, "People rave about

Aspen. What did you like the most about it?" Show an interest in the buyer, not an interest in telling the buyer about yourself. This is subtle but powerful. It's basically the difference between, "Would you like to see the slides of my vacation?" and "May I see the slides of your vacation?" Those two questions have enormous qualitative differences in the responses.

4. *Never Allow Yourself to Be Placed on the Defensive.* This dynamic is entirely within your control. If the buyer blurts out, "So, what is it you think you can do for us?" do not respond with a litany of your vast potential. Instead try, "I'm not really sure, to be honest. If you could tell me some of the issues you're facing, that might serve as a logical starting point for both of us to make some decisions." If you're asked, "What do you charge?" the proper reply is, "It's impossible to answer that, since I have no idea yet what you need or if I can fill that need. Why don't we start there?"[4]

5. *Co-Opt Predictable Objections.* Have certain responses prepared to deflect potentially uncomfortable questions. If you've never worked in the industry and the prospect asks, "What have you done in our industry?" be prepared to respond, "Actually, I've worked with a wide variety of issues you're facing within several industries, and I can bring the breadth of what they do to your situation. For example, your customer response issues are analogous to those of the airlines, and at United we created an approach that. . . ." If you know you have potential vulnerabilities (for example, geographic distance, small size firm, unknown to the buyer previously, and so on) then it's mandatory that you prepare responses to co-opt potential objections.

6. *Exhibit Great Patience.* Significant relationships may require significant time. Some prospects are hard to reach at first, may be aloof, or may simply be very private. Don't force the issue. Keep the prospect talking *and do not attempt to fill silence yourself.* The more you say to "fill dead air" the stupider you'll

---

4. When prospects insist that I at least give them a range for my services, I tell them it would be from $50,000 to $1,000,000. They either laugh or sit there in stunned disbelief, at which time I say, "Look, if we can exchange some information and discuss some objectives, I can have specific investment options to you by courier tomorrow. Is that sufficient?" It always is.

Chicke Fitzgerald is the president of MTech Strategies, Inc., of Mariet-ta, GA. She has a young daughter. From 1998 to 2000 her revenues increased from under 100K to over 700K. She specializes in the travel technology area.

Q. What's behind your startling growth?

A. The single key factor in my success is my network. Since going out on my own in 1995, I have not had to solicit any business. All of my business is generated by word of mouth and relationships. My best clients are Ernst & Young and Ericsson Wireless. Ernst & Young calls me in as a subject-matter expert on travel-related consulting opportunities as a part of their sales team. If the business is secured, I then put a team of subcontractors together to fulfill the work, in addition to my own participation. This allows E&Y to keep their staff lean, but still have the depth and breadth to offer their clients in the travel technology area. Ericsson uses me as their outsourced marketing and business development department in the travel arena as opposed to staffing this area with full-time people. I also maintain a large card file of contacts that I have made throughout the years and I do my best to keep in touch with individuals who could possibly generate new business for me. I also make sure that I attend all of the key conferences in my industry and have recently published a study on the trends in my industry for the 21st Century. This study will secure my posi-

sound. Let the prospect take the conversation in a comfortable direction for him or her, and wait for your opportunity to engage in some relevant discussion. I once had a series of breakfasts with a hospital CEO over nine months before he was ready to talk about any kind of project together. Subsequently, I was award-ed several projects over a two-year period. It's better to have two years' of work at a later date than no work more quickly.

tion as an industry expert. This book, coupled with the demand for my time by my clients, has allowed me to double my daily fees. I had previously been undercharging for my services.

Q. Is there anything you'd do differently?

A. If I had it to do all over again, I would have left corporate America and gone out on my own much earlier. I didn't really understand the worth of my experience in the marketplace and had long been self-conscious about my lack of an advanced degree. As it turns out (for me and Bill Gates!), the lack of a degree has not hindered me at all. I occasionally think about going back to school to obtain an executive MBA, but each time that I look at my daily fees, I ask myself whether it would really be worth it to me to do so.

Q. What is your major unaccomplished goal?

A. My major achievement that I still hope to reach is to broaden my practice beyond the travel and transportation field to include other areas of specialty. I have done some work in the healthcare and retail sectors, but by and large, my practice still centers around eCommerce in the travel arena. One of my goals is to be home with my family more, and if my practice were broader, there would be more business available to me locally to help me achieve a better balance in my life and my practice.

7. Close One Step at a Time. Remember that a sale is really the result of a small series of "yeses," so be clear about what you want to accomplish tactically at any given time. Try to close on each small "yes," one at a time. If you gain more than one, good for you, but few people are able to meet a buyer for the first time and walk out with a contract. A more realistic series of "yeses" may look like this:

- Agreement on phone conversation
- Agreement on meeting to get acquainted
- Agreement on second meeting to discuss issues
- Agreement on third meeting to gain conceptual agreement
- Conceptual agreement on objectives, measures, value
- Agreement to review proposal
- Acceptance of proposal

That's a minimum of seven "yeses" in a very aggressive sequence.

8. *Offer Alternatives Every Time.* Always be prepared to provide options, even for such mundane things as meeting sites and venues. The more a buyer is faced with "yes/no" decisions, the more likely it is you'll get a "no" or the buyer will procrastinate. But the more the buyer has a range of options that are all agreeable to you, the more you'll hear a "yes." In fact, your odds of gaining a small "yes" from point seven above increases by about tenfold. Don't push the client into a room with one door.

9. *Look Around in Awareness.* Be absolutely current on the news in general, not only in the industry. If a buyer says, "Did you see what happened in Rome?" or "Can you believe that playoff game yesterday?" he or she is indicating a strong personal connection with the event. This is your opportunity to ask about the buyer's opinions and views on the event and to do so being informed enough to say, "Those landmarks in Rome have been the subject of bitter confrontations for some time," or "How could anyone have expected such a rash of injuries to key players so early in the game?" Relationships tend to be best established on non-business issues, when possible.

10. *Know Thy Prospect.* Finally, be acutely aware of the buyer's style and comfort zone, and try to respect them. I'm not talking here about neuro-linguistic abracadabra, or INTJs or Drivers or a low D or any other of the pseudo-psychological nonsense. I mean that the more comfortable the buyer, the better your chances of quickly building a relationship. Consequently, if the buyer wants to chat, chat; if the buyer wants to talk business, talk business; if the buyer uses the easel, you use the easel; if the buyer says, "Let's go get some coffee," go along and drink some unless you have a toxic allergy to the stuff. Go with the flow at the outset.

Relationship building is strongly dependent on your being an object of interest to the buyer. Otherwise, you're simply someone who wants something. Provide value early, in your suggestions, opinions, ideas, and even humor. If the buyer finds you interesting, you will *accelerate the relationship.*

I talk to consultants all the time who tell me that they can't break into the large firms or deal with sophisticated buyers at high levels because they lack graduate degrees, large company experience, experience in that industry, a staff and appropriate resources, line management experience, and a host of other "lacks." When I ask how it is that these buyers so quickly determine those perceived shortcomings, I'm told: "Well, I explain it to them." This is still another good reason for getting the buyer to talk, rather than talking yourself.

But it's even more vital to be willing to go on the offensive. Your position has to be that the client is actually far better off dealing with you.

WHY SIZE DOESN'T MATTER (IN FACT, WHY SMALL IS OFTEN BETTER)

One of the most chronic complaints or fears is that small firms or solo practices don't have the "heft" needed to service large client organizations effectively. Yet, I've made my living as a solo in that exact marketplace.

Here are the kinds of arguments that you have to be prepared to discuss, should the issue arise, and what to say to the prospect:

1. *You always deal with the principal.* There is a huge benefit to the buyer in always having access to the "top gun," the person who can make decisions and take action immediately. *That person is you!* Working collaboratively with you has a significant advantage, which you should highlight.

2. *Our overhead is very low, hence, our fees reflect that.* You do not have scores of offices, advertising, company cars, and vast legions to support. Hence, your fees are much, much lower.
3. *We are immediately responsive.* You can provide the client with your home phone, cell phone, and private e-mail, and thus guarantee a certain level of responsiveness (I guarantee ninety minutes. No one ever abuses this, but the knowledge that the service is there provides tremendous value).
4. *Our approach is tailored to need, not "off the shelf."* You don't use "models" and matrices and other proprietary formulas and attempt to force clients into your mold. Each client is distinct, and each client merits a distinct intervention, which you can provide because you haven't invested millions is a "system" or methodology that you have to commercialize.
5. *You aren't paying our people to learn the consulting business.* We don't use junior partners, new MBAs, or interns. If we must subcontract, it will be with a few other seasoned people, like myself.
6. *There are no conflicting priorities from dozens of other clients.* We only take on a few clients at a time, so our attention is undiluted. Also, there is no chance of competitive clients, and we can guarantee you that we will not take on a direct competitor, avoiding the discomfort of having completely separate teams working on your accounts.
7. *We can sign non-disclosure, non-compete and other documents readily.* You are not dealing with many people, so confidentiality if further safeguarded. We have no turnover here.
8. *Attendant expenses will be less.* Our travel, administrative, and support expenses are small, because few people will be working on your project and we are not concurrently training newer staff.
9. *We need you as much as you need us.* Each of our clients is highly important to us. We can't afford to have a poor relationship or an ill-conceived project. This is truly a collaborative, win/win effort.
10. It's about value and results, not quantity and size. The outcomes are what are important, not the alternatives. We will be least disruptive to your ongoing operations while obtaining the exact same project results.

Size doesn't matter, and small size—"boutique" firms, if you care to be trendy—can be an advantage over the monoliths that descend on the client with

While working with the CEO of Calgon on a general retainer, he called me into his office just prior to 4 p.m. on a Thursday afternoon.

"Alan, I've got a compensation meeting doing on downstairs in the conference room, and it's been going on every Thursday at 4 for five weeks. Go down there and find out what's going on, why it's stalled. I hired a big shot comp firm, but they can't seem to get my people on board."

"Fred, I know next to nothing about compensation practices."

"No, but you do know about people, conflict, and facilitation. Tell me what's not working in that meeting."

I spent the next two hours amid Fred's six vice presidents, who all knew me well enough to disregard me, and the compensation firm's junior partner who was assigned to the project. She was totally unable to facilitate, cajole, order, or otherwise influence the six very disparate interests in that room, each of whom had a favored compensation formula.

At 6 p.m. I reported back to Fred.

"I bet you were sold this project by the managing partner in Pittsburgh," I ventured.

"Yes, he and a senior partner from New York spent two days with me."

"Well, you've got a very junior person down there utterly intimidated by your big guns, who are shooting up the landscape."

"What do you suggest?"

"Fire the comp firm and tell your people that they have 48 hours to come up with a comp plan, or you'll have to impose one that none of them is likely to love."

Two days later, Calgon had a good comp plan with strong ownership from the division heads and had saved a pile of money on its compensation consulting project, which was being billed by the hour and didn't have an end in sight.

a hundred junior partners, all of whom are there to try to learn the client's business before being able to contribute to it.

The value you bring to a large client and a high-level buyer has nothing to do with size and everything to do with value and the quality of the perceived relationship. You are providing your past experiences and current expertise to improve your client's future, as shown in Figure 1.1.

Consultant's Past	Current Intervention	Client's Future
• experiences	• coaching	• higher productivity
• education	• survey	• lower attrition
• accomplishments	• redesign	• higher morale
• development	• workshop	• improved image
• travels	• retreat	• better performance
• work history	• etc.	• greater market share
• beliefs		• greater profit
• victories/defeats		• more growth
• risks/adversity		• more innovation
• experimentation		• problems solved
		• happier customers
		• superior service

Process Flow

⟶

Figure 1.1. What Is My "Value Package"?

USING THE SPRINGBOARD TO OTHER POTENTIAL CLIENTS

Once you've taken the innovative and energetic actions required to meet and develop relationships with high-level buyers in major organizations, don't let go. We're all too prone to pat ourselves on the back and begin implementing our great piece of business, maybe spending the money on the way back from the client.

But the key is, *once you're inside a client organization, take advantage of the springboard.* Springboards increase the ability to leap. And while there is no denying the importance of the current piece of business to your cash flow, there's also no denying the direct and ancillary benefits it can generate for your practice. Even larger firms seldom fully exploit the springboard phenomenon.

So, ironically, be acutely aware that the moment when you've successfully completed a wonderful sale is also the moment to build other wonderful sales.

This isn't called greed. It's called marketing.

There is a prevailing myth in consulting that you can't market while you deliver and you can't deliver while you market. In smaller firms, the belief in this myth severely delimits growth and empties the pipeline of potential business. In larger firms, the belief creates massive overhead in the form of larger staffs and resources to separately sell, deliver, market, develop methodologies, and so on.

RULE 5

A current client is valuable in a large number of ways, and immediate income is only one of them. Ironically, the most powerful marketing you can accomplish is when delivering a large intervention, and the cost of doing this is virtually nil.

Here, then, is how to use the springboard without doing a belly flop.

TEN TECHNIQUES FOR SPRINGBOARD MARKETING

1. At the outset, in your proposal or confirming letter, establish that you'd like to rely on the buyer for a testimonial, reference, referrals, or blurb for one of your publications if the project is completed to the buyer's satisfaction. In this manner, you've set the stage for the help, and you don't have to raise the issue later.[5]

---

5. Note the use of a "choice of yeses" here, too. The technique is ubiquitous and highly effective.

2. Ask the buyer if there are trade associations or professional groups that you might address. Sometimes the buyer may hold a position such as programming chair and can at least introduce you to the right people.

3. Ask whether the buyer or a significant manager would be interested in co-authoring an article based on the project, subject to the organization's policies and guidelines.

4. Ask whether the internal house organ would care to run an interview or an article about your work.

5. Reach out to other true buyers you meet in the course of your work and offer value. This is not self-promotional. If you run into the vice president for European operations, suggest that you've learned things on other assignments that might merit a lunch together sometime.

6. Join internal task forces and committees as appropriate. I've seen consultants become accepted as "one of the team" and repeatedly asked to participate in additional projects (requiring additional proposals). Figure 1.2 shows one way to determine which meetings are best for you to join.

7. Meet with the buyer repeatedly. Don't abdicate that relationship. In larger firms, this is always a danger because the rainmaker moves on too early, leaving only implementers on the job. In smaller firms, the rainmaker becomes preoccupied with delivery. Set up a series of meetings to deliver *good news* as the project progresses. Establish a reliance on you, so that the buyer actively thinks of you for additional projects.

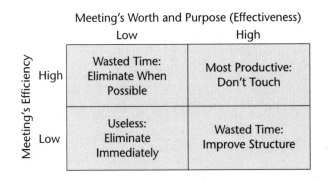

Figure 1.2. Matrix of a Meeting's Usefulness for You

The Ultimate Consultant

8. Obtain permission to use the client's name, logo, and endorsement as appropriate. As opposed to point one above, seek approval immediately to cite the organization as a client to add to your literature, website, and other promotions.

9. Provide value on issues beyond your project. During one engagement I found clear evidence of a hostile work environment in a remote location, despite the fact that I was there to conduct focus groups on another issue entirely. I reported this to the buyer as my ethical obligation, and not only was he immediately grateful, but he asked if I could work with his human resources department to remove the problem and create an educational program for management. I could and I did.

10. Think of the fourth sale first. Look down the road at anticipated client needs, the client's customers, and the changes in the environment that are probable. Once you are onboard, productive, and developing sound relationships, you will automatically have the inside track on future business. Think about what you have to put in place now to ensure that future.

There is a "discounting principle" at work in major organizations with consultants. Once you're trusted and productive, the cost of replacing you with another consultant—and the cost to that other consultant to develop a relationship that can overcome your current one—is almost prohibitive.

Use the springboard as soon as you enter the pool. You'll make quite a splash.

One Last Time: This is a relationship business, meaning the one-on-one interaction with a true buyer is the critical factor, no matter what size the company. Assiduously pursue and develop those relationships, and then exploit them for mutual success.

THE ULTIMATE RULES

Rule #1. Evolve so that you develop relationships with more and more powerful buyers. This is not always hierarchical. A director of sales sometimes has a larger budget and higher value needs than an executive vice president of human resources. Find important organizational contributors who control large budgets.

Rule #2.   The best way to "infiltrate" a large organization is by targeting a specific buyer. Don't become tangled up in committees, resource centers, or "auditions." Ironically, you have to be clear first on what you can accomplish for the organization and then find the buyer who has a commensurate need.

Rule #3.   This may sound counter-intuitive, but you will build relationships faster by confronting a buyer and questioning basic premises than you will by doing a "soft shoe" and trying to be innocuous. Low-level people are easily threatened; high-level people are readily challenged and enjoy the joust. Get on your horse and charge.

Rule #4.   Relationship building is strongly dependent on your being an object of interest to the buyer. Otherwise, you're simply someone who wants something. Provide value early, in your suggestions, opinions, ideas, and even humor. If the buyer finds you interesting, you will accelerate the relationship.

Rule #5.   A current client is valuable in a large number of ways, and immediate income is only one of them. Ironically, the most powerful marketing you can accomplish is when delivering a large intervention, and the cost of doing so is virtually nil.

Jim Kwaiser is a consultant on family businesses, a tough market, assisting clients in areas such as conflict, communication, and strategy. He markets himself as a family business dealing with family businesses. His company is C.H.A.L.L.E.N.G.E.S., Inc.

Q. What single factor accounts most for your success?

A. Learning how to network effectively with the people who do business with the people I want to do business with!!! This eliminates cold calls. We network with attorneys, financial planners, insurance agents, and accountants who deal with family businesses. Our networking people introduce us to the key family members, who trust their judgment, and they are more receptive to us.

Q. What would you do differently if starting over?

A. What would I do differently? Zero in on my "passion" first. I always loved dealing with families in business, but because I had such a strong sales and operations background I started consulting in sales and operations first. It was only after I realized that I wouldn't be truly happy until I worked primarily in the family business market that I made the change.

Q. What major achievement is yet to come for you?

A. I really want to help all family businesses successfully move from one generation to the next without destroying the family relationships and also keeping the business together. I hope that by finishing a book offering practical solutions on the C.H.A.L.L.E.N.G.E.S. families in business face we can reach more of them. We will continue to help them one at a time as well until we get to them all.

Value-Based Fees

*If You're Charging by the Hour
or Day, You're an Amateur*

One of the fundamental problems besetting the consulting profession is quite simply how to charge the client. The "traditional" approach of charging for the time spent solving the client's problem is adopted from the "sister professions" of accounting and law, where the approach has served to seriously delimit the ability of accountants and lawyers to earn money and create real wealth for most of the last century.

Aggravating the issue and stifling any innovation was the emergence of the pre-merger mania "Big Eight" accounting firms into the consulting field, with Andersen eventually fielding the largest consulting force in the world. The problem is that all of these firms (now merged to five at this writing and inevitably heading toward implosion into two or three) have an audit mentality etched into their corporate psyches, which neatly and stubbornly demands that every job title have a commensurate connection to a rate for billable hours.

There is hope. Andersen has been a client of mine over the years with the goal of a few practice heads to change their method to value-based fees. The baby is alive and, thus far, hasn't been smothered.

It's astonishing to me that I still have to deal with fees in a sophisticated work for successful people in the field, but the empirical evidence quite clearly supports the fact that even highly successful consultants are working too hard and earning too little. To put it another way, about 80 percent of the people reading this book are undercharging for their value, because they are charging for their work instead.

When I attend consulting conferences, I still find sessions devoted to "How to choose the right hourly rate" and "When to raise your per diem," presumably provided by the top authorities in the field. Clearly, my work is still cut out for me.

THE CONCEPT OF VALUE-BASED FEES

The first thing to understand about value-based fees is that they are the fairest and most equitable arrangement *for the client.* This is an essential concept for two reasons: First, it removes the onus of the inaccurate idea that value-based fees unduly reward the consultant; second, it provides the leverage to convince the client that these fees are in the client's best interests.

Value-based fees are best for the client because:

- There is never a "meter running" with the inevitable pressure to "find something for the consultant to do" as long as the meter is ticking.
- The client does not have to make an investment decision every time the client may deem the consultant's help necessary.
- The client's employees can freely call on the consultant without worrying about increasing costs or going to the boss for approval each time.
- The consultant can take on more work within the project's scope without the risk of the client perceiving self-aggrandizing increases in the hours required.
- The best interests of the consultant are to finish the project quickly, not to stretch it out or fill projected time even though it is no longer necessary to spend that time.
- There is a fixed cap on the investment right from the outset.

Everything is about value, not about fees. If the discussion is about fees, then you've lost control of the discussion.

Vignette

> The first sale is always to ourselves, and it's often the toughest sale of all. I have an exercise in my mentoring program in which I ask a consultant to look in the mirror and say affirmatively, "The fee is $50,000." Many of them begin to laugh, and one woman said, "The fee is $35,000!"
>
> "What happened to $50,000?" I asked.
>
> "I couldn't go to fifty," she explained.

Value-based fees are possible when the consultant focuses on the output, not the input. A focus group, survey, executive coaching, workshop, or department redesign are all commodities that can be "shopped" for the lowest price. But improved teamwork, higher sales, reduced attrition, and faster customer response time are business outcomes that are worth a high premium. The buyer must see a fixed investment resulting in a clear and impressive set of outcomes; too often, however, the buyer sees a clear fixed cost and only vague benefits.

Figure 2.1 demonstrates how a buyer would normally view most consulting projects, with vague benefits assumed from the tasks to be performed (consultants love calling these "deliverables," which further compounds the crime) and escalating costs resulting from increasing hours. However, the graphic on the bottom shows a more intelligent proposition for the buyer: A fixed cap on the investment with clear and demonstrable benefits to the business as a result of the engagement.

The point here is to provide the buyer with a clear picture of return on investment. Once you do that, high fees lose their impact when compared to the impressive business results the client will enjoy. However, even low fees

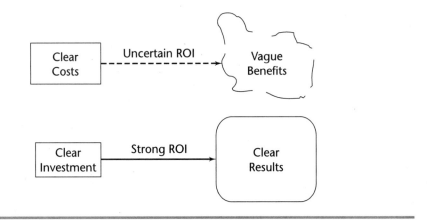

Figure 2.1. Costs vs. Outcomes

provide an obstacle when the client perceives only a commodity—a training program or an employee survey—being implemented.[1]

THE KEY TO HIGH FEES IS NOT TO MENTION FEES

The proper sequence of events with a prospect is depicted in Figure 2.2:

- Create shared values
- Build a relationship
- Gain conceptual agreement

1. This is yet another excellent reason to stay out of the human resources department of virtually any organization. Not only do HR people focus on tasks and are usually not an integral part of the company's strategy, they also have very little credibility in terms of delivering measurable business improvement. They would rather revel in "open meetings" and "power sharing" than get dirty trying to improve customer retention or the speed of R&D commercialization.

- Submit a proposal
- Implement the project
- Solidify and build on the relationship

Shared Values.   I'm not referring here to states rights versus federalism or public versus private education. I'm talking about shared values and philosophies about fundamental business principles. For example, I don't believe in downsizing as an anodyne for lousy decisions in the executive suite, and I refuse to work on projects that throw thousands of people out on the street. I make no value judgments about whether you do or not, but I know that I won't, so any prospect asking me to help maintain morale while they downsize is not one that I'll work with. Unless there are shared values about the underlying business principles, the project will not be successful because the consultant will not be able to adhere to the client's wishes.

RULE **7**

The best response to the premature question, "How much will this cost?" is "I don't know." The best response to the follow-up question, "When will you know?" is "If you can provide me with the information I need, I can have all the details, including investment options, to you tomorrow. Is that agreeable?"

Relationship.   The relationship with the economic buyer—the person who has budget and can sign the check—must be one of peers jointly determining whether they choose to work together. The relationship must include honesty and candor, as well as the willingness to confront each other and to admit errors. It needn't be—and probably shouldn't be—a social or personal relationship, but must be a comfortable business collaboration, not between buyer and seller, but between peers and colleagues. It is critical to establish a strong relationship prior to seeking conceptual agreement.

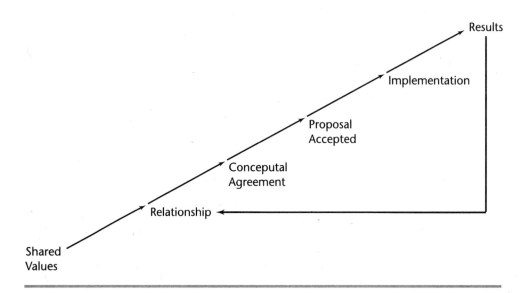

Figure 2.2. The Success Sequence

Conceptual Agreement. This means gaining agreement in concept—philosophically—with the buyer on three issues:

- What are the objectives (business outcomes) to be achieved?
- How will we measure progress and success?
- What are these outcomes worth to the client?[2]

This step is the heart of the value-based process. If you can gain agreement with the buyer on the outcomes, the metrics, and the worth of those outcomes, then fees are academic. Making the buyer a collaborator in the determination of value is a subtle but extremely powerful device to ensure that fees are regarded merely as intelligent investments. If you gain conceptual agreement, you should be successful in over 80 percent of your subsequent proposals, because they will be summations of conceptual agreement and not explo-

---

2. See Appendix A for sample questions to elicit responses in each of these areas.

While working with one of the consulting functions of Hewlett-Packard, we found that the unit—already under pressure to increase profitability—could substantially increase profitability by doing not a whit's additional work or by acquiring one new client if it simply changed to a value-based fee structure from its current hourly configuration. When this was tested with clients, citing the benefits to the client, there wasn't a serious objection to be heard.

The problem was internal, because HP's accounting system demanded that billable hours multiplied by rates for those hours be placed—literally—in certain boxes on the spread sheets. The apotheosis of lunacy occurred when, during a case study using value-based fees, one of the consultants complained that the size of the new fees would not fit in the boxes provided by accounting!

The problem was solved in what I call the "rational self-interest" approach to bureaucracy. We agreed that the next sale would be value-based and that the accountants would be told to figure out how they wanted to report the $600,000 that couldn't be subdivided into the neat boxes. If they rejected the contract, the consulting team would go to senior management and ask for a decision as to whether to make the boxes somewhat bigger or to turn down the business.

The contract went through, and profitability began to soar.

---

rations of buyer acceptance. It is essential to base conceptual agreement on the strong relationship previously developed *and never to submit a proposal prior to gaining conceptual agreement.* Otherwise, your proposals become negotiating documents.

Proposal Acceptance. This document is now simply part of an intelligent sequence leading to the collaboration, and not a pivotal negotiating point. The proposal should summarize the conceptual agreement and, for the first time, specifically provide the client with options for implementation (methodologies)

Jim Webb, CMC, generates seven figures in revenues annually for Kepner-Tregoe, Inc., a forty-year-old firm that specializes in analytical thinking skills and corporate strategy. I worked for this firm for eleven years and learned the consulting business while watching a true genius, Ben Tregoe.

Q. What is your greatest asset?

A. Relationships. I do not believe that an executive will bring in a consultant, especially in the area of business strategy, unless there is a large element of trust.

Q. What would you do differently if you did it over?

A. As a business strategy consultant, I started out with a large blue-chip firm whose economic engine was primarily driven by information technology. Should I have it to do all over again, I would have started out with a consulting firm whose primary focus was strategy consulting.

Q. What is the major achievement you have yet to accomplish?

A. Write a best-selling book and hit the lecture tour.

and the investment each requires. Ideally, each "value package" should have an increased investment so that the buyer can determine just how significant an outcome is desired and how much investment is necessary to achieve it. *This is the first time a buyer should see the fees, and then only attached to the business outcomes as the appropriate investment.*

Implementation and Results. The project can now be implemented using the buyer's preferred option of those you've provided, and the results generated, per the conceptual agreement gained earlier, will serve to reinforce the relationship because you are delivering as promised (or more than promised), reaffirming the trust and collaborative nature of the relationship.

The key to high fees is not to mention fees. When a prospect presses me and says, "Alan, at least give us a range," I reply that it will be between $50,000 and $5 million. The buyer laughs (usually) and I've established a beginning sum in the buyer's mind in that I just might not be kidding at the lower end. But then I make an offer that is never, ever refused: "If you can spend thirty minutes with me to provide some information about outcomes and impact, I can provide a proposal within forty-eight hours by courier. It will have every detail, including timing, logistics, and your investment options. Is that reasonable?"

It's always reasonable, and it launches the discussion into the areas I want to explore.

If the client says, "Every other consultant has used an hourly (or daily) rate, which we find useful to control costs and compare services," then respond, "I hear that from many of my new clients, and this is why I'm so successful. Here are the benefits to you that my single fee provides and which overcome the disadvantages to you of time-based fees." (See the list above.)

THIRTY-EIGHT WAYS TO INCREASE YOUR FEES, BEGINNING TOMORROW

1. Establish Value Collaboratively with the Client.   It's imperative to reach agreement with the buyer as to the real worth to the organization of achieving the business outcomes specified in the objectives. This should be done

A woman in my mentoring program—Joan—presented a case in which she was having difficulty obtaining the level of fees she felt was warranted for her financial sales skills interventions. She agreed to try the value-based approach, and we decided to role play it prior to her next major appointment with a senior vice president at a major bank. I played the buyer.

After very effective relationship building, Joan expertly elicited my objectives, suggested measurement devices from her experience (a nice touch), and successfully extracted from me the worth to the bank of achieving these heightened sales results. But before she could tell me a proposal would be on the way, I asked her point-blank and very assertively, "What will this cost? Surely you have some idea, since I've given you all this information and you've done this before. I'd like to know while you're here."

Joan, caught in the headlights, stammered, "Well, it's probably going to be about $25,000, but we can do it for less if that's a problem."

interactively (not by e-mail or letter) and should result with the buyer literally nodding in agreement as you summarize the quantitative (retention improvement) and qualitative (better teamwork) worth, which you can then reiterate in your proposal.

2. Base Fees on Value, Not on Task. Never base a fee on your doing something. Always base it on the client achieving something. Tasks (surveys) are commodities. Value (market share) is a unique client improvement. Also, never base fees on per head (numbers of people in a workshop or survey) basis, which tends to drive the client to limit participation.

3. Never Use Time as the Basis of Your Value. The toughest obstacle for consultants to overcome is to disregard their time. They tend to believe that the client will abuse their time, or that the time a client demands is time lost elsewhere. In truth, clients don't abuse time if there are clear, delimiting objectives, and the time you would be spending with your feet propped up watching a *Seinfeld* rerun doesn't count. Conversely, you can't feel guilty just because you only had to show up four times to complete a $74,000 project (which has happened to me frequently). You must shake the "time ghost." Your value is in your talent, not in your showing up.

4. *Don't Stop with What the Client Wants. Find Out What the Client Needs.* Every client knows what he or she wants, but few know what they need. Never stop with the buyer's presentation of "the problem." Probe deeper, and find out why that problem is perceived. For example, most clients who

from the TRENCHES

Shayne C. Gad, Ph.D., runs a sole practitioner firm called Gad Consulting Services, specializing in the regulatory aspects of drugs, medical devices, and dietary supplement safety. He's fifty-one and works for about forty clients a year, having "launched" himself in 1994 when his biotech job disappeared. His revenues are a hair shy of half a million annually.

Q. What personal traits were most important in moving from organization man to consultant?

A. Flexibility and dependability. Broad skills and being a quick study. That is as much as I can boil it down.

Q. Would you do anything differently, knowing what you now know?

A. I would have started at a higher hourly rate and would not have wasted money on traditional print advertising (money spent on such would have been better spent if I had taken it as singles and burned them to keep warm in the winter).

Q. What is the major achievement you have yet to accomplish?

A. Just continue to do as I am. I have hit all my goals and targets (OK, it would have been nice if just one more client had paid on time and I had thus earned $500,000 in revenues in one year!)

The CEO of a specialty equipment manufacturer called me in from a referral from a peer. The CEO wanted a good consultant who could evaluate the business acquisition process.

"What we need," he told me in short order, "is a first-rate sales training program that will speed the acquisition process and obtain more new clients."

"Why do you want this?" I asked.

"Because we have 25 percent uncontrolled attrition, and we're bringing in about 25 percent new business, so we're on a treadmill and our profits are flat."

"What on earth in 'uncontrolled attrition'?"

"We lose clients to plant closings, government regulatory changes, and competitive technology that we don't possess."

"I've never heard of that. How do you know? Is that an industry norm?"

"We don't know if it's a norm, but the sales force suspects that it is. In fact, the salespeople took the survey of former clients that produced the uncontrolled attrition focus."

"Let me ask you something. If clients were leaving because of poor service, do you really think the sales force would report that in their survey of attrition causes?"

There was now a long silence. The CEO finally said, "What are you suggesting?"

"I'm suggesting that I conduct a quick study of your former customers to determine whether you just might be throwing good money after bad."

I found, of course, that 90 percent of the attrition was caused by poor service in the former clients' perception, and I could then do no wrong for that client. We fixed the service problem and the sales management problem, never did do any sales training, and I earned over $400,000 for refusing to respond to the client wanting a $50,000 training program that wouldn't have helped.

want training programs really have needs that are only partially addressed (or not addressed at all) by training, which all too often is an easy way of throwing money at the problem instead of actually trying to understand its causes. (See the case study on the previous page.)

5. Think of the Fourth Sale First. Fees Are Cumulative, Not Situational. Don't be greedy. Even on a value basis, the goal is to develop a relationship and implement successful projects that will lead to years of work. View your larger clients strategically, and anticipate how you can be of help over the years on a variety of projects, not just for the present on a single project. Over 80 percent of my business has been repeat business, and most of the rest has been by referral. The cost of acquiring new business from scratch seriously decreases margins.

6. Engage the Client in the Diagnosis. Don't Be Prescriptive. The client perceives much greater value when you and the buyer are jointly diagnosing the issues, instead of you prescribing some off-the-shelf medicine. Internists make much more money than pharmacists because they are so much more valuable in diagnosing illness. And when the patient is involved in the diagnosis and resultant course of treatment, the quality and success of the treatment are greatly enhanced. One simple way to do this quickly: Provide a "process visual" and let the buyer decide where the organization belongs. See Figure 2.3 for an example. Ask the buyer to profile the organization for each factor.[3]

7. Never Voluntarily Offer Options to Reduce Fees. In a frenzied attempt to close business rapidly, many consultants build in automatic fee reductions, based on numbers, multiple assignments, and other factors. The only option I ever recommend is a small discount for the client to pay the entire fee at the time of project acceptance, and that's mainly for two reasons: You have use of your money from the outset, and the client cannot cancel the project.

8. Add a Premium if You Personally "Do It All." Often a contract will have a provision that says the consultant will do everything required, but

---

3. This chart first appeared in the author's book *Making It Work* (Macmillan), later republished as *Best Laid Plans* (Las Brisas Research Press).

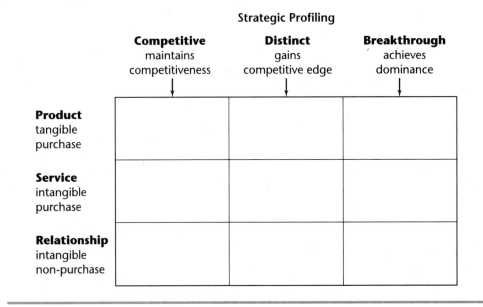

Figure 2.3. Strategic Profiling from the Buyer's Perspective

if subcontractors are used the fee will increase to accommodate the extra expense. Presumably, the extra help will speed the project completion. I do just the opposite. I tell the client that the fee is for the entire project and I'll decide on the subcontracted help as needed. However, if the client wants me to do all of the work in order to keep a single "filter" in place or guarantee a single qualitative source, then there is a 10 percent premium on the fee. In other words, it costs more if I'm the only one to work on the project, not less. I'm the talent, not the subcontractors.

9. If You're Forced to Consider Fee Reduction, Reduce Value First. Sometimes fee reduction is a reasonable request. On those occasions, never reduce the fee without making a commensurate decrease in value. Take out the international part of the study, or remove the post-survey discussions with management, or eliminate the written reports. Sometimes a client will say, "We can't afford to lose that," and will concede the fee, but in any case you don't want to be seen as someone who has a padded fee awaiting reduction.

Avoid early discussions of fees, period. Explain that it is not in the buyer's interests to off-handedly quote fees, or that it's unethical for you to do so. Whatever it takes, focus on value alone until you have conceptual agreement.

10. *Always Provide an Option That Is over the Budget.* Sometime you'll be told the budget, and it's reasonable, so always provide one option that is above the limit. There will still be two or more options within the budget limitation, so you're not risking anything but just may be creating much higher profits. I lost a piece of business to a competitor once who came in over budget but offered far more than the buyer had specified. I didn't have to learn that lesson twice.

11. *As Early as Possible, Ask: "What Are Your Objectives?"* This is the "question guaranteed to result in higher fees" (QGTRIHF). Always begin with objectives, because they focus the buyer on results (not costs) and provide you the opportunity to pursue real needs (not wants). There is nothing easier, or more valuable, than starting the process by stating, "Can we begin with what you'd like to accomplish as a result of this project?"

12. *Broaden Objectives as Appropriate to Increase Value.* If a buyer says, "We need better market share in the Northeast," I always ask, "Wouldn't you want greater market share everywhere?" If the buyer says, "My team needs better delegation skills," I inquire, "What about the skills of their reports in accepting delegation, and the culture of the organization in supporting empowerment?" It's relatively easy to broaden the objectives—and, consequently, raise the fees— by asking a few innocent questions.

13. *Ensure That the Client Is Aware of the Full Range of Your Services.* Prospects will sometimes jump to a conclusion about your "specialty," or they may have been misinformed by a reference source. If you're talking about a customer survey, for example, don't be reluctant to drop into the conversation that "One survey we conducted was immediately before we ran a strategy retreat, which provided contemporary feedback for the strategy process."

14. If Something Is Not on Your Playing Field, Subcontract It.   My rule of thumb is this: If the predominant aspects of the project are not within your competencies, then refer it elsewhere. But if the predominant parts are within your competencies, then subcontract what you can't handle. It's the overall relationship that counts, not individual mastery of every implementation element.

15. Always Ask Yourself, "Why Me, Why Now, Why in this Manner?"   If the buyer has a raft of choices, you're less valuable, but if you're one of the few with the expertise or repute, you're much more valuable; if the client can wait without a problem, that's one thing, but if the window of opportunity is closing, that's quite another; if the client can do this internally, that's easy, but if an external consultant is mandatory, that's different. By asking these questions you'll know your intrinsic value in setting the appropriate fee.

16. Use Proposals as Confirmations, Not as Explorations.   Don't submit a proposal until you have conceptual agreement on objectives, measures of success, and value to the organization. Otherwise, the proposal becomes a negotiating document, and the options you have listed will be the point of departure to negotiate downward. I hit over 80 percent of my proposals, but I send out far fewer than most consultants because of my method of using them.

17. When Asked Prematurely About Fees, Reply, "I Don't Know."   Don't be cornered. Simply tell the buyer that you can't quote a fee until you have more information—in fact, it would be unfair to the prospect to do so—but you can have the options ready within twenty-four hours. When consultants allow themselves to be forced into fee quotes prematurely, they almost always quote too low a fee, and the prospect expects to negotiate down from there.

18. If You Must Lower Fees, Seek a Quid Pro Quo from the Buyer.   In the real world, you'll sometimes want a piece of business and will accept a lower fee to get it. Even then, suggest an accommodation wherein the client guarantees to provide referrals, or videotapes one of your presentations for your use, or provides products and services for free or at cost, or places you in front of a related trade association. There is usually some barter that is attractive to both parties.

19. *Don't Accept Troublesome, Unpleasant, or Ugly Business.* A prospect who is unethical, ornery, nasty, or otherwise unfriendly won't magically metamorphose as a client. Bad prospects are bad clients, and the only thing worse than no business is bad business. No matter what the fee, these clients will cost you more than you keep.

20. *When Collaborating, Use Objective Apportionment.* You may divide the client business into acquisition, methodology used, and delivery, for example. That means that if I sell the client, my technology is used, but you deliver, I get two-thirds and you get one-third. Use whatever formula you like (some people feel the acquisition aspect deserves more weight), but use something that clear and objective too so that the ground rules are clear for revenue sharing.

21. *Any Highly Paid Employee Must Bring in New Business.* Whether on salary, bonus, and/or commission, high pay is justified for new business acquisition. Delivery, research, and support are commodities for which you should subcontract. In fact, it's a buyer's market, since those abilities are in huge supply. Don't pay people for delivering your business acquisition unless it's on a pay-for-performance basis.

22. *Seek Out New Economic Buyers Laterally During Your Projects.* This is part of the "springboard" from Chapter 1. The time to market is always the current time, so be on the lookout for opportunity as you are implementing. This is neither unethical nor illegal. It's simply smart business.

23. *It Is Better to Do Something* Pro Bono *than to Do It for a Low Fee.* Don't ever be pegged as a low-priced option. If there's something you're dying to do, or a cause you feel more than merits your attention, than do it for free as part of your pro bono work. Don't allow yourself to be pegged as a "cheap resource."

Rule of Thumb: NEVER do pro bono work for a profit-making entity.

Tom was a member of my mentoring program for six months in 1998. He had a staff of six, two administrative people and four professionals. He was the sole rainmaker. His firm was generating in excess of $600,000 in revenues, of which Tom was keeping about $90,000 after all was said and done. The staff performed "research" when not delivering, and they weren't delivering unless Tom was selling to fill the pipeline.

Tom was overweight, smoked heavily, and traveled about 70 percent of the time. His staff was demanding more benefits, and he was considering giving the professionals a piece of the business to keep them happy.

My advice was to fire everyone and use strictly subcontractors. Tom felt an obligation to his staff, and I felt the obligation actually went the other way. He had spoiled them all and created a group of demanding whiners. Tom promised to consider my advice seriously in another year, once he "dug himself out of the current hole" he perceived.

About six months after Tom left the program, I learned that he had suffered a fatal heart attack while working late one night. He was forty-six.

---

24. Fees Have Nothing to Do with Supply and Demand, Only with Value. Don't listen to the "experts" who tell you that you can raise fees when demand exceeds supply, which is a formula to work harder, not smarter. My ideal year is one in which I work for ten minutes for a client who is ecstatic and pays me $5 million. (My wife says that if I can work for ten minutes I can work for twenty minutes.) Raise fees when the value you provide justifies it.

25. If You Are Unaware of Current Market Fee Ranges, You Are Undercharging. When you network and talk casually to clients, try to find out what the general ranges are for a variety of projects. This kind of market intelligence will help you implement your strategy, whether you choose to be the Cadillac of the market or the Taurus. Just don't choose to be the Yugo.

26. Psychologically, Higher Fees Create Higher Value in the Buyer's Perception. I call this one "The Mercedes-Benz Syndrome." Buyers believe they get what they pay for, which is why McKinsey, IBM, Rolex, and Ferrari don't enter into price negotiations. No one says, "This is the cheapest consultant I could find, and I'm proud to have him!" Instead they say, "This person is costing us a fortune, and we were lucky to get her, so listen up!"

27. Value Can Include Subjective as well as Objective Measures. When an executive says to me that a given result would be "priceless" or "invaluable," I move on. That's good enough. A high-level buyer's relief from stress, anxiety, unpleasant situations, a poor image, safety concerns, and similar pressures is worth a great deal. Go with that.

28. Introduce New Value to Existing Clients to Raise Fees in These Accounts. Suggest that a client consider using the traditional customer and employee surveys as a device to get customers together with employees who never otherwise see them to create a greater sense of accountability. Offer to combine the annual performance evaluation process directly with the periodic succession planning system. Don't simply sit back and do the same thing every year.

RULE 10

Setting fees successfully at high levels is about your self-esteem in justifying and articulating the value you are providing for the client. The good news is that you control this. The bad news is that you control this.

---

29. Do Not Accept Referral Business on the Same Basis as the Referring Source Does. A colleague might refer business to you in a client system in which the colleague is paid by the hour or day. Don't accept the same terms. Immediately educate the buyer that you and your colleague work differently and that your arrangements will be somewhat different. This will protect your fee ranges, avoid refusing the work, and prevent you from being branded as a per diem consultant.

30. When Forced into Phases, Offer Partial Rebates to Guarantee Future Business. When the client insists on a phased approach to a complex project (for example, needs analysis, design, pilot, implementation, monitoring, and so on) that the client won't buy into all at once, then offer a rebate from the fee for the prior phase on the succeeding one if the buyer commits before the prior phase is completed. This tends to dissuade buyers from looking for alternatives at every new phase, using your work from the prior phase.

31. At Least Every Two Years, Consider Jettisoning the Bottom 15 Percent of Business. All of us are burdened by business that made sense at one time but not now, business that is accustomed to too much service for too little money, and business that is comfortable but unchallenging. We can't reach out unless we let go, and we must let go of non-productive, low-potential business. I've seen large firms dragged down by these anchors. Refer the business to someone who will appreciate it and handle it even better than you.

32. Start with Payment Terms Maximally Beneficial to You Every Time. For example, explain that your policy is full fee in advance. If the client finds that unacceptable, then offer 50 percent on acceptance and 50 percent in forty-five days (no matter what the length of the project). But if you start with nothing down and gradual payments, I can guarantee that you'll wind up searching for your fees well after the project is over, which means you've received much less money than someone else getting the same fee paid in advance. Beneficial terms to you equal higher profits.

33. Offer Incentives for One-Time, Full Payments. You never know until you ask. By offering a modest (5 to 10 percent) discount for payment on acceptance, you just may put a six-figure check in the bank tomorrow. *Note:* Some organizations have rules in their accounts payable departments that any accepted proposal or contract that offers a discount mechanism must be accepted with the discount.

Because we can never be sure of our successes until we understand their causes, I decided one year to ask my largest single buyer in my largest single account—Merck—why he always paid in advance for projects that were in excess of $200,000.

"I'll bet you think it's because of your discount," he smiled.

"Well, yes," I stammered.

"It's not," he explained. "It's that by paying you in advance, I can't have my project cancelled, no matter what."

I had ignored my own advice about the buyer's best interests. Company upheavals and poor results couldn't endanger his own plans and success because he had already paid me! I had a legitimate customer benefit that I hadn't realized. I now work that into all implementation discussions!

---

34. Never Accept Payment Subject to Conditions to Be Met upon Completion. Conditions change. Buyers get hit by beer trucks. The project is never quite "finished." If you allow yourself to fall into this trap, you deserve what you get (or what you don't get). You don't buy an oven with the agreement that you'll finish paying after it has cooked its last meal. Don't allow yourself to be fried in this dilemma.

35. Focus on Improvement, Not on Problem Solving. Everyone can solve problems, and problem solving is a commodity. But few people can systematically "raise the bar" and improve performance of already stellar operations. Yet that's where the value is. It's a question of the all-stars improving still further. Orient yourself to innovation, not problem solving, and the worth of your project will be commensurately higher. See Figure 2.4.

36. Provide Proactive Ideas, Bench Marking, Best Practices from Experience. Don't become "industry bound." Demonstrate value to the buyer by bringing to bear experiences in other industries and in other conditions that can con-

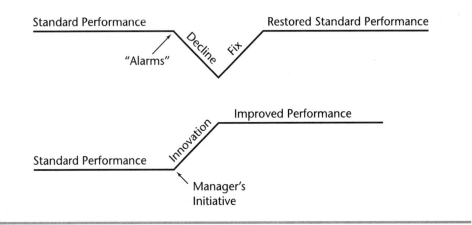

Figure 2.4. Problem Solving vs. Innovation

tribute to improving the current client's condition. Allow your "weaknesses" to actually be your strengths.

37. Practice Stating and Explaining Your Fees. Remember my "student" trying to state fees in the mirror. You have to be confident when they do come up for discussion. Practice your responses so that you're neither sweating profusely nor losing eye contact.

38. Always Be Prepared to Walk Away from Business. Few devices will raise fees as much as this one. Never be anxious. If you're at an impasse, simply say, "I've enjoyed meeting with you, but I don't think I can undertake the project given what you're offering. Let's stay in touch." Often, you'll be stopped before you're even out of your chair. But just as the client can say "no," so can you. Don't be afraid to reject business until it's in a form that's most advantageous for you.

One Last Time: Here's a bonus, the ironclad rule about how to raise fees. If you want to raise fees, then raise your fees.

THE ULTIMATE RULES

Rule #6.   Everything is about value, not about fees. If the discussion is about fees, then you've lost control of the discussion.

Rule #7.   The best response to the premature question, "How much will this cost?" is "I don't know." The best response to the follow-up question, "When will you know?" is "If you can provide me with the information I need, I can have all the details, including investment options, to you tomorrow. Is that agreeable?"

Rule #8.   Collaborating with the buyer to establish project outcomes, measures of success, and *value* to the organization will result in higher fees than any other approach to billing, hours, services, or support that you've ever employed.

Rule #9.   Avoid early discussions of fees, period. Explain that it is not in the buyer's interests to off-handedly quote fees, or that it's unethical for you to do so. Whatever it takes, focus on value alone until you have conceptual agreement.

Rule #10.   Setting fees successfully at high levels is about your self-esteem in justifying and articulating the value you are providing for the client. The good news is that you control this. The bad news is that you control this.

Steve Grove in the principal at S. Grove and Associates, LLC, founded in 1991. Today they have twenty-four employees in three offices providing accounting and consulting assistance to a wide variety of businesses, generating fees in the low seven figures.

Q. What's your key success factor?

A. My key factor to success in my mind is honesty. The word "honesty" covers a broad range in business, but I feel it is essential to work with people in the most up-front and honest way that you can. I know that the truth is not always the nicest part of any situation, but it gives you a good place to start. It can be as simple as bidding on a job and being honest about your costs and your need to make a profit—and the customer not caring about our costs or profits. It can go deeper into the truth about a particular organization that may need to sell or close down. I grew up as a scout, I am an eagle scout and remain involved. As corny as it may sound, I try to follow those practices and principals in my daily life. Holding your honor to truth and honesty makes you an attractive commodity to some. I also believe that you need to deal with employees in the same way. They may not like the truth, but at least they know it. I know that employees always say they want to know everything; then they typically complain about perceptions that they don't agree with. However, I do believe it's a good way to start.

Q. What, if anything, would you do differently if you could?

A. If I had to do things differently, I would examine my pricing structure much more carefully. I would also screen my clients much better back at the start, as I am now. Knowing where to say "Yes" and "No" are important parts of business, and I wish I'd had the experience nine years ago to understand that. I have put myself through a lot of problems that I didn't have to have. Stringing clients along and allowing them to hurt you financially is never good anywhere. I would be much more careful in my hiring practices and confront the employee issues much sooner and more quickly, Consultants tend to move emotionally due to the changing nature of their business. We tend to want to believe that things will just take care of themselves and that people will be good and share our goals, but this isn't true. You need to be your best advocate, and that takes careful time and thought.

Q. What have you yet to achieve?

A. The one major achievement I have yet to accomplish is to see my organization grow into a self-sustaining one where the other leaders are able to act and react in the way that I would. As we have grown through the years, the complicated issues have grown. To be able to walk away from a business for a bit of time and rely on the management and staff to run and keep things going is a major issue for me. I see that we are growing toward this point and soon may be there.

CHAPTER 3

Marketing and Publicity

Creating Gravitational Pull

The point of no return for success in this business is about three years. At that point, most of us have run out of our original contacts, friends, and family and are now relying on acquiring new business based on the quality of our work and the effectiveness of our marketing. A great many people and firms are "three-year wonders," which abruptly collapse when the key, single account they are relying on disappears or the magical buyer "from the old days" finally retires.

Successful consultants over the longer haul are engaged in one of two types of marketing:

1. They have implemented both active and passive marketing techniques that suit them and their practices very well and that they continue to evolve consciously.
2. They have unwittingly and accidentally stumbled upon effective marketing techniques that they don't appreciate and that can evanesce at any time.

Some consultants tell me that "I'm a consultant, not a marketer." To which I reply, "You are a marketer, just a lousy one."

Marketing is the active promoting and publicizing of why the buyer needs and requires your particular products and services.

Marketing is the creation of need. *Selling*, on the other hand, is the demonstration that your alternative meets that need. However, effective marketing can create a need for you and your expertise. In that case, the marketing effectiveness co-opts the need to sell. When a buyer says, "Alan, we've heard great things about you and read some of your books, and you're the person we need," I no longer have to sell myself or my approaches.

RULE 11

Outstanding marketing will also create the beginnings of a relationship and embrace the sale itself. That's why intelligent, constant marketing is the secret to long-term success in consulting.

There are three questions you need to answer every year or so, because your practice inevitably changes with greater exposure, more learning, varying clients, and new passions:

1. What is the added value I currently bring to clients? How does my firm improve the client's condition?
2. Who, specifically, is likely to pay for that value? Who are my true economic buyers?
3. How do I reach them? Where to they spend time, to whom do they listen, what do they read, how are they influenced?

Once you know the answers to these three questions, you can continually organize and evolve your marketing plans. And those plans should be both strategic and tactical.

- Creating a "brand" identity: a logo or catch phrase that reminds buyers that you are the source for a particular need, for example, "The Performance Pros."
- Creating a "presence" in the public mind: attaching your name to an annual conference or event.
- Maintaining ongoing communications and information flow through a newsletter, magazine, or other periodic contact.
- Establishing credibility and visibility through the use of the media: articles, interviews, columns, and so forth.
- Creating an expertise "vehicle" in the form of a cassette, video, or product.

Some Tactical Uses and Alternatives

- Creating a website that allow for visitor interaction in the form of purchases, enrollments, requests, chat rooms, and so on.
- Circulating a product catalog regularly to a growing mail database.
- Appearing as a speaker at trade conventions, management meetings, symposia, or other public forums.
- Creating new press kits and brochures periodically to give potential and past buyers new "looks" at your services.
- Doing a radio or print interview specifically to promote a seminar, workshop, consulting approach, or product.

CREATING A STRONG GRAVITATIONAL FIELD

When I discuss effective marketing with veteran consultants, they often reply, "Oh, I've done that already." Newer consultants tend to say, "I've done that, but what else should I do?" The point is that when you're doing something right, *keep doing it.* You may evolve your approaches and move from some techniques to others, but effective marketing is about perseverance and continuity.

Consequently, I've created a "gravitational field" theory, which I've found provides a diverse array of options to successful people. You can determine what you're already doing well, what you're doing but could be doing better, and what you're not doing at all and should consider starting. My advice is to always make sure you're engaged in two activities that may be outside of your comfort zone. If you don't care for public speaking, give it a try, because it is probably a marketing avenue that has great potential and that you haven't exploited. If you are discomforted by having a "product," then grin and bear it and create just one to see what happens.

At this stage in my career, I'm engaged in every single aspect of the gravitational field. It's like a well-diversified stock portfolio: When some areas are down (not bringing in much business), others are soaring (attracting a great deal of business). I've chosen the particular elements that appear in the gravitational field because, over twenty-eight years in this business, I've found them to be the most powerful in terms of cost-effectiveness and credibility.[1]

The elements, shown in Figure 3.1, are not in any particular order. Their attractiveness, import, and effectiveness will vary for each of us based on the nature of our practices, our own strengths and preferences, and the nature of our clientele. Nevertheless, I've found that all of them can be applicable to virtually any practice, depending on your own initiative and energy.

So, herein are the formulas for sophisticated marketing and creating one's own perpetual "gravity" that attracts business to you, moving clockwise around the chart. You'll appreciate in quick order how much they interrelate and support each other, creating a powerful synergy, which is why you're well-advised to engage in as many as possible.

PRO BONO WORK

Pro bono work for marketing purposes should have the following characteristics:

- A cause or objective in which you believe and wish to support
- Relatively high-profile non-profit or charity
- Public events and media coverage

---

1. Let me point out here, for firm principals or partners, that your people should feel as if they own their part of the business, and that they should aggressively pursue many of these components. This is not a question of "waiting for corporate" to provide marketing. Every consultant should be engaged in marketing. If they can't or won't do this, you may have the wrong people.

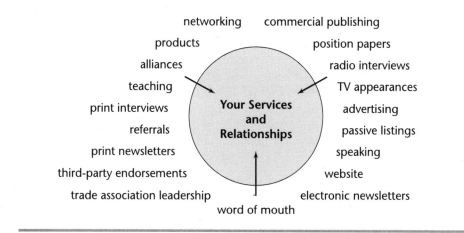

Figure 3.1. The Marketing Gravitational Field

- Significant potential buyers or influencers are volunteers and/or key figures (for example, the editor of the local newspaper, the general manager of the electric company, the senior vice president of a major bank)
- Involvement will be interactive, not individual

Seek out a leadership position or fill a difficult position in the organization. Typically, someone to do fund raising, manage volunteers, and handle publicity is vitally needed and these jobs are tough to do well. You want a high-visibility position, one in which you can rub elbows with your potential buyers and influencers. Take on the dirty, difficult, and desultory jobs, but do them extremely well. Make reports at the meetings, give interviews to the media, and shower credit on your colleagues.

When the time is right, suggest to the executive you've worked alongside or the publisher you've supported that it might make sense to have lunch some time and compare notes about your two organizations. Pro bono work like this automatically builds relationships and allows others to see your abilities on neutral turf. That's why you should do the tough jobs and do them well. Excellent organizational ability, strategies, management of others, fiscal prudence, and similar traits translate well into the needs of your pro bono colleagues.

Pro bono work is especially powerful for those living in fairly major markets and who wish to reduce their travel and work closer to home. I've done work for everyone from the League of Women Voters to a shelter for battered women to local theater groups.

Rule of Thumb: You should be engaged in at least one pro bono activity each quarter.

RULE 12

THE most powerful single aspect of market credibility is a commercially published book. I was aghast when I found that the people calling me in to help with strategy had acquired my strategy book but not read it, but I got over that when their check arrived.

COMMERCIAL PUBLISHING

There is no stronger credibility statement than a commercially published book, period.[2] For successful consultants endeavoring to reach the next level, this may be the shortest route.

Early in my career, I published books that addressed the issues I wanted to be hired to consult about: innovation, behavior and motivation, strategy. Later in my career, I published books that capitalized on my established expertise: marketing, consulting, speaking professionally. An entirely new career was launched for me when I published *Million Dollar Consulting,*[3] which established me as a "consultant to consultants."

---

2. Self-published books serve many objectives, including passive income streams, but they are not credible in terms of establishing repute.

3. McGraw-Hill, 1992, revised and re-released in 1998.

Rick Betterley runs Betterley Risk Consultants, Inc., risk management consultants, based in Sterling, MA. His revenues nearly doubled between 1997 and 1999.

Q. What is the single key factor in your success?

A. Ability to change the focus of my practice as the client market needs changed.

Q. What would you do differently if you did it over?

A. Nothing.

Q. What is the major achievement you have yet to accomplish?

A. Making our subscription-based publication a real business (as a strong second revenue leg and an equity builder).

What part of your existing practice would you like to propel forward, or what new aspect would you like to create?

Writing a business book is not like writing a novel. You need a topic, ten or twelve chapters, and a half dozen key points supported by facts, stories, and anecdotes in each chapter. If you don't believe me, pull any ten random business books off the shelf and take a look. Create a treatment for the book, which should take about a week or two, and get it off to an agent or a publisher.[4]

---

4. For an excellent book on how to get published, see *Write the Perfect Book Proposal: 10 Proposals That Sold and Why* by Jeff Herman, Deborah M. Adams (John Wiley & Sons, 1993). In the interest of full disclosure, Jeff Herman has been my agent on several books. For an example of the components of a treatment, see Appendix B in this book.

Another aspect of commercial publishing involves articles and interviews in the popular and trade press. You should be circulating article query letters and manuscripts regularly. Get used to the rejection; it happens to all of us. Successful consultants in particular, with a raft of client experiences and case studies, should be able to create powerful, vivid pieces that, in turn, will draw interested readers to want to know more.

Try to include offers in your articles of research studies, visits to your website, faxed responses to questions, and so on, enabling readers to continue to connect with you in more and more personal ways.

Whether you enjoy writing or dread the thought of it, you are lax if, at this point in your career, you are not publishing on a regular basis.

Rule of Thumb: You should be publishing one article per quarter, meaning you should be proposing four articles per quarter in different publications. (Set a goal: Create a book treatment in the next ninety days and send it to a publisher or agent.)

POSITION PAPERS

I often refer to these as "white papers." These are powerful tools that can be used for the following purposes:

- Content in your press kit
- The basis for articles to be published
- The basis for booklets
- Web page content
- Handouts at speeches
- Giveaways for inquiries

Position papers are two-to-six-page discussions of your philosophy, beliefs, findings, experiences, and/or approaches. They *are not and should never be* self-promotional. Instead, they should provide credibility through the impact of their ideas and the applicability of their techniques.

Try to provide as many pragmatic and immediately useful ideas as possible. The best position papers are applicable, not esoteric. The reader should

Persistence is as important as talent in publishing. Many editors gleefully accept what another has scornfully rejected. Sometimes it's a matter of whether the editor hit traffic that morning, had a fight with a spouse, or is in desperate need of something to fill a hole in the publication. When I questioned one editor who had accepted one of my book proposals and already paid the advance what she advised about a tricky part of the chapter I had submitted, she aloofly told me that she hadn't actually read it, but she had bought "the concept."

In other words, she needed a book on the subject, and mine had come along at the right time. So much for quality control.

My best seller, *Million Dollar Consulting,* was rejected fifteen times when it had the working title *Confessions of a Consultant.* One day I got a call in my car from my agent, who was sitting across the desk from the senior editor at McGraw-Hill.

"Alan, I'm sitting here with a possible deal," he said calmly.

"Jeff, you mean they like the book?!" I exclaimed.

"No, they hate it, just like all the others."

"Are you calling to torture me?"

"They hate the book, but they love how you've built your practice. They want to know if you can write a book about growing a practice."

"Of course. In about three days, actually."

Jeff was momentarily off the line. When he returned, he said, "OK, we've got a deal. I told them six months if they're lucky and we can get the papers signed this week."

Never worry about rejection. Some day I will get some publisher to take on *Confessions of a Consultant*!

come away from them saying, "I'd like to apply this, and I'd like to hear more from the author."

Position papers are one of the absolutely most economical, high-impact, and versatile aspects of the gravitational field. Right now, you probably have sufficient experience and ideas to create several dozen. Create some short ones that are "plain vanilla" and straightforward and some longer ones with graphs and charts.

Rule of Thumb: One white paper every month.

RULE 13

The broadcast media are there to be used. There is a huge "expert vacuum" created by a plethora of talk shows, news shows, and commentary programs. If you can't get on one, you're simply not trying.

RADIO AND TELEVISION INTERVIEWS

You should be doing radio and even television appearances at this point in your career. They are relatively easy to do, as there is a constant need for fresh voices and faces to provide expert commentary on issues ranging from management fads to business etiquette to how to retain key talent.

Sources for publicizing your availability for interviews are listed in Appendix C. These publications charge a fee for listings, ranging from bimonthly ads (very helpful in you're promoting a book, for example) to annual, full-page descriptions in books sent to every assignment editor, talk show host, talk show producer, reporter for major media sources, and related others in the country. Some also duplicate the listings online.

As with the entire gravitational field, don't evaluate media interviews in terms of number of "hits" or new business. Regard them strategically as an ongoing part of your major thrust to create recognition and higher levels of credibility. Some radio appearances are worthless in terms of short-term business, but you never know who will hear you and pass your name on, or what other media professional might then invite you to a more appropriate setting.

Radio interviews, with rare exceptions (for example, National Public Radio and some major syndicated shows), are all done from your home over the telephone. Television shots are done in the nearest local affiliate. For a memorable interview (most TV shots are only five to eight minutes, while some radio interviews can last for an hour), follow these rules:

1. Provide the interviewer and/or segment producer with detailed background about you, including pronunciation of your name, and key "talking points" or questions to ask.
2. Research the topic so that you can quote a few dramatic statistics and anecdotes. The media love pithy sound bites. In fact, practice short responses to all questions so that more questions can be accommodated.
3. *Always* have two or three points in mind that promote you that you can work into responses, no matter what the question. Do not rely on the host to promote you, no matter what the promises. For example: If the question is, "Alan, what's your opinion of large-scale downsizing and its impact on our society?" answer this way: "One of the reasons I'm asked to work with executives from top-performing organizations is that they want me to help them *retain* key talent, not throw it away. So let me answer from their perspective. . . ." If you've written a book, then say, "As I point out in Chapter Four of my newest book, *Good Enough Isn't Enough, . . .*"
4. Obtain a tape. Usually, asking the station in advance will do it, but always back it up with another taken from the actual airing by a friend. Splice these tapes together for a "highlights" reel of your media work, which will sell more sophisticated media outlets and just might get you on national TV. Such a tape is also quite impressive with prospects.

Radio and television work requires a promotional investment for ads and listing, but it's well worth it when you've reached the stage where your experience and accomplishments make you an "authority."

Rule of Thumb: Appear in a minimum of one major listing source with at least a half-page ad annually.

Cher Holton, Ph.D., CMC, CSP, is co-founder and president of The Holton Consulting Group, Inc., of Raleigh, NC, which works on the "human side of quality."

Q. What is the single key factor in your success?

A. This is tough. It's so difficult to separate one specific thing as the key factor. I'd say persistence, ability to listen to clients and be responsive, and luck. Being focused, and loving the area I specialize in would be up there, too—along with staying on the cutting edge in terms of my expertise area. And I can't leave out the ability to build strong relationships and get referrals. Finally, my prior experience in the corporate world was invaluable for my perspective.

Q. What would you do differently if you did it over?

A. I would network with consultants much more successfully than I did, much earlier in my career! I would also start out with a much better system for charging clients on a value basis rather than a daily rate. (Luckily, I never got hooked into an hourly fee—daily was bad enough!) I'd also do a better job of follow-up. I lost a lot of potential business, I'm sure, because of my inconsistent follow-up. (And I'd start publishing a lot sooner.)

Q. What is the major achievement you have yet to accomplish?

A. Write the best-selling book on team relationship development—and become the consultant of choice for Fortune 100 companies when new teams need that jump-start. (And win a world championship as an amateur dance couple with my husband, Bill!)

ADVERTISING AND PASSIVE LISTINGS

"Passive listings" are those that appear in certain "buyer's guides," trade association resource lists, and similar literature. They are relatively inexpensive and can be surprisingly effective (and startling in terms of calls coming out of the blue). For consultants who want to stay "in the neighborhood," the local phone book's business section is a viable tool, because some people actually look under "management consultant" or "business consultant" for sources.

Here are some trade associations that produce listings that appeal to the human resources and training communities and produce leads throughout the year:

- American Society for Training and Development
  1640 Kind Street, Alexandria, VA 22314
  703/683-8100

Probably a "must" for those focusing on training and related human resource issues. Publishes *Training & Development*, a monthly magazine. Hosts national events and local chapter meetings. Produces a buyer's guide.

- Society for Human Resource Management
  1800 Duke Street, Alexandria, VA 22314
  703/548-3440

The society provides extensive benefits and offers and publishes the monthly *HRMagazine*. Hosts national events and local chapter meetings. Produces a buyer's guide.

- Training Magazine
  50 South Ninth Street
  Minneapolis, MN 55402
  612/333-0471

The best publication in the training field, with controversial articles and critical reviews. Accepts freelance submissions (no payment) and ads. Produces a buyer's guide.

Rule of Thumb: Find the three or four listings that best reach your highest potential buyers and invest in a major presence annually.

SPEAKING ENGAGEMENTS

Early in people's consulting careers, I advocate that they speak wherever and whenever they can to improve credibility and visibility. However, for the experienced consultant, professional speaking is not only a key gravitational pull but is also extremely lucrative.

CASE STUDY

For four years I had paid $125 for a modest six-inch listing of my services in the Buyer's Guide of the American Society for Training and Development. No one ever called or wrote.

One day, I received a call from a mid-level manager at the American Institute of Architects in Washington, DC. She said that they were seeking consulting firms to help with a reorganization of their structure and membership services and asked if I'd care to send materials.

I said yes, but indicated that I'd like to meet the buyer. She told me that qualified candidates would meet with a screening committee, and that body would determine who would meet the decision maker. In this case, the potential was sufficient for me to meet with the "gatekeepers." I was chosen for the committee review, along with five much larger firms; made my presentation; and was chosen to meet the buyer.

The result was a $156,000 contract and a project that had a major influence on the future of that organization.

I've never had another serious inquiry from the ASTD listing, but I'm there every year (except now my investment is $500 for a fancier placement with my logo). You never know where the next high-potential lead will come from, and I want to ensure that my "gravitational field" is at full strength at all times.

Most consultants are lousy speakers because they become wrapped up in their methodology and the content of their message. But the fact is that audiences need to be captivated and even entertained a bit if they are to accept any message more easily and readily.

Moreover, the keynote spot at major conferences or in-house company meetings provides a terrific platform for hundreds (and sometimes thousands) of potential buyers and recommenders to establish the beginnings of a relationship with you at one time. This isn't the place to go into the details of developing a professional speaking career, but we can examine a few of the needs and benefits because the synergy with consulting is so powerful.[5]

1. As a keynote speaker or concurrent session speaker, you should continually cite your experience and other organizations with which you've worked, so that the audience can think about how you might be helpful to them. *Always make it clear that you are a consultant who happens to speak at such meetings, and not a speaker who also consults.*
2. Provide handouts with your company's name and full contact information.
3. Obtain a participant list of everyone in your session.
4. Come early and stay late, so that you can network with the organizers, senior management, participants, exhibitors, and others.
5. Charge a high fee for your speaking, just as you would for your consulting. I suggest a three-part fee of increasing amounts for keynotes, half-days, and full-days.

I used to speak for free as a method to publicize what I do. Then I realized that not only were others being paid, but that the speakers doing the most important spots were always the highest paid. Today, it's not unusual for a client to say, "I'd like you to address our annual meeting; then let's explore how you can work with us to implement the theme."

Here is an excellent resource if you want to find out which associations are holding meetings, who the executive director is, what the themes will be, who will be in the audience, and what the budget is (can you ask for anything more?!).

---

5. For those interested in pursuing speaking as a professional strategy, see the author's book *Money Talks: How to Make a Million as a Speaker* (McGraw-Hill, 1998).

- National Trade and Professional Associations of the United States
  Columbia Books, Inc.
  1212 Washington Avenue, Suite 330, Washington, DC 20005
  202/898–0662

Rule of Thumb: You ought to be speaking at least once a month in front of groups that include potential buyers.

RULE **14**

It's great to be smart, but it's equally important to persevere. By exerting as great a gravitational pull as your resources and talents permit, you'll ensure leads from the widest possible sources, some of which will be surprising. I'm constantly amazed at how stupid I was two weeks ago.

WEBSITES AND ELECTRONIC NEWSLETTERS

At this stage, your website should be state-of-the-art from a marketing standpoint, not necessarily a technical one. It's not the bells and whistles that matter, but the "draw" and appeal for potential customers. More and more I find I'm telling prospects to "Be sure to visit my website," only to hear "That's where I just came from."[6]

---

6. Many consultants are under the misconception that a website replaces a brochure or press kit. You need them both. Printed matter is more easily passed around and shared. Many people like the kinesthetics of print material. And there are those for whom access to the web is not convenient, not possible, or unappealing. You need sophistication in both areas.

A high-powered website should follow these tenets:

- Sufficient search engine presence using appropriate generic and specific key words to drive people to the site
- A user-friendly initial page, with immediate appeal and options for the visitor
- Easy navigation and no "traps" that force visitors to hear more about your methodology than they'd ever need to hear
- Immediate value, in the form of articles to download, links to related, high-quality sites, tools and techniques, and so forth
- An opportunity to contact you easily at any time
- Products to purchase (preferably your own)
- A compelling reason to return and to tell others about the site

By posting an article each month (still more utility provided by the position papers discussed earlier), new lists of techniques, and other value-added additions, you create a site *useful to the visitor.* No one hops in their car to read highway billboards, and no one is interested in visiting sites to hear people talk about themselves. Develop and upgrade your site with the potential buyer in mind. (And visit the sites of your colleagues and competitors to understand what they do well and how you can do even better.)

Electronic newsletters are wonderful means by which to reach more and more buyers, because readers routinely pass excellent newsletters along to colleagues as a favor. Start with your current database, create a sign-up spot on your website, and offer the newsletter in your signature file on your e-mail.

An excellent electronic newsletter should do the following:

1. Be brief—on average, no longer than a single screen.
2. Be non-promotional and simply carry your contact information at the bottom.
3. Enable people to subscribe and unsubscribe easily (which is also required by law).
4. Contain high-value content that is immediately applicable for most readers.

5. Go out at least monthly, and on the same day. Consistency and constancy are everything.
6. Be copyrighted.

One of the people in my mentoring program began with a modest list and soon had thousands of subscribers to his sales-skills newsletter, which addressed "sales acceleration." He closed a piece of business with a bank in Toronto that he never would have even spoken to without someone in the bank finding the newsletter and realizing that their loan officers needed this particular kind of sales help.

Commercial list servers can automatically deliver the newsletter and add and delete subscribers for less than $50 per month.

Rule of Thumb: You should have a newsletter of some kind, either a monthly electronic one or at least a quarterly print version.

WORD OF MOUTH, REFERRALS, AND THIRD-PARTY ENDORSEMENTS

All of us need to keep fueling the "buzz" that surrounds our names and our approaches. I've found that consultants become blasé about endorsements and testimonials after a while, but they are our stock-in-trade.

In every single engagement, ask the client for a referral, a blurb for a product you're creating, to serve as a reference, and or to provide a testimonial letter (which is simply a "choice of yeses"). If you don't ask, they generally don't happen.

Write letters to magazines and newspapers that rely on your credibility for the point you make, pro or con, relative to a recent article. Stand up at business, social, civic, and professional meetings to make your point. Take controversial and "contrarian" stands if you must.

Once you have an established reputation, it's far easier to maintain the momentum of word of mouth, which is a powerful lead source. But we often don't bother any longer, which is ironic when it's now easier than ever. And this leads into other parts of the gravitation field. It's likely, for example, that some of your high-level buyers can place you in front of the trade associations to which they belong as a featured speaker at the next convention or meeting. Are you pursuing these connections?

Rule of Thumb: Your current, active clients should be providing a minimum of one testimonial and three highly qualified referrals every single month.

TRADE ASSOCIATION LEADERSHIP

At this point in your career, when you may feel that you're not getting anything out of professional associations and trade associations (and justifiably so, because most member will be at a lower level) it's time not to abandon them but to use them differently. It's time to take a leadership position.

In the first place, the association and its membership can use your expertise and experience. In the second, it's a good way to "pay back" the profession that has been so kind to us. But, third, the visibility will be a tremendous source of gravity.

You don't have to take on time-consuming national duties. You can simply serve as an officer at the local or chapter level, head a committee, organize an event, or sponsor an initiative. Whatever it is, your status within the industry will be enriched. I find that many of my referrals come from other consultants who feel they can't handle the assignment and hope that I will either reciprocate some time or involve them in the project, both of which I'm quite happy to do.

Because very few capable people ever seek these offices, it's almost guaranteed that you can be as responsible and as visible as you choose.

Rule of Thumb: You should at minimum belong to the Institute of Management Consultants and be known to your local membership, presenting a session at least once a year at a scheduled meeting.

CLASSROOM TEACHING

You will establish an entirely new circle of references and contacts through teaching part-time at a university, college, or extension program. And you're now in a position to do so with a minimum of difficulty.

You can claim the title of "adjunct professor" in most cases and arrange to teach an evening a week. Or you can work through an organization such as the Institute of Management Studies, which provides day-long sessions around the country through local chairpeople. (It's located in Reno and San Francisco).

The ideal is to teach at the graduate level, where you will be challenged by students and receive a diversity of opinion that you might not in business life.

These positions add immeasurably to your ability to become published, gain credibility at higher and higher levels, and receive references from the university (and, in some cases, from the students).

You can almost always find a junior college or trade college to start out if you're uncertain and want to test the waters easily. For seven years I was on the extension faculty at Case Western Reserve University in Cleveland and received several pieces of business as a result.

Rule of Thumb: At least teach as a guest lecturer three of four times a year at local institutions or by contract at national sites.

RULE 15

When you are more successful than you've ever been, new doors open that were stuck closed before. Don't be afraid to give them a kick, no matter how many times you were denied entry in the past. The best revenge is in exploiting those opportunities now.

ALLIANCES AND NETWORKING

I've placed these two together for discussion purposes because alliances are often the result of effective networking. Interestingly, and short-sightedly, experienced consultants sometimes feel that their networking days are behind them. But that's only if you see networking as a tactic instead of as a marketing strategy (and strong aspect of gravitation).

Among those who constitute networking potential for you are:

- buyers
- media people
- key vendors
- mentors

- endorsers
- meeting planners

- recommenders to buyers
- bankers
- key advisors
- high-profile individuals in your business

- trade association executives
- community leaders

Networking is far easier than ever with the advent of e-mail, voice mail, and other communication alternatives, but nothing is as effective as the face-to-face interaction that allows personal chemistry to develop. If possible, networking should be done in person, then followed up or reinforced through other communications avenues.

Here is a sequence for networking, whether at a trade association meeting, civic event, business conference, recreational outing, or nearly any other activity that you know in advance you'll be attending.

1. Learn who will most likely attend the event. Obtain a participant list, a brochure, or the names of the committee members, or make an educated guess. Prepare yourself for whom you're likely to encounter, and create a "target list" of the best prospects. For example, if you know the local business page editor is attending a charity fund raiser, you may want to make his or her acquaintance so that you can eventually suggest an article. If the general manager (and a potential buyer) for the local utility is at the dance recital, you may want to try to identify him or her and begin a casual conversation during intermission.

2. Begin casual conversations during the gathering to both identify those targets you've chosen and to learn who else might be there who could be of help. For example, you might want to introduce yourself to another consultant whose web pages you think are excellent to explore whether he might make his web designer's number available to you, or approach a local designer because you'd like to understand how she might work with you, even as a novice.

3. Introduce yourself without describing anything about your work and simply listen. If in a group, which is likely, don't attempt any personal networking. *Wait until you can find the person alone later and approach him or her one-on-one, preferably where you will have a few minutes in private. That's all you need.* Don't talk to someone while your eyes work the rest of the room, and talk only as much as required to get the other person talking. You want to hear about the person and his or her views and preferences.

4. When you're able to spend a few minutes one-on-one, offer something of value, based on what you've heard. For example, if the person is a potential buyer who has mentioned the problem she's having with attracting and retaining good people, suggest a book that you would be happy to pass along or a website, which you'll send by e-mail, that has articles on

the subject. If the person is a graphic artist, ask permission to give his name to some people you know who need literature designed. The key here is to provide value to the other person.

5. In the event you're asked what you do, practice providing very succinct responses. Here's a dreadful response:

   "I'm a consultant who focuses on the interactions of teams, especially cross-functionally, raises sensitivity to synergies possible in greater collaboration, and implements processes to enhance team connectedness. I use instruments such as. . . ."

   Here's a terrific response:

   "I assist clients in improving individual and organizational performance." (If the other person says, "That's a bit vague. How do you do that?" then you reply, "Well, if you tell me something about your organization and the issues you're facing, I'll show you how the approaches may apply specifically to you."

6. Exchange a card or somehow gather the other person's contact information so that you can send the promised material or information. At a minimum get a phone number and e-mail address. DO NOT provide brochures, materials, or any other gimmicks or "stuff." No one wants to lug around material at any kind of event, and this stuff usually winds up in the nearest discrete garbage can.

7. Immediately, the next morning at the latest, deliver what you promised. If you're providing the other party as a resource to someone else, then copy that person on the e-mail or correspondence or mention to them that you've given their name to the individuals you had mentioned.

8. In a week or so, follow up to see whether the material was helpful, the reference worked out, the prospects called, or whatever. Ask if there is anything further along those lines that might be helpful. Then summarize or reaffirm your offer of further help with a letter accompanied by your promotional material and literature. Suggest to the other person that you thought he or she might want to learn a little more about you and what you do.

9. In a few weeks, send still more value in the form of a contact, potential customer, article of interest, and so forth.

10. If the other party replies with a "thank you" for your latest offer of value, then get back to him and suggest a brief meeting, breakfast, lunch, or other opportunity to get together at her convenience. Simply say that you'd like to learn more about what the person does and also get his or her advice about what you could do. If the person has not responded with a "thank you" of any kind, then wait one more week, call to see whether he or she received the additional value you sent, and then suggest the meeting as described above. (An active response simply enables you to shorten the waiting time.)

Rule of Thumb: You should be networking at some event at least twice a month, and you should establish at least one useful contact from each one.

THE ULTIMATE RULES

Rule #11. Outstanding marketing will also create the beginnings of a relationship and embrace the sale itself. That's why intelligent, constant marketing is the secret to long-term success in consulting.

Rule #12. THE most powerful single aspect of market credibility is a commercially published book. I was aghast when I found that the people calling me in to help with strategy had acquired my strategy book but not read it, but I got over that when their check arrived.

Rule #13. The broadcast media are there to be used. There is a huge "expert vacuum" that is created by a plethora of talk shows, news shows, and commentary programs. If you can't get on one, you're simply not trying.

Rule #14. It's great to be smart, but it's equally important to persevere. By exerting as great a gravitational pull as your resources and talents permit, you'll ensure leads from the widest possible sources, some of which will be surprising. I'm constantly amazed at how stupid I was two weeks ago.

Rule #15. When you are more successful than you've ever been, new doors open that were stuck closed before. Don't be afraid to give them a kick, no mat-

Nick Miller is the founder of Clarity Advantage, which specializes in sales acceleration. Over the past couple of years the company has grown rapidly from mid six figures to the magic million mark.

Q. What's the key to your success?

A. Focus—concentrating marketing, selling, and delivery on a specific set of problems and a small number of industries, enabling me to command respect and to bring long perspective to my clients.

Q. What would you do differently if you began again?

A. When I started my business, I didn't write a business plan or accumulate enough seed capital to get through the bad times. Unfortunately, the bad times started immediately. The projects on which I'd expected to depend disappeared in the middle of the 1991 recession. So, I would have been more thoughtful about the plan. Second, I changed my idea for the business about every eighteen months for the first six years of the business. Every time I did that, I lost momentum and money. So I would have been more thoughtful about staying focused and being patient enough to let the strategy work.

Q. What's your major unaccomplished achievement?

A. I'd like to enjoy my success, be a hero to my kids and a terrific partner for my wife. That's the biggest one. There are specific objectives I have in my business life—to write books, to do more coaching work, to establish income from products—but they pale in comparison. I've worked so much for so long, and they've gotten the short end of the deal.

ter how many times you were denied entry in the past. The best revenge is in exploiting those opportunities now.

Final Thought: Perpetual gravity requires perpetual motion. To keep your gravitational field strong, you have to provide the energy and attention continually to attract interest continually.

Branding and Celebrity

A Brand in the Hand Beats Feet on the Street

There's celebrity and there's celebrity. Madonna is a brand and so is Coca-Cola.™ But there are myriad "brands," monikers, identities, and connections that differentiate a great many people who are not household names, *but are readily known to the people who most likely can purchase their services.*

Cold calls don't work in the consulting business. That's why we've discussed the "gravitational field" in prior chapters—techniques to attract people to you, which enhance your business prospects and also change the buying dynamic in your favor. Perhaps the ultimate gravitational pull is a brand name or association.

The irony is that so many consultants who have worked so hard and produced such dramatic results have not attempted to create the necessary cachet.

Let's follow a logical progression of establishing a brand, exploiting the brand, and then extending the brand to you, personally, which creates celebrity.

WHAT IS A BRAND AND WHY DO IT?

I think that any brand has the following common elements:

- It is a clear label of identification, associating some product, service, outcome, or benefit to you (or your firm).
- It is commonly known among those groups that constitute your buying demographic.
- It is a recurring theme in your literature, presentations, website, and other promotional materials.
- It creates a "Mercedes-Benz" sense in the mind of the buyer, so that you are, even prior to forming a relationship, considered the elite of the field.
- It is contemporary.

There is a woman, Nancy Friedman, who billed herself and now her company as the "Telephone Doctor."® I knew that if I simply searched for "telephone doctor.com" on the web, I would turn up her website (which I did). If a client of mine needed telephone sales development, I would automatically think of her and her company, even though we've never met.

I've been known by the following brands:

- Million dollar consultant
- Ferrari
- Contrarian

The "million dollar" moniker came from my best-selling book, *Million Dollar Consulting*. I drive a Ferrari and use the name on my private e-mail, and the car has appeared in some ads with me. Many of my articles and books, as well as my speeches, include a decidedly contrarian tone to the conventional wisdom on most subjects.

RULE 16

A brand doesn't have to be totally unique and singular. It must simply serve to drive people with a particular need to your particular alternative.

You probably already have some brand opportunities at this stage of your career, whether you've formally identified them or not. Here's a process, though, to help determine what your current or potential brands may be:

1. List the three most dramatic outcomes that clients derive from your work.

   _____

   _____

   _____

2. List the three most powerful services you provide.

   _____

   _____

   _____

3. List the three most compelling client needs you foresee in the next two years.

   _____

   _____

   _____

Now, combine the three sets of responses around a common strategy. Here's an example:

1. List the three most dramatic outcomes that clients derive from your work.
   a. Enhanced teamwork across functions and disciplines
   b. Alignment of individual objectives behind corporate objectives
   c. Focus on customer needs, not internal perceived inequities

2. List the three most powerful services you provide.
   a. 360° reviews and feedback
   b. Executive coaching and counseling
   c. Facilitation of teams and groups

3. List the three most compelling client needs you foresee in the next two years.
   a. Cross-cultural and global synthesis of operations
   b. Enhanced e-commerce and Internet marketing
   c. Acquisition and retention of talent in a dwindling labor pool

Given these responses, I might decide to use my expertise in communications and group work, combined with cross-functional teamwork and the need for organizations to work with wider diversity in both their employee base and customer mix, and create any of the following brands:

- Rejoicing Through Diversity
- The Team Coach
- The Global View
- Communicating Across Boundaries

You get the idea. The key, here, is the combination of what outcomes you know that you are capable of generating, what competencies you bring to the client, and what future needs are likely to be.

If this exercise is hard—or too vague because you're adept at many things—ask a trusted group of advisors to help you. (You can also ask your clients.) You can try to create an advertising listing or a promotional sheet. Force yourself to focus on those issues. Another way to look at your potential brand is to ask:

CASE STUDY

A very good sales trainer was stuck in the usual rut of competing on price for the commodity he found himself selling: sales skills training based on number of days and/or number of participants. We determined that the solution was to create a brand that centered on a preferred client result, not on the methodology.

He developed a newsletter called "The Accelerator," which focused on how to increase the velocity of sales, thereby collapsing closing times and increasing the profitability of new business acquisition. The newsletter took off like wildfire, and he began to receive calls from all over the United States and Canada.

He was then in a position to name his own fee as more and more companies demanded the *outcome* he provided, and his *methodology* was no longer the center of attention.

1. What will future clients most need for their businesses?
2. What are my competencies that relate to those needs?
3. What am I most passionate about?

I'm passionate about toy trains, but my clients have no need for expertise in the area. I have the competency to play racquetball but, again, no need among future clients. Some of my prospective clients have auditing needs, but I don't have the competence, and some need front-line supervisory training, but I have no passion for it.

However, many future clients will need help assimilating, aligning, and synthesizing cultures after mergers and reorganizations. I know how to do that, and I love that type of consulting. So that is where I need to be, and that is the basis for my brand: aligning cultures.

RULE 17

A brand doesn't have to be "cutesy." While some phrases and mottoes may be effective for drawing attention, sometimes clear and simple English does the trick nicely.

HOW DO YOU ATTAIN A BRAND WITHOUT PULLING A MUSCLE?

Simply coming up with something "catchy" doesn't do the trick. In fact, sometimes plain English works best. The vital element, though, is to communicate your brand consistently, loudly, and comprehensively, so that as many people as possible hear about it again and again.

Consistency.   Every marketing expert you ever talk to will have his or her own ideas about marketing clout, but they will all agree on one thing: Consistency is everything in attempting to get a message across.

- Place your brand in your signature file on all your e-mail.
- Insert the brand in an appropriate place on our letterhead.
- Create one sheet with your brand promotion for your press kit.
- Include it in your speeches and presentations.

Broadcast. You should publish articles expressly on the brand and its applicability to clients. If the brand involves global marketing, then publish on the glob-

George Silverman is president of Market Navigation, Inc., of Orangeburg, NY, specializing in creating "runaway word of mouth" for customers who want to accelerate sales growth. His two-person firm generates well over a million dollars in annual billings.

Q. What is the key factor behind your stunning revenue growth?

A. A single one doesn't come to mind. The ones that do are: having a purpose, goal, direction, and raison d'etre. Working with the right people. Total honesty. Writing in small chunks, regularly, newsletter articles and books. Always trying new, high-payoff things and realizing that only a few of them need to work.

Q. Is there anything you would have done differently?

A. Let my expertise show sooner. Realize that clients have very little time to think, so I am their "designated thinker." Write my books sooner. Get started on my organized development of my speaking career sooner. Get someone to manage the details of my business and my projects so that I could concentrate almost exclusively on what I do best and like to do best. Know that it's not only OK, but essential, that I follow my passion.

Q. What's left to accomplish?

A. Becoming a well-known speaker, author, and marketing consultant.

al marketplace. If you're a contrarian, then publish on why reengineering hasn't worked, or why rewards actually punish people. Pursue radio and television interviews that provide you a forum for your views and your brand promotion.

Simplicity. A brand must be simple to understand and easy to apply. You can't make the potential buyer work too hard. "Team Molding: Creating Great Teams from Great Talents" is far better than "Integrated Synthesis: Making Optimal Work Units from Individual Contributors." The "Telephone Doctor" is a good example, as is "The Friendly Skies" of United Airlines.

Perception. Perception is reality. When I was a kid, I wore $12 sneakers in which I ran down the street, played tag, shot baskets, and, generally, hung around. Today, there are racquetball shoes, cross-training shoes, jogging shoes, and shoes you wear to change from one pair of specialized shoes to another, and they all cost $120 a pair. The "athletic shoe" industry (AKA: "sneakers") has done mammoth work in managing the pubic perception of their product. You have to do the exact same thing. People spend an extra $20 on "free range chicken," even when there is no evidence whatsoever that it's better than any other chicken, free or imprisoned. Perception is enhanced through assertive promotion.

Support. Testimonials and endorsements of your brand image are powerful marketing devices. Don't simply accept an accolade such as, "Alan helped us with our teamwork and realignment to the extent that the organization is more productive than ever before," but try for, "Alan and his 'Team Growth' approach were the most powerful resources we've ever utilized for forging new collaborations within our organization." If you don't have a product name or service trademark, then try this: "Alan Weiss is Mr. Teamwork. No one else can forge teams as rapidly, especially among people who have never shown an interest in working together before."

In this fashion, you can have more than one brand. In fact, I strongly advise it, because brands can fall out of favor or prove to be ineffective. This is a side of branding that few people speak about, but it happens when:

- A new technology usurps all existing approaches. McKinsey or Boston Consulting Group could introduce a revolutionary strategy formulation process tomorrow that might render all other approaches obsolete or unattractive.

- The brand develops a bad repute, through no fault of your own. If there were a backlash toward diversity in the workplace, for example, being tied in to diversity training would be catastrophic.
- Uniqueness disappears. So many people begin providing so many services in the area that you get lost in the crowd, no matter how singular your brand once was. Focus groups and executive coaching, to name two areas, were once the province of a few specialized firms, but today they are conducted by everyone and his dog.

In addition, the reason for the exercises above that help to develop a brand is that you want to avoid fads. It is suicidal to have your brand affixed to such things as open meetings, open book management, left brain/right brain thinking, mind mapping, accelerated learning, and so on. These approaches had their fifteen minutes in the sun and are gone or forgotten.

RULE 18

Brands should be connected to compelling, future client needs. In this way they avoid the "flavor of the month" syndrome and the inevitable disappearance that follows the early euphoria.

THE FINE ART OF CONTRARIANISM

One of the easiest and most profound ways in which to stand out in a crowd is to turn against it; to move in the opposite direction; to stand like a rock amid the current. This is contrarianism.

One of the first business articles I ever published was called "Why Quality Control Circles Don't Work," and it was published in something called "Training News" at a time when people were falling all over themselves to implement QC Circles, which had become the hit of the month. The editor told me that he loved the reaction to the article—both from a small group who felt there was finally a voice of reason and from a larger group who wanted me tarred and feathered—and wondered if I'd like to do a column on a regular basis.

The result was "Revolutions," which ran for six years until the publication was purchased. I wrote seventy-two columns, many of which I still use as reprints today, each one with its own counter-trend aspect. Hence, I became known as a contrarian.

This is a prime example of a body of work gaining a brand for the originator. I had never specifically thought of myself as a contrarian, but the sobriquet applied and stuck as I continued to produce the columns. On many occasions I'm booked to speak—not because I'm what the audience wants to hear, but rather because the buyer wants to shake up the audience. Organizers have happily placed me on the general stage to tell large groups of human resource professionals why their profession is on the decline due to their actions and inactions, for example. I'm then called in to consult with HR departments, with the understanding that the organization is hiring a bit of a maverick who is guaranteed to tell the truth, no matter how painful or unpopular.

There are other examples of contrarianism, perhaps not quite so contrary:

- Use a process, not content, approach. Don't try to be the expert in the client's product or service, but do try to be an expert in the processes (conflict resolution, decision making, performance evaluation), which can be applied cross-industry.
- Push back at client basic premises. If the client says that customer attrition can't be reduced any further, ask "Why not?" If the customer says that staff reductions are inevitable, say, "What about other options?"
- Focus on diagnosis, not prescription. Don't arrive with an off-the-shelf response, but rather with a series of questions to engage the client in a joint diagnosis of the problem and mutual decision about solutions.
- Insist on working with line management. Don't settle for an evaluation, gatekeeper, or human resource intermediary. Establish yourself as someone who consults with front-line management.

I'm not suggesting that everyone should be a contrarian. I am suggesting that you can readily establish a brand when you're willing to step out from the mainstream and perhaps incur some discomfort and wrath along the way. It's tough to sort out all the potential resources active in the mainstream, but it's relatively simple to identify the ones that have stepped out of the crowd.

You will not establish a brand quickly or definitively by being "one of the

The Drevenstedt Group is a seven-year-old operation focusing on dental practice management in the Southeast, growing at better than 10 percent a year. President and founder Linda Drevenstedt began her career as a dental hygienist.

Q. What are the keys to your success from square one?

A. Marketing, marketing, marketing. I have an old Howard Shenson tape set that I used to model my business. I always have marketing plans and goals, even when I am overbooked. I never stop marketing. My main source of clients is my speaking. When I began the business, I would speak for free just to get in front of dentists. I always got at least one client with every speaking engagement. Sometimes it was not immediate. I always make up a "Keeper" handout with my contact information on EVERY page. I always use an evaluation form that allows them to request a complimentary telephone appointment to discuss their practice problems and to be placed on my mailing list. That list has been building for years and consists of everyone who has seen me in person as a speaker. Those dentists on the list get my mailings of upcoming seminars. The complimentary telephone appointment becomes my sales appointment. Early on I learned to get the leads with the speaking, but I wasn't closing sales. I took sales

crowd." The brand only reflects who you are and what you accomplish. The more outstanding and unique the person and the accomplishments, the more powerful the brand.

CAPITALIZING ON YOUR BRAND

Word-of-mouth is critical for brand capitalization. You've heard of mnemonics, which is the technique of using one idea or word or phrase to remind you of

training from a master consultant in my field. It was the best money I've spent. I use speaking as my main marketing. I now speak for a fee only, except for the dental schools in my area. I now force exposure by producing my own seminars. The mailings generate name recognition and "branding" for me here in the Southeast.

Q. What would you do differently, if given the option?

A. I would move into office space sooner. I am still in my home with two people showing up every day. Our business plan has included a move as an objective for the last two years. The move is not coming quickly because I want to have enough room for a small training room without a big drain on overhead.

Q. What is your greatest unachieved goal?

A. A major achievement in my business plan for the year and into 2001 is to start a training school for people who are non-dental to learn to run a dental practice. There is a tight hiring market here, and we need more trained personnel for many practices in our area to grow. I am currently replacing an associate consultant who left, so I have put the training school on the back burner while I handle lots of clients.

another. You've also heard a brief few bars from a certain piece of music and been transported back to a singular moment in time associated with that music. (Some people report that particular aromas provide the same kinds of instant associations.) That's how you want your brand to be recalled by others.

I tell people that I improve individual and organizational performance. Robert Middleton, an expert in catch phrases and marketing ideas and president of Action Plan Marketing in Palo Alto, CA, tells people that he helps service businesses attract more clients. You need a quick "hook" that describes your benefits memorably, clearly, and oriented toward the buyer. (If I said that I "provide skills training" or Robert stated that he "analyzes service firm performance," neither of us would have half the business that we do.)

Your brand should, then, meet these five criteria:

- Brief, concise, crisp
- Memorable; stands out in a crowd
- Provides strong outcomes to the buyer
- As generally applicable as possible; non-specific
- Effective in diverse media

Brief, Concise, Crisp.   The brand has to be clear. "Telephone Doctor" is terrific, but "telephonic communications enhancement" is not; "strategic outcomes" is clear, but "core capabilities audits" is not as clear.

Memorable; Stands Out in a Crowd.   "Sales skills" is clear, but it is also quite common; but "sales acceleration" is rather memorable. "Managing diversity" is in widespread use, but "rejoicing in diversity" creates more cachet. "Accurate overnight shipping" is descriptive, but "absolutely guaranteed to get there the next day" is a knockout—and is clearly FedEx.

Provides Strong Outcomes to the Buyer.   "Better recruiting" is always nice, but "higher quality hires retained for life" has a certain zest to it. "Performance evaluation experts" is an accurate description, but "aligning individual objectives behind corporate strategy" has much more punch.

As Generally Applicable as Possible; Non-Specific.   Ironically, brands don't have to be highly niched. Both mine and Robert Middleton's leave plenty of room to maneuver, although mine is even broader than is his. But why preclude buyers prematurely? "More responsive phone center response" is impressive, but why not "more responsive customer service" as a wider net? "Programming solutions while you wait" is cute, but "technical solutions while you wait" is cute and broader.

Effective in Diverse Media.   Make sure that your brand can be well-represented in the spoken word, in print materials, on a website, in a recording, on a wall chart, and so forth. Elaborate visuals are seldom effectively translated into language. One of my clients used an egg analogy, complete with yolk, white, shell, even albumin. (This must be the only consulting brochure in the world featuring albumin.) It's a meticulous analogy, but not one that is conveyed readily in any other context. (And it requires great patience to assimilate.)

Find out, through introspection, a review of client results, and the advice of trusted others, what you do well and turn it into a statement that fulfills the criteria above. Then keep chiseling at it until all that's left is solid rock. Here's an example of the sequence, from generalized service down to brand:

1. We help clients in the healthcare industry deal better with the tough times caused by government regulation, insurance changes, patient demands, and other turbulence in the industry. (Not brief, not memorable, not outcome oriented.)
2. We help clients in the healthcare industry to maximize profits while maintaining the quality of patient care. (Getting there, but might be more memorable and more generalized.)

CASE STUDY

There is a trend in the training and development community to form huge holding companies of diverse firms. These efforts have been well-funded—and historically unsuccessful.

The Times Mirror Group, for example, purchased Zenger-Miller, Learning International, and other firms. Provant burst into existence by purchasing over a dozen small training companies. Publishers such as McGraw-Hill and Prentice-Hall have tried similar strategies.

The problem is that two bad things immediately happen in these attempts at forming conglomerates in this business. First, there is little or no synergy in either methodology or historical results among the various organizations. Second, their unique marketing strength, their brand, is subsumed into a new corporate amorphous identify.

Not one organization has ever been financially successful in creating a large mega-company out of smaller training firms. Once the smaller firm's unique strength was removed—its market brand—the whole actually became less than the sum of the parts.

3. We improve the fiscal health of clients in the healthcare industry. (Probably good enough and on target.)
4. We improve the health of our clients and their patients. (Evokes fiscal improvement and quality of care improvement and is generalized.)

RULE 19

Brands can go too far, and represent a generic service or product, rather than your firm. If you don't believe that, just look at the troubles that have surrounded terms such as Kleenex,™ Kodak,™ Formica,™ Jell-O,™ and others.

TESTING AND PROTECTING YOUR BRAND

You can obviously protect your writing through copyrights and certain titles and descriptions through trademarks, service marks, and registration. But the surest protection is to ensure that your brand uniquely points to you as the source and cannot be utilized by others.[1]

Your responsibility is to promote your brand, to be its most ardent supporter, and to become, de facto, the celebrity and expert about what you offer.

Test your brand by carefully observing people's reaction to it:

- If you're talking to someone while networking, offer your brief description *and then pause without offering anything further.* Listen for the next question. Is the person in the dark, muttering, "Oh, that's nice," and then turning

---

1. This is particularly important because not everything is guaranteed protection by law. For example, most people don't realize that a book title cannot be copyrighted, and someone could publish "Gone with the Wind" or "The Grapes of Wrath" tomorrow, so long as the content was different.

desperately to find someone else, or does the person respond, "That's fascinating; my boss would love to meet someone like you."

- If you're using it on the website, offer a feedback opportunity. Cite your brand briefly, and then provide the opportunity to ask for more information. Assess how many visitors exhibit further interest and precisely what kind of information they request.
- If you have print materials, offer a fax response to readers for more information.
- If you are making a speech, evaluate how many people come up to you when you're done and request more details, how many business cards you're given, and what types of people are showing the interest.
- If you're simply in casual conversation, innocently insert your brand into the discussion and see whether the other party chooses to pursue it or not. Find out whether it causes instant interest or immediate ennui.

Use the brand in your advertising, listings, brochures, promotional literature, and exhibits. Ensure that it's attributed to and identified with you. "Oh, yeah, that's the person who does the cross-cultural work. I've heard all about it." You're ultimately successful when your brand becomes excellence itself.

OBTAINING CELEBRITY STATUS

The ultimate brand success is when "Madonna" or "Cher" or "McKinsey" or "Andersen" is good enough. Years ago, people thought that Kodak was film itself and that all film came only in yellow boxes. "IBM" on a computer was once reason enough to buy it, and the old adage, "No purchasing manager was ever fired for buying from IBM" immortalized the quality associated with that brand. (In more recent times you could make the case that "No CEO was ever fired for bringing in McKinsey to formulate strategy," which speaks not only to McKinsey's repute but also to the desperate need for consultants to shore up weak executive knees.)

Frequently, people who are introduced to me will respond, "Ah, Summit Consulting Group, I've heard of you. You have a great reputation." I'm often positive that they don't know for a second what we do or how we do it, but they do remember dimly reading something about or from us, attending a conference at which we spoke or were quoted, or listening to colleagues who did speak of us. We've achieved that kind of word-of-mouth celebrity.

Does that make me a "celebrity"? Not in the sense of Di Niro or Pacino, but certainly insofar as my business community is concerned.

RULE 20

Celebrity is the natural result of the progression from various brand identification to personal identification within markets that constitute your business future.

And that is the key. As you develop a cachet about yourself, *the brand becomes you.* One of my favorite testimonials comes from Judy Jernudd in Los Angeles, who says, "Alan is the rock star of consulting."

There is an old progression among movie stars that supposedly runs in this sequence:

1. Get me a young, bright actor.
2. Get me that guy who did the last bit for us.
3. Get me what's his name.
4. Get that guy George Jones.
5. See if Mr. Jones is available.
6. Get George Jones.
7. Get a young George Jones.

The sequence for consultant celebrity might be:

1. Get me a consultant for my merger and acquisition work.
2. Get me that firm that did the last project.
3. Get me the woman who represents that firm.
4. Get that Marie Smith.
5. Find Marie Smith.

The difference for consultants is that age doesn't matter and, if we continue to do the job well, neither does fee.

You are a celebrity when the brand becomes you. That occurs when you're sought out as the featured speaker because people want to hear you and the organizers want your name on the brochure, not your company, not your specialty, and not even your topic. That occurs when a client asks for your help and trusts you to determine whether you're the right person for the job. That occurs when a publication wants an article from you and tells you that the topic and length are up to you. That occurs when an Internet site wants to feature you in a live interview. That occurs when a publisher indicates that any book idea from you will merit serious attention and, by the way, do you have an agent?

TEN WAYS TO PROMOTE CELEBRITY

1. Promote the Brand Yourself.   First, get over it. If you don't toot your own horn, there is no music. It is not egocentric or arrogant to draw attention to yourself as the representative of your firm's products and services. On a grand scale, Lee Iaccoca virtually pioneered this concept—and saved Chrysler in the bargain. The CEO as celebrity has become a too-common affectation, but is nonetheless a fact of our times. The first sale is always to yourself, and you have to be comfortable "carrying the brand." In sports, this is called being a "franchise player," meaning you're the one the fans come to see.

2. Use Your Name as Much as or More Than Your Firm's Name.   People don't request Summit Consulting Group, Inc., for their keynote speeches, they request Alan Weiss. Your name and photo should appear prominently in your materials, website, promotional packages, and so forth.

3. Acquire Professional Help.   I've gone through five professional photographers during my career, as my needs have grown more sophisticated and my personal celebrity has increased. People are influenced by first impressions and the care you take in your own image. My publicity shots are now taken by a professional in New York who specialized in actors and politicians. He makes me look better than I've ever looked, and I can use all the help I can get. Similarly, I've matured through several stages of graphics designers. When an offi-

I had completed three years of work with a $400 million dollar Midwest manufacturer, covering about five different projects. In October, the CEO called me in to discuss plans for the following year.

"What kind of projects do you have in mind?" I asked.

"Alan, I'm not sure at this point. I only know that there will be plenty for you to do, and we need your smarts around here. You're an added dimension to my management team, and I want to ensure I can call on you whenever I need you. What's fair to you?"

"Well, how about a retainer? We can do it by the quarter, or half-year, or full year. Obviously, the longer the period, the more economical for you."

"Let's go for the full year," he said. "What fee would be fair?"

I had done a lot of work for this company, and I simply took an average of the past two years. "What about $100,000, paid in advance, to cover the entire year?" I said, with relish.

"Not enough, given what you've done," said the CEO. "Let's say $130,000, and we'll shake on it."

That is one of the few times in my life that I've been speechless, and it was much later that I realized that I had become the asset. I was the brand.

---

cer at a new client, the American Institute of Architects, told me that "your materials don't effectively represent the quality of the work you actually provide," I had my entire "look" changed within thirty days. Invest in the best.

4. Aggressively Pursue the Media. Make it a goal to do four radio interviews a month, two print interviews a month, and one television show every quarter. An appearance I made on CNN, shot at my house, prompted calls from around the country and also provided a video that is a powerful promotional tool. I beat out another consultant for a job across the country when one of the executives noted, "This is the guy who was on CNN."

5. Publish a Book.   Find an agent, put together a professional treatment, and get a book into print. It may be the only book you ever publish or the first of a string. But it's important to establish that level of credibility and to have your name on the spine alongside that of a major publisher. It doesn't matter whether the book isn't a wild success or whether people who contact you haven't actually read it. It is simply a mammoth credibility statement.

6. Adopt a Set of Rules or Principles.   Become known for a position on certain issues. For example, I always cite "The 1 Percent Solution," which is also the name of one of my tapes, explaining that if you improve by 1 percent every day, in seventy days you're twice as good. A consultant named Jeff Davidson talks continually about "breathing space" and has written a book about it. Enable people to identify a set of rules, or philosophy, or business principles with you, personally. No one can think of reengineering without thinking of Michael Hammer, for instance, or one minute anything without Ken Blanchard.

7. Become Associated with Other Celebrities.   Seek to share the speaking platform with others who have celebrity recognition. Co-author articles with them. Collaborate on a study or project. Celebrity by osmosis is not uncommon. There are many people on game shows and hosting events whom I've never heard of except by their appellation, "television personality." (O Henry wrote a fabulous short story about a "man about town," and what exactly was a "man about town," only to find out that he was one.)

8. Host or Sponsor Events.   Lend your name to a fund raiser, a scholarship, a building project, or any other good cause. Make sure you're listed as a donor in brochures and programs. Volunteer to underwrite a speaker or a prize for a trade association.

9. Develop a Separate Internet Site from Your Firm.   Use it to promote you. Highlight your publications, public works, speaking, philosophy, and personal approaches. Create at least a parallel focus on you, personally.

10. Begin a Personal Newsletter, Written and/or Edited by You.   Make this your private preserve, and encourage free subscriptions. Develop a following of people who want to read about what you, personally, have to say, and initiate

Chuck Sennewald's practice analyzes organizational and operational strengths and weaknesses in protection programs, security, and related litigation. He's actually trying to scale down his practice to about a quarter million in revenues, but is having a hard time doing so.

Q. What is the single key factor behind your success?

A. Probably the fact that I was published. My book, *Effective Security Management,* added credibility to my credentials as a "Security Management Consultant."

Q. What would you do differently if starting out again?

A. I celebrated my twentieth anniversary last November and thought about this very question. My answer: Nothing.

Q. What is the major achievement you have yet to accomplish?

A. To self-publish and then market the book on the Internet (my website is *www.shoplifting.com*)! I have four books, but all were handled by a major publishing house. I'm presently working on one (have completed the writing), but the daunting challenge is to do the many, many tasks required to actually bring a book to market. It's an exciting but tough job, at least for me.

an interaction with those readers. The ideal vehicle for this is an electronic newsletter. Mine grew from forty names to over one thousand in the first three months alone, through word of mouth.

Sophisticated marketing entails the use of a brand (or multiple brands) to draw people to your expertise. But the ultimate consultant parlays that "draw" into personal celebrity, which is really the ultimate brand. Although none of us ever really stops marketing, once people are drawn to us by name recognition alone, the rest is easy.

THE ULTIMATE RULES

Rule #16.   A brand doesn't have to be totally unique and singular. It must simply serve to drive people with a particular need to your particular alternative.

Rule #17.   A brand doesn't have to be "cutesy." While some phrases and mottoes may be effective for drawing attention, sometimes clear and simple English does the trick nicely.

Rule #18.   Brands should be connected to compelling, future client needs. In this way they avoid the "flavor of the month" syndrome and the inevitable disappearance that follows the early euphoria.

Rule #19.   Brands can go too far and represent a generic service or product, rather than your firm. If you don't believe that, just look at the troubles that have surrounded terms such as Kleenex,™ Kodak, ™ Formica,™ Jell-O,™ and others.

Rule #20.   Celebrity is the natural result of the progression from various brand identification to personal identification within markets that constitute your business future.

Final Thought: If you have the opportunity to jump immediately to personal celebrity, do so. You can always establish individual brands from that much more powerful platform.

CHAPTER 5

Passive Income

Making Money While You Sleep

To address one of the questions I've been asking successful colleagues in "From the Trenches" throughout the book, I would do two things quite differently:

1. Capture and nurture a database of all contacts much earlier and much more diligently.
2. Create products and passive income sources much earlier.

I've addressed the first point elsewhere, and it's immediately remedial, in that all of us can improve on that instantly with today's technology. But the second point is more problematic, and I've seen top consultants ignore this huge source of exposure and income.

I was of the rather pristine belief that a consultant was rather "soiled" by products (these I imagined, wrongly, to be the sole form of passive income), which were commodities, after all, and not sufficiently abstract or elite. I also rather pragmatically believed that one couldn't have an effective product until the brand was established, with the resultant credibility and visibility.

Let me define "passive income": Passive income is revenue generated through previously established channels that does not demand a "close" by you interactively *and* does not require that you leave your home or office.[1] Passive income is important for a wide variety of objectives.

Ten Great Reasons to Create Passive Income Products and Services

1. Major and alternative source of income, which can add to your revenues in good times and replace lost revenues in bad times. Generally, if your passive income declines for a given period, the problem is not serious, because there are no ongoing costs associated with the income channels.
2. An extremely high-margin proposition, boosting the bottom line disproportionately with the commensurate revenue generation.
3. Important source of marketing, credibility, and visibility. An element in the "gravitational field."
4. Can form the backbone of joint alliances and collaborations.
5. Can create a separate and salable equity business, particularly attractive to sole practitioners whose consulting practices are not readily salable.
6. Global and cross-cultural business, ideally suited to e-commerce and Internet marketing.
7. Can provide for expansion business in already "saturated" accounts, or business in organizations in which traditional services cannot be sold or are unaffordable.
8. Tend to open up new practice areas and disciplines.
9. Can be used as value-added elements to increase existing fees.
10. Can provide a significant basis for supplemental retirement income.

---

1. The ultimate passive income is interest and dividends from investments, but I'm talking strictly about products and services here, as this is not meant to be an investment guide.

RULE 21

You must always view passive income sources as key benefits for clients, first and foremost, and they will then be most effectively marketed. If, however, they are viewed as merely consultant income streams, they will provide only minimal profits.

COMMERCIAL PUBLISHING

In the world of business publishing, a book earns back its costs at about 5,000 copies (that is not a typo: only five thousand copies); at 7,500 the publisher will consider another book from the author, and at 15,000 copies it's "let's do lunch."[2] Most business books, however, die on the vine.

As noted earlier, commercial publishing is important for credibility. Your name on the spine alongside a major publisher creates instant veracity in your areas of expertise; hence, your early books should be on subjects that are intrinsic to your consulting work. But my point here is a very different one.

Ordinarily, an author will receive between 5 percent and 15 percent of sales as royalties, depending on a myriad of factors, including volume, discounts, book clubs, overseas sales, returns, and so on. (The IRS code is easier to understand than most publishing contracts.)[3] And if you used an agent, 15 percent of what you are due will first be due to him or her. This is, trust me, no way to get rich.

However, when the publisher formally declares a book out of print, the author (if intelligent or with the help of the agent) can take advantage of a contractual element called "reversion of rights." This allows the author to take back all rights and publish the work, using the original formatting, art

---

2. At this stage, for example, after more than fifteen commercially published books, my best-seller remains *Million Dollar Consulting,* which has probably sold about 80,000 copies over a period of eight years.

3. My current, wonderful publisher for this series, Jossey-Bass, of course excluded.

work, and other elements, if so desired, changing only the name of the publisher to the author's designated company. In most cases, the original publisher will sell to the author the plates and film necessary to print the book at cost (usually a few hundred dollars), although there is never a guarantee that they've been retained in good shape.[4]

Now the fun begins. To publish two thousand copies of a hardcover book, including jacket art, exactly like the original, will cost about $8,000 to $10,000, depending on the printer, the size of the book, and your negotiating skills. Assuming that this book sold for $25 or $30 at retail (which is why I advocate only reprinting as a hardcover, not as a paperback), your profit per book will be $20 to $26, or about a whopping 85 percent.

Assuming you keep the references up to date when you reprint (which is why two thousand is the maximum print run I recommend), the work will be timeless. By retaining the ISBN number and informing *Books in Print, Amazon.com,* and other sources that you are now the publisher, distributors will come to you for the book (you can be listed on the Internet booksellers within a day, for example).

My policy is to keep every single one of my books "alive." I continue to sell my very first book, *The Innovation Formula,* first published in 1988. Recently, a client ordered four hundred copies of my book on behavior and motivation, first published in 1990.

My rule of thumb is that senior people in consulting should be producing a book every two or three years.

 RULE 22

Writing a book is not a mysterious, arcane event. It is a project not unlike any consulting assignment, involving planning, time management, execution, feedback, contingencies, and disengagement. Excellent business books rely most heavily on examples, which any veteran consultant should have in abundance.

---

4. I recommend that each time you reprint you update examples, references, dates, and so on to keep the book current, updating its copyright each time.

I was asked by Merck early in my career to conduct focus groups on the acceptance of diversity within the organization. These studies continued for many years, and I was engaged by other firms to do similar work.

Consistent with my publishing "gravity," I began to write articles on my diversity work and findings, offering recommendations on how to maximize the acceptance of diversity and overcome the resistance to it. Eventually, when I had about twenty published articles and position papers, I decided to create a product.

The result was *Rejoicing in Diversity,* a fifty-six-page booklet, deliberately titled to stand apart from the traditional "managing diversity" approaches. Only about half the booklet is text, with each of those pages offering a discrete, pragmatic technique. The opposing pages contain "keys" to success and ideas to remember. The design embraced both a quick read for supervisors and managers and also a tool for the use of workshop facilitators.

The booklet sells for $7 and costs $1 to produce at a commercial printer. It is now in its third printing. Many firms that are too small to engage my services buy copies for all their employees, and many firms that have engaged my services have done so after receiving a copy of the booklet.

I've done analogous works in the areas of ethics, leadership, innovation, and professional services marketing. Books from this series of five are ordered every single day of the year.

SELF-PUBLISHING

Self-publishing is even more lucrative than commercial publishing because, from the outset, the high-margin profits belong to you, not a publisher. But there are nuances to self-publishing that make all the difference.

First, never self-publish for ego purposes. There are so many vanity books extant that you could cry for the forests they destroyed. No one of any consequence ever believes that a self-published book makes anyone an author, just as no one of intelligence believes that someone who buys air time on a local cable channel is a "talk show host."

And therein lies my second admonition: Don't self-publish books, self-publish other kinds of products.

The types of products that lend themselves best to self-publishing are those that don't involve a need for a commercial publisher's imprimatur, can be printed inexpensively, are pragmatic and immediately useful, have no time limitations or planned obsolescence, and can generate high margins (either through individually high prices or great volume). These print products include (we'll deal with audio and video separately a bit later):

- Booklets: Choose a topic within your expertise
- Instruction Manuals: "A guide to troubleshooting System 4"
- Systems: Blueprints for a project management approach
- Employee Handbooks: "How to stay healthy on and off the job"
- Newsletters: Sent in hard copy or electronically by subscription
- Cards and Mnemonics: Safety reminders that are posted
- Evaluations and Tests: How to value your business for tax purposes
- Forms and Guidelines: Recruiting questions to ask and avoid
- Industry or Market Reports: What to expect from consumers

Inside Tip: In many cases, trade associations will enter into an alliance with you to market these products to their members at a discount, will underwrite all or part of their cost, or will pay for a customized version. Because trade associations are in the education business as one of their fundamental member benefits, they are prime sources for product sales and/or distribution channels. If you have a trade association as a client or speak for one, it is negligent not to propose products for their members. This is a win/win/win equation.

AUDIO AND VIDEO

To some of you, audio and video products are going to sound far-out and even unprofessional. You're free to skip this segment. But for those of you who stay, you're apt to find a trove of potential income.

The general business population learns in a variety of ways. That we know. Yet despite that knowledge, consultants have not bothered to exploit the gamut of learning methodologies. There is no reason not to exploit all of

Tom Atkins helps businesses and non-profits evaluate risk in the property and liability insurance areas, so as to assure business viability and continuation.

Q. What's the best part of the job?

A. Enjoying the professional practice and the fact that I believe in what I do. I have great fun at it. I look forward to coming to work. This tends to make me work hard and long for the benefit of my clients, as well as making me a good advocate for the services of the firm.

Q. Anything you would have changed if you could have?

A. Since I am happy with what I do, and since the remuneration (low six figures) is more than adequate, and since I am happy with the location of my practice, I would not change anything in the past. I personally have not kept up with technology as much as some of my associates and some of my clients. This is causing a bit of a problem in the game of catch-up. If I had it to do over, I would have spent more time on technology (computer) skills in the past five years.

Q. Any unachieved aspirations?

A. In my field, I am close to the top. I do not want to run a business. I am fifty-six and have no mountains to climb at this time. But I am sure things may change in the future.

them, because the technical prowess required to implement can be hired by the hour!

Every single time you give a speech, you should arrange to have it professionally taped (which right now means DAT, but could mean something else by the time you finish this chapter, given the rate of technological change). Such taping is no big deal and will cost only a couple of hundred dollars or so. In many cases, the sponsoring organization or client is doing this anyway, so you merely have to request a master as a condition of your appearance (a request which is never denied—this recording is of your intellectual property).[5] For best results, always try to have the audience reaction captured in the microphones, so that laughter, applause, questions, and reactions are spontaneously captured.

For another couple of hundred dollars you can have a professional editor remove dead air (audience exercises), enhance the sound levels if needed, provide a voice-over introduction (the event introducer is dreadful 99 percent of the time and should be edited out), instructions to turn to side two, and a voice-over at the end. You can also add generic music for a small fee.

Because you're not going to update the tape contents, you can reproduce these in larger quantities with commensurate price discounts if you like, and tape reproduction is a highly buyer-friendly, competitive industry. You can have as few as a thousand tapes made with printed labels and cases for less than a dollar a tape, meaning that your total investment in recording, editing, and duplication will be about $1,500 to $1,800. If the tapes sell for $12 each, that is a profit of about 70 percent, and all further costs will be for duplication only, meaning a margin of about 90 percent forever after.

Moreover, if you combine three to six tapes in an album with a workbook or two from the print materials listed earlier, that album can sell for anywhere from $75 on up. (An alliance partner and I sell a set of twelve tapes and a one-hundred-page workbook for $150.) I no longer sell individual cassette tapes, since my strategy is to provide high-quality, high-priced products, so I promote a series of albums.

Note that audios used as products should almost always be derived from appearances before live audiences, and not be studio products. Although some of the major audio publishers do use studios and choreographed readings, the best tapes (and the most forgiving, as your listeners will not be expecting perfection but are content being a part of the "live" event) for our purposes are live recordings of us in front of clients presenting practical advice and techniques.

---

5. Whenever an organization requests that your talk be recorded, give permission provided that you are given two masters for your files and that you retain copyright and rights to further use the recording for commercial purposes without restriction. Under these conditions, try not to use dated references or examples that may make the content obsolete at some future point. For specific techniques, see my book *Money Talks: How to Make a Million as a Speaker,* McGraw-Hill, 1998.

As an ancillary use, these very inexpensive cassettes can readily be included in press kits, given away as marketing promotions, be used as takeaways at conventions, and so on.

The best audiocassettes are generally thirty minutes on each of two sides. Why? Because thirty minutes equates to most commuters' drive time, one way.

Video sells well (if done well) because it is useful for individual study as well as group discussion and workshops. Even more so than audio, video is only effective if done before a live audience. There are studio quality presentations that are excellent, but they are basically "talking heads" or dramatic vignettes, and that is an aspect of production that requires major investment and time.

from the
TRENCHES

Patrick Lucansky, Jr., works for The Highland Group, generating in the low seven figures for this full-line consultancy with an emphasis on manufacturing, pharmaceuticals, biotech, and medical devices. The firm's revenues are in excess of a hundred million dollars.

Q. What is the key to your approach?

A. First, I identify the client's driver goals, which are supporting the corporate vision. Then I match my firm's talents and goals to theirs. This goal alignment allows the client to see that I have listened to their needs and demonstrated how we can meet them through a mutually beneficial project.

Q. What would you have improved on from the beginning?

A. I would spend more time interviewing and analyzing the data.

Q. What achievement is still unmet?

A. The major achievement I would still like to accomplish is to build a sector from the ground up. I have always been involved early on but never at the very beginning.

Some clients will video a presentation for remote sites or for posterity, and that is your best source.[6] Alternatively, you can arrange for your own production crew, which will run from about $500 to $1,500. (If you hear that a video shoot costs a minimum of $5,000, leave immediately and make sure your wallet is still in your pocket or purse.) Always use two cameras, one for audience reaction shots, which make a good video into an outstanding one. The camera on you should pan, provide closeups, and frame you at varying distances.

A good video is usually forty-five minutes to an hour in length. Your production people will take care of the assorted FBI warnings and so forth, and you should plan a voice-over introduction as well as an on screen textual introduction, and a similar arrangement for the closing.

Just to take an arbitrary example, a video on effective sales skills, shot before a live audience, with interactive questions and answers, can be a highly effective corporate product. But that same video, modified slightly to emphasize individual influence, can be a very powerful personal purchase. Hence, a single product handled well can apply to your traditional marketplace and to an entirely new one.

A single video can sell for $49 to about $89, depending on content, length, and your repute. But combined with print and/or audio materials, the package can sell for anywhere from $99 to $299. Once you create these products, the combinations and permutations are vast.

RULE 23

Try never to duplicate materials among your books, audiotapes, and videos. You don't want customers deciding which alternative best presents the material, but rather to realize that there is new material on each medium.

---

6. Another technique: If the client has video capability but is not choosing to use it, offer a discount in return for the technical assistance. It's no problem for the client, because the capability is already present.

NEWSLETTERS

Newsletters can be used for excellent marketing and publicity purposes, especially electronic versions. But I'm talking here of print newsletters of high value sold on a subscription basis.

If there is anyone out there who still doesn't believe in value pricing, be aware that some high-end newsletters—I'm thinking of one that caters to the IT profession, for example, published by Kennedy Information in Fitzwilliam, NH—charge over $900 for annual subscriptions. You only need a hundred subscribers for that endeavor to begin to get really interesting.

I know, you're not a publisher, and there are marketing costs, and it's a lot of work, and blah, blah, blah. The facts are these: You can write a high-quality, four-page or eight-page newsletter, have it printed at a local franchise printer in two- or four-color, and mail it monthly or bi-monthly for relatively little money and, once you're organized, little time. And that newsletter can demand a subscription price of anywhere from $98 to $198.

Let's approach this another way. How many quality names are now on your database? By "quality" I mean that you've interacted with them, they've purchased something, they are clients, they are prospects, or they in some way know and support you. I'm going to choose the arbitrary number of 2,500, which I know is low for many of you, but I want to be conservative. (My quality list right now has about four thousand, and I've been a laggard in this area.)

If 15 percent of those people were willing to subscribe to a newsletter that you produced, and you charged $198 for a monthly publication, the gross revenue immediately created is $74,250. Subtract operating costs of $1,000 per issue (printing and mailing) and one-time start-up costs of $3,000 (design and promotion), and the first year profit is about $60,000. Assuming more of your quality base signs up the next year, word spreads to others as the issues are distributed, and an effective conversion (renewal) base the second year, and you will be building a $100,000 profit in short order without leaving your office.

If it's so simple, why doesn't everyone do it? Because only consultants who possess this unique combination are really in a position to do it:

- Unequivocal track record of success
- Name recognition (branding)
- Significant list of qualified potential buyers

- Ability to reach out quickly to unknown potential buyers
- Ability to create and maintain an interesting publication

Ironically, when consultants reach this unique juncture of capabilities, they seldom consider using them for this type of passive income.

Newsletter Nuts and Bolts

Of course, this isn't one of those Judy Garland and Mickey Rooney movies where the kids say, "Let's put on a show!" What does it take to produce a money-making newsletter?

1. Choose a general theme about which you have high passion, significant expertise, and the belief that there is great need among potential readers.

CASE STUDY

Several years ago I decided to enter the newsletter market with a publication I called *The Consultant's Craft.* It was an eight-page, two-color bimonthly, focusing exclusively on practice management. Over a hundred people quickly signed up from my mail list at the time, and I began to promote it on the Internet and at my speeches.

As the newsletter passed 250 subscribers not quite a year later, I was approached by Kennedy Publications, which published *Consultant's News* and dozens of other newsletters. They offered a deal to buy out my newsletter, pay me to continue to write for it and serve as editor, and to collaborate with them on a number of books and seminars.

The Consultant's Craft became the monthly *What's Working in Consulting,* I've published the first two in a series of books with Kennedy, and we've launched and conducted a seminar series around the country. I continue to write half of the new newsletter, which has a wider distribution than ever, as well as develop further projects.

I had not known that these options were open to me a few years ago, and I'm constantly searching for new ones that I probably don't know about today.

It may be a consulting expertise (quality, programming, conflict, time management) or a more generalized business expertise (hiring, practice management, investing). Those three factors are essential: you believe in it, you know a lot about it, and people need to hear about it.

2. Choose your frequency. Monthly is best, bi-monthly will work, but quarterly is not valuable enough and bi-weekly will kill you.

3. Ask your graphics designer to create a common layout that your local printer will use every time and simply insert your copy. These are called "mastheads" and "banners," and means that your printer can actually print large volumes of the two- or four-color layouts ahead of time at very low prices. DO NOT attempt to create the newsletter yourself on your computer, no matter how sophisticated your software or templates.[7]

4. Invite others to contribute so that you don't have to write everything. A good formula for eight pages, for example:
   - Two pages written by you
   - Two pages of quick factoids, paragraphs, and items
   - One page by a regular contributor
   - One page by a different contributor each month
   - One page of letters from readers
   - One page used for notices, subscription advice, address changes, etc.
   - Photos and graphs to brighten things up

5. Create three issues in advance before you begin, and try to stay that far ahead of yourself. Schedule your own writing time as you would normally schedule anything, and set deadlines for the others.

6. Use either your printer, a mailing house, or your local hourly subcontractors to stuff and mail the newsletters. Have a special, lower rate for two-year subscriptions (many people take advantage of these) and specify your rates for overseas mailing, as you will have international requests.

7. Secure an ISSN number (analogous to a book's ISBN number) for the newsletter so that it can be easily found by those who have heard of it.

8. Aggressively promote the newsletter on the Internet (but don't distribute it that way) via search engines, linked sites, and your own site, and offer a complimentary copy to anyone interested.

---

7. Even if you're a technical genius, the point here is to minimize your time investment and have others do the legwork.

> Newsletters are not only high-potential passive income in themselves, but they offer springboards to other options, such as product promotion, consulting sales, speaking, and other services.

Finally, the newsletter should never be self-promotional. It should provide only constant value to the reader. The more you focus on the reader's needs, the more loyalty and word-of-mouth you'll develop. However, you can use the mailing itself for inserts about your other products and services, and you should expect to begin to see consulting leads develop from the dissemination of the newsletter. Passive income can easily lead to active income, if you so desire.

OFFSITE ADVICE

I want to conclude this chapter with the most fascinating income possibilities of all for experienced, successful consultants. I'm going to roughly label this as "offsite advice."

For many years, people approached me to serve as a mentor. Initially flattering and unrefusable, these requests soon deluged me, to the point where I had to turn everyone down or I would have had to give up my own practice. Yet several people were persistent and well-intentioned, and I knew that I could considerably boost their careers.

At that point, my formal mentoring program was born: The Private Roster Mentor Program. For a set fee paid at initiation of the process, I work with individuals and/or small firms over a six-month period. Personal meetings are not part of the process (although they can occur if someone happens to live nearby or someone wants to fly in at his or her own expense). I take on twelve to twenty people at any one time, depending on their level of sophistication. About a quarter of the participants have been brand new to the profession, and the balance of the sole practitioners have had existing practices ranging from

$75,000 to well over a million dollars. I've had "mentorees" from everywhere from Australia to Switzerland and deal almost exclusively by e-mail, phone, and fax.

Over the first five years of its existence, the program has generated in excess of $700,000 in fees alone, and that's not counting business referrals and product sales, which easily raise the figure to over $1 million. The mentor business is conducted entirely from my home, with no attendant expense whatsoever—and not one penny ever invested in marketing.

A Second Example. Many of you reading this have been involved with executive coaching, either as a discrete business or as an adjunct to a project that required one-on-one work with some key people. Coaching has become a very hot field, and not one likely to cool off soon, because it is ego-driven ("What, you don't have your own coach? My company pays for mine, and he's one of the most expensive around.") and based on very real problems for current executives age forty-five to sixty-five, such as:[8]

- Relative unfamiliarity with high technology applications
- Unaccustomed to, uncomfortable with, instantaneous communications
- Poor frame of reference to diverse workforces
- Poor frame of reference to diverse customer bases
- Unsure about dealing in a truly global economy
- Stunned by workplace issues of AIDS, single mothers, addiction, and so on
- Facing increasing transient workforce of little inherent loyalty
- Facing pressures from new and unprecedented competitors
- Forced to cater to increasingly educated and demanding consumers

My list could go on. The point is that the underlying reasons for the need for personal and personalized assistance is growing, and the internal options for filling that need—human resources—are unthinkable, both in terms of credibility and confidentiality.

---

8. Just a random pass through this week's business mail provides a direct-mail piece for a full-blown coaching conference sponsored by Linkage, a convention group in Massachusetts, and a feature article in *Fortune*: "Do You Need a Coach?" by Betsy Morris (February 21, 2000, page 144).

Hence, external coaches are not about to go away, and this is one beauty of a growth industry. Who better to fill it than experienced consultants? And while you can certainly coach interactively in the executive's office, you can also do it (with greater discretion) by phone, fax, and e-mail. In fact, the ability to call the coach at home on a Sunday night is an extremely valuable option. (I'm talking about planned calls when necessary, not about your being paged at the opera or ball game.)

RULE 25

You might not desire passive income, as such. But if you desire more control over your life, and fewer airplanes in it, passive income is the best technique to gain that control without sacrificing life style.

At the moment, anyone can be a coach, and the coach "certification programs" are ridiculous. After all, who certifies the certifiers? Sorry, but finishing a mail-order course on coaching skills can't take the place of a seasoned consultant who has been in the trenches with executives for years and years.

My website offers a coaching service for management. I don't promote it aggressively, but it's there and accessible. There is zero cost of acquisition. I'll still coach executives onsite under the right circumstances, but now I have a "passive" option as well. The business brings in six figures.

TRANSITIONING TO SOFTER LANDINGS

There are other methods to gain passive income, and perhaps I'll do an entire book on this subject alone some day. My suggestion to you is that at some stage of your success you may want to consider working less hard, travelling fewer miles, and exerting less effort, but without sacrificing the life style or abrogating the commitments you've proudly established. That is an achievable set of goals if you consciously rethink your income streams, moving from "feet on the street" to the comfort of your home or office.

You don't make this transition overnight, and you may not choose to make it 100 percent. But through an intelligent combination of products and services, you can begin to build a significant six-figure income from activities that do not demand that you leave home. One of the keys to success is to start these at some comfortable point at which they can gradually build, and you don't feel the pressure to make them a success immediately.

My best-selling book was rejected fifteen times; it took me a year of thinking about it to launch my first newsletter; I was heavily engaged in mentoring before I realized the income potential; I'm sure there's more I'll learn tomorrow, because I'm constantly surprised at how stupid I was two weeks ago!

What is the percentage of your income that flows in via e-mail, fax, and phone? How much of it *is not* dependent on you being at a certain place at a certain time? How much would you like it to be?

I'm not suggesting that the normal progression of success is to give up interactive consulting to become a product czar. But I am strongly recommending that you diversify your income stream so that you can take time off, weather time of client inactivity, and gain more control over how you choose to invest your time.

When I first hit seven figures, I realized I was travelling about 80 percent of the time. By focusing on my interventions, I reduced it to 65 percent, where it plateaued. I realized that my basic business model had to change if I wanted to stay off the road that amount of time. Last year I traveled about 15 percent, and my wife was usually with me. And last year my passive income, for the first time, exceeded all other income.

My objective is for passive income to represent about 75 percent of my overall revenues, so that I can simply carefully select whatever consulting and speaking assignments please me and turn down the rest. And, if I so choose, I can simply not take on any assignments for a few months. This year we'll be taking five major vacations. I'm not saying this is the way you have to do it, but it sure makes sense to me.

THE ULTIMATE RULES

Rule #21. You must always view passive income sources as key benefits for clients, first and foremost, and they will then be most effectively marketed. If, however, they are viewed as merely consultant income streams, they will provide only minimal profits.

Darrel Raynor, MBA, is president of Data Analysis & Results, Inc., of Waxahachie, TX. His per client revenues have ranged from $800 for a day to over a million over eighteen months, dealing in the recovering of "failing or flailing" software.

Q. What is the single key factor in your success?

A. Networking: actively HELPING people without the thought of direct tit-for-tat help from them. Done over a period of years, helping others is what built my business.

Q. Would you do anything differently if you started over?

A. Not commit more than forty hours per week for more than a month at a time. This would enable training, marketing, networking, administrative, and other things to take place at the same time as important consulting engagements. This would have reduced the cyclic ups and downs I experienced early in my practice. I also would have started my non-profit, The PC Donate & Retrofit Clearinghouse, years earlier. It has been great fun to help others.

Q. What major achievement have you yet to accomplish?

A. Successfully managing a project that will bring lasting good to humanity. An example might be: Helping the Carter Center eradicate a disease, helping Habitat for Humanity plan the yearly work build blitz, or helping a third-world country increase its communications infrastructure.

Rule #22. Writing a book is not a mysterious, arcane event. It is a project not unlike any consulting assignment, involving planning, time management, execution, feedback, contingencies, and disengagement. Excellent business books rely most heavily on examples, which any veteran consultant should have in abundance.

Rule #23.   Try never to duplicate materials among your books, audiotapes, and videos. You don't want customers deciding which alternative best presents the material, but rather to realize that there is new material on each medium.

Rule #24.   Newsletters are not only high-potential passive income in themselves, but they offer springboards to other options, such as product promotion, consulting sales, speaking, and other services.

Rule #25.   You might not desire passive income, as such. But if you desire more control over your life, and fewer airplanes in it, passive income is the best technique to gain that control without sacrificing life style.

Final Thought: Consider your practice the way you would your investment portfolio. How diversified are you in terms of streams of income? The best time to establish increased diversity is when you are strong and can afford to invest your time in additional products and services.

Joint Ventures

When 1 + 1 = 64

There is a particular parasite that plagues successful consultants. According to all reputable studies, it never afflicts anyone making less than six figures, but can become nearly debilitating if untreated by the time you pass a half-million. Disability insurance does not cover it, and many otherwise thriving consultants have lost time, business, repute, and momentum to it.

The disease is commonly known as Why Don't We Collaborate? or WDWC?

My experience is that, when other consultants suggest that we collaborate, what they're really suggesting is that I take money out of my pocket and put it into theirs. Frankly, I'd rather be hit up for a loan or an outright gift. In over fifteen years in my own practice, a consultant has come to me *with an existing piece of business and the offer to share in it in return for future consideration exactly once.* That's right, in a single moment in time a bright, ambitious guy asked me to work on a project he had sold, share

119

in the revenues, teach him something, and perhaps consider him as a future subcontractor or better should I be sufficiently impressed. I was and I did.

But on the approximately 3,500 other times that WDWC? was proposed[1] to me over the last decade, the hopeful and naïve (or scheming) consultant just wanted a handout. To walk up to someone you've never known (or, worse, send them an e-mail), shove a card at them, and suggest that the two of you are perfect to work together "on the right project" is either so stupid or so amateur that I scarcely know where to begin with it.

But I'll try.

FORMING PARTNERSHIPS WITH COLLEAGUES

My philosophy is that 1 + 1 must equal 64 or so. By that I mean that collaboration with colleagues—other consultants, irrespective of their earnings compared to yours—must generate exponential growth, not arithmetic growth. Just as a single $100,000 sale is more lucrative and time-effective than ten $10,000 sales or four $25,000 sales, $250,000 managed and implemented alone is more profitable and time-effective than $500,000 managed and implemented by two. In fact, that quarter of a million solo is probably better than $650,000 generated by two.

Here's why. True collaborations—not those that require only an exchange of business cards and the lie, "Let's get together"—whether effective or not, all require the following requirements:

- Frequent, often prolonged, and time-consuming communications between the partners (the more partners involved, the worse this is by a factor of ten).
- Common support mechanisms. If you have staff, both will be used in often duplicative jobs. If you don't, you'll have to arrange for some, because you'll need a common approach and you're not going to do your partner's administrative work, nor will he or she do yours.

---

1. This is not a random number or hyperbole. I speak about fifty times a year, and an average of two inquiries arise each time, either from the audience or from someone who has read about me. Then add in people who read my books and visit my website. Multiply that over just the last ten years of my practice.

- More intense prospect and client planning. You have to ensure that your game plan is understood, responsibilities are allocated, and every prospect communication is shared thoroughly.
- Lengthy decision making. Neither of you can decide anything of substance about a client or marketing strategy without the other's concurrence. This delays everything from sending a report to updating a website.
- Non-business issue interference. When you work alone, you don't have to worry about employee discontent. Once you have staff, you experience absenteeism, fringe benefits, office gossip, and the joys of "people management." When you have a collaborator on an equal footing, you also inherit his or her staff problems, personal issues, and other liabilities.
- Egregious errors you can't control. It's one thing to blow up an account yourself, but it's quite another when you were doing fine and the collaborator blows it. Moreover, your E&O insurance isn't going to cover your colleague, but you might find yourself sucked into a morass not of your making.
- Possible unfair loss of business—getting "juiced" as we used to say on the streets. Your collaborator may just decide that things have too much potential to share with you, or that your participation is no longer required to guarantee success, or that the mortgage payments are falling behind. Just because you act professionally doesn't mean the collaborator will. (And no amount of legal contract will prevent that. Generally, the longer the contract, the less the trust. If I can't simply shake hands and trust the decision, then I don't enter into an agreement. No piece of paper is going to overcome my gut instinct.)

RULE 26

Make it your practice to collaborate only when the other party offers a piece of business to you that is attractive and profitable. If you follow this rule diligently, you'll never go to jail for murdering a partner.

I refuse to offer anyone a piece of business I've attracted and sold. I will subcontract parts of it that I can't—or choose not to—handle, but that is clearly on a subordinated basis and usually at an hourly or daily rate (because sub-contractors rarely read my books on value pricing, thank goodness). I will allow people to participate in my business as a learning experience *at no remuneration*, especially if they want to engender a relationship. That's right: If you want to see how I operate and maybe demonstrate to me that you're a viable partner, then you invest in that endeavor, which means working on my project at your expense. I've had quite a few takers.

CASE STUDY

A woman who told me she would work on a joint project for us calls to tell me that she has spoken to the vice president of a major photography man-ufacturer, and he is ready to hire a consultant for some direly needed organization development work.

"I mentioned your name, and he said he'd be happy to talk to us. But you have to call him to set things up. Would that be all right? Here's his number."

I told her that I'd be happy to call. The executive ignored my first two calls, so I made a third one at 8:15 in the morning and got lucky. He told me that he had indeed spoken to the woman, and that he'd told her there were some company issues that needed work. He was willing to have external consultants send in their materials and daily rates, but they should go to his director of organization development, in human resources. He went on to say that there was no urgency, and that they generally chose the most cost-effective outside help, although he never personally met with consultants prior to their being hired.

I told him that I wasn't interested in bidding on anything, but could I include him, personally, on my mailing list, which was designed for execu-tives. He graciously said "yes," probably to get me off the phone, and that was that.

He's still on that list, and I've never done business with that company or with that woman.

The sad fact is that most people trying to secure business do not under-stand the process, misread or mishear what transpires, and delude them-selves about prospects' interests. That's why they need to collaborate with a pro. Other than that, they do great.

The way to frustrate WDWC? right at the outset is to have a "wall." My "wall" goes like this:

> "I'm sorry, but partnering is no less a relationship business than is marketing consulting services. I don't partner with people with whom I haven't a relationship, and there is no incentive for me to establish one. But if you bring a piece of business to the table for us to jointly work on, that would tell me that you're serious. I'm not trying to be mercenary, but I have to know who is capable of generating business at my level."

That ends most conversations, which it is intended to do. Some people do believe that I'm mercenary, and that's all right with me. Too much of my time was once wasted on people who, bright and enthusiastic as they seemed to be, simply wanted a free ride to learn the business, gain entry to key organizations, use my repute, and possibly earn some money in the bargain.

Nice work if you can get it, but you're not going to get it from me.

If people who wanted to collaborate were really adept at securing business for themselves, they wouldn't have to engage in WDWC? (It's much like all of these "successful" consultants and speakers I encounter on the Internet who are trying to sell an old computer or purchase a second-hand printer. When you're truly successful, you donate old stuff and buy new, and you're not constantly groping for bargains. A consultant in my mentoring program told me recently that at a convention she shared a room with a "highly successful bureau owner." I gently had to explain that a "highly successful bureau owner" would probably not only not be sharing a room to save money, but would have a suite to herself.)

RULE 27

If you're being pitched a story of how successful your potential collaborators are, take a hard look at how they dress, what they drive, where they live, and where they've been. Successful people don't drive dented old cars, and even their casual clothes are impressive. Shallow? No, prudent.

Here is the crucible for evaluating potential peer collaborators.

Ten Criteria to Test Peer-Level Collaborators
1. Does the person have a personal track record? What is his client list like? What kind of work has she done to date?
2. Does he have references? Will clients vouch for her? Can credentials be authenticated?
3. What is his repute? Has she published? Does he speak at conferences? Has anyone you know heard of her?
4. What's his image? Does she have an impressive website? Does his business stationery impress you?
5. What's her professionalism like? Does he use the language correctly? Does she dress well? Does he practice proper business etiquette?
6. What are her abilities? Does he provide an expertise or methodology that you don't have yet that compliments your own set of skills and offerings?
7. What are her credentials? Does he have academic, business, professional, and/or experiential credits that make you proud to collaborate with him?
8. What's her experience in collaboration? Has he done this before with others? Does she have a preferred model? Does he recognize the potential pitfalls?
9. What's the value added? Overall, do the two of you make a *significantly stronger* entity for a given piece of business than you do separately? Will the prospect appreciate that?
10. What's your gut reaction? Are you comfortable with the person personally, and do you enjoy him or her? Would you be comfortable relying on his judgment in your absence? Would you trust her with your wallet?

Overwhelmingly, collaborating with colleagues once you've established a highly successful practice brings diminishing (and sometimes punishing) returns. However, because you're also in a position to call the shots, if you use a tough set of criteria such as that suggested above, you might just be able to separate out that one golden opportunity from the legions of WDWC?

Charles Ritz is a regional manager for Communication Management Specialists, LLC, in Norcross, GA. This telecommunications consulting firm generates in excess of $20 million annually, a four-fold increase over a three-year period.

Q. What is the single key factor in your success?

A. Empowering each employee down to the lowest level to develop new business and manage the new business that they brought in.

Q. What would you do differently if you did it over?

A. Research client history more in-depth before signing a contract.

Q. What is the major achievement you have yet to accomplish?

A. Increase company earning past $100 million a year.

FORMING ALLIANCES WITH LARGER ENTITIES

I've found that success enables you to leverage your abilities through working with larger entities. This is an opportunity that does not present itself too early in most careers, so when it is viable it should at least be considered.

By "larger entities," I mean any of the following, and this list is hardly exhaustive:

- Larger consulting firms
- Universities and colleges
- Private and/or non-profit educational organizations
- Client companies
- Sponsoring organizations
- Alternative learning (for example, eCommerce)

Larger Consulting Firms

There is, of course, always someone bigger than you are, and therein lies some great potential business. I've often filled a temporary role in larger firms that didn't have my expertise on board and couldn't afford to acquire it full-time. We had a marriage made in heaven. Some firms have asked me to focus on a single client, others on an industry, and some on internal development (for example, I would create a function for them, put it into action, and leave).

There are two key positions for this pursuit in larger consulting firms: the managing partner or CEO and the practice managing partners. You can establish relationships with these people in any of the following manners:

- Publish in the media, including *Consultants News, Consulting Magazine*[2] and other publications that reach this audience
- Speak at trade and professional association conferences where they congregate
- Arrange for common clients to introduce you, either under the guise of coordinating work, or simply as an honest favor
- Network and request common acquaintances to arrange an introduction
- Send them something of value, and offer to stop by "the next time you're in the neighborhood"

Larger firms are still fixated on billable hours, but that shouldn't present a problem because you're not an employee. You can simply cite your fee, and the firm will tend to either include it somehow in client billings or pay for you out of internal funds. (Never agree to collaborate with a larger firm on the basis of billable time.) If the firm asks that you make your own arrangements with the client, then do so, explaining to the firm and the client that you are not using the same time-based billing for various reasons.

The bottom line is that it can't hurt to establish relationships with key people in the mega-firms, and that these collaborations, should they develop, are always a good bet for you both financially and in terms of repute.

---

2. Both published by Kennedy Publications, Fitzwilliam, NH. By way of disclosure, I edit another of their publications, *What's Working in Consulting*.

Coldwell Banker, the giant realty firm, featured me as a keynote speaker at their annual conference of top performers. I was placed there by a speaker's bureau, since Coldwell wanted to try something different and not have an industry specialist drone on about "location, location, location."

The spot was so successful that Coldwell asked me to appear at four other events. But, equally important, they asked if they could hire me to appear before their own clients and prospects.

Coldwell organized a six-city "road show" that featured me, a futurist, and a Coldwell executive. The audience were the commercial customers and prospects whom Coldwell cherished, and with whom they sought to solidify their relationships. The morning sessions were billed as educational and developmental and, although there were a dozen Coldwell people present to network and shmooze, there was no overt selling or promotion. The audience was simply treated to some entertaining and enlightening development on the probable future of the business climate and the techniques to be innovative in exploiting change.

Every single remark I heard about these mini-conferences was highly positive, and I began more actively seeking them out elsewhere once Coldwell so expertly educated me about their existence.

Universities and Colleges

Major educational institutions have entered the consulting and training fields with a vengeance. They are looking for alternative sources of revenue beyond tuition and fund raising, have a residual talent base, possess facilities that are underutilized, and have a vast "reach" to alumni, local businesses, and the media. They constitute a potentially powerful marketing machine.

However, they often don't possess the right amounts of expertise, pragmatics, and/or flexibility, thereby creating the need for high-powered consultants to partner with them. Regard universities with these programs and these goals as huge distribution networks and regard yourself as the product or service. It can be a marriage made in heaven.

Find the executive director of the management extension program, or the vice president of business programming, or whatever the equivalent officer title may be. Overwhelm that person with references, experiences, *and both the additional added value you can bring to the program as well as the existing needs that you can fill.* Approach this from the standpoint of university greed. They want to maximize income. You can help them. In the bargain, you can maximize your own income. (If you have professional staff, you can assign someone permanently to this marketplace.)

In some cases, it's sufficient simply to fill a "faculty" spot in the extension programs several times a year. The deal is almost always that you get paid for the instruction, and any consulting business that ensues is purely between you and the client organizations. The university benefits from the ongoing company tuition to the programs and from the enhanced reputation of bringing you together. I worked for seven years in this manner with Case Western Reserve University's Weatherhead School of Management, which has an excellent reputation. I brought first-rate instruction to their program, and I gained instant credibility with their clients through my association with the program. Everybody wins.[3]

Once Again: When you're successful, and clearly represent a value-added proposition, these collaborations are relatively easy to foster.

RULE 28

Ironically, higher-level collaborations are far easier to develop if you parlay your current level of success and experience into a value-added proposition for your potential partner. It's like a bank loan— much easier to secure when you don't need it as much.

---

3. An interesting side note: The conventional Case faculty demanded that X percent of the teaching slots were reserved for it, because the outside instructors were so much more popular and pragmatic that clients began to request solely outside faculty. Case had a devil of a time accommodating the politics and the performance.

Private and/or Non-Profit Educational Organizations

There are some little-known but interesting organizations floating about, such as the Institute for Management Studies (IMS) with offices in San Francisco and Reno. The organization works through local chairpeople—usually retired executives, consultants, or professionals of some sort—who enlist local organizations on a subscription basis. They then bring in speakers to day-long events for front-line supervisors, middle management, or senior executives.

The IMS pays the speakers, albeit not a fortune (at this writing, about $5,000 for top draws, but some people may be booked a dozen or more times a year). However, any business that ensues is completely that of the speaker, so you are, in fact, being paid to market yourself through your developmental presentation for the audience to anywhere from fifty to one hundred fifty potential recommenders or purchasers. Besides the more than dozen chapters in the United States, the IMS has quite active chapters in London and Amsterdam, provides publicity about books written by its faculty, and publishes a substantial course catalog. Some of the faculty are not immediately recognizable, but others are well-known authors and consultants.

The American Management Association supports a raft of conferences, as does the Young Presidents' Association. There are scores of for-profits that market similar events, such as Linkage in Massachusetts, which runs major conferences on human resources, high-tech, consulting, and a variety of other topics. In all of these endeavors, the benefits include: The speaker is publicized, there are print brochures, there is usually a book store that will carry your products, networking is prolonged and of high quality, and potential business (let alone hefty improvements to your data base) can be mined. And, in most cases, you'll also be paid for your contribution.

You can become a long-term, regular contributor or a situational participant, depending on your expertise, your passion, and your availability. No matter what involvement you choose, these organizations present viable joint venture possibilities.

AND NOW A WORD FROM OUR SPONSOR

Client Companies

Often, your own clients can represent joint venture partnerships, which are especially valuable because the relationship has already been formed and nurtured, trust is present, and you should be able to move with some alacrity.

Here are three major forms of client joint venturing that any successful consultant can consider:

Sponsorship as a Featured Speaker

Merck has paid the bill for me to appear in front of trade associations that otherwise couldn't afford my speaking fee (for example, Health Industry Distributors Association). In so doing, Merck gets excellent publicity, the association can acquire top speakers, and I have the opportunity to appear in front of hundreds of health industry executives and business owners. On another occasion, Merck sponsored my appearance on a panel for a non-profit in Washington, DC, which educates congressional staffers.

The CEO of Cologne Life Reinsurance, a client at the time, was also a member of the programming committee for the American Council of Life Insurance and supported my appearance at their annual meeting attended on two consecutive weekends by 250 life insurance CEOs and COOs. I would have paid them for that opportunity.

To take advantage of sponsorship as a speaker, let your buyer know that you are a professional speaker as well as a consultant, find out what trade associations the client company belongs to and/or supports, and offer to play a role that will both help the trade association and cast your client in a favorable light. The fee arrangements should be secondary to the win/win/win marketing potential.

Sponsorship as a Consultant

Many organizations supply their own executives on a "lend lease" basis to non-profits, government agencies, charities, and similar public bodies. Some will also pay for the services of a consultant to help those organizations. This might be for a prolonged and profound project or for short-term simple assistance. In either case, your clients will pay your fee, just as if you were helping them, to help the organization being supported.

This approach enables you to support your client's pro bono activity, legitimately provide your talents for the non-profit, and meet a wide variety of potential buyers. (It's often a good idea to provide a discount on your own fee in the spirit of the endeavor.) The non-profit's board, directors, management, and clients will all have the opportunity to see your work, or at least reap the rewards of it. You may also receive some valuable media publicity.

Andrew Sobel focuses on strategy formulation and implementation for high-tech clients, taking on just one or two at a time. His partner is a marketing professor at Emory's Goizueta Business School. Andrew came from MAC and Gemini and currently generates over seven figures in business.

Q. What's the key reason for your current success?

A. It's a tossup: (1) Ability to identify and convincingly articulate the most important, overarching issues or themes that impact a given problem my clients are facing—"big picture thinking"; (2) ability to view the world from my client's perspective—to wear his hat, to empathize, to tune in to his hopes, concerns, and goals.

Q. Anything you would do differently?

A. I co-founded MAC's international practice and lived in Europe for thirteen years. When I repatriated in 1994, it was really difficult—I had been a superstar in Europe (country and office head, on the management committee), but I probably didn't have my head bowed low enough when I returned to this country! I left to start my own firm a year later. I should have either done a better job of re-ingratiating myself into the U.S. organization, or I should have left a year earlier! It was the year from hell, let me tell you. Afterwards I learned that "repatriation" is harder than "expatriation."

Q. What is your greatest unachieved goal?

A. Becoming a well-known speaker and author as opposed to just another management consultant. I'm hoping this will happen over the next year or so, as I have co-authored a book to be published by Simon & Schuster later this year.

I worked with a small business trade association—a market in which I would never ordinarily play a role—because I was subsidized by Peat Marwick, Fleet Bank, and the *Providence Journal,* all clients at the time. As a result of the work I performed, several small business asked for my help individually, which I provided on a discounted basis because they were all within an hour's drive and no marketing or travel costs were associated with the projects.[4]

To take advantage of this opportunity, inquire at your client's about their involvement with pro bono community work. In larger organizations, there is often a community outreach operation, which may be housed in the public relations department. In smaller organizations, the principals may actually be board members or highly visible supporters of certain causes. Let the proper people know that you'd be happy to play a role, and volunteer to allow your name to be used in publicity and press releases.

RULE 29

You don't know until you ask. Many organizations support and sponsor a myriad of activities, but don't ask external consultants to become involved on the assumption that it would be an unfair request or interpreted as a condition of maintaining the consulting assignment. You have to volunteer for this duty more often than not.

Joint Venture on Products and Services

In many cases a client will see a market opportunity that can be uniquely exploited through your talents. By establishing a joint venture, you and the client can both prosper.

---

4. An interesting "reversal": By doing pro bono work for the president of the University of Rhode Island and his staff, I was recommended for a paying job with a small business owner who relied on the university president for recommendations.

For example, a client once realized that a set of customer quality control forms could be used throughout the industry without a loss of competitive advantage. I was asked to develop them, using the client's own customers as a "laboratory." Once completed and tested, they were sold through an industry trade association with the client and me sharing the profits. In many cases like this, determinations such as who owns the copyright, the supply or revisions from year to year, customization for certain usage, and other considerations will influence payments and royalties. A simple contract can take care of all of that nicely. In many cases, the client will actually cede all rights and income to you, if you develop the prototype for no fee for the client's initial use. This can be especially valuable in areas such as training and development activities.

If you don't believe that these ventures can be big business, consider for a moment that firms such as Disney, 3M, and others have launched their own separate training and quality businesses because of the success (and publicity) of their internal efforts, and that every major audit and accounting firm eventually entered the consulting business, branching out from there to outsourcing, training, and other areas.

To explore these areas, examine areas of client need that also represent widespread industry need, but not on a competitive basis (areas such as safety standards, documentation approaches, public relations—Merck, for example, writes the "Bible" of desk reference medical information, which every other pharmaceutical company and health organization uses in common, and Cologne Reinsurance is known for publishing the key underwriting guide in the reinsurance industry). Find the entrepreneurs within the organization and network with them. In some cases, there may even be a business development unit charged with innovative start-ups.

These synergistic opportunities abound. They are initiated through the same kind of relationship building that we should be doing with our clients. And they can be just as lucrative—both in terms of income and marketing—as any client relationship. They need only start with your initiative and, occasionally, a missed lunch.

Sponsoring Organizations

There are organizations that actively sponsor consultants, trainers, speakers, facilitators, and others as outreach programs to their customers, community, and media sources. For example, an athletic shoe manufacturer might sponsor

Kennedy Publications publishes unique periodicals and reports in the consulting profession. It was founded and run for many years by its maverick owner, Jim Kennedy, who began with *Consultant's News.* I made it a practice to stay in touch with Jim—who could be cranky on his best days—and always provided complimentary copies of my books and other products. Occasionally, I would provide an article or his staff would review a speech I delivered at an industry conference.

When Jim sold the business, I made sure to touch base with the new executives, Wayne and Marshal Cooper. Wayne and I agreed to have lunch (he inadvertently stood me up, which created a bizarre but funny beginning to the relationship) and we both quickly saw the wisdom of several joint ventures.

As a result, Kennedy bought my newsletter, *The Consultant's Craft,* and offered me the editor's position on the replacement, *What's Working in Consulting.* We published two high-end, extremely successful books, *How to Write a Proposal That's Accepted Every Time* and *How to Market Professional Services: From Anonymity to Celebrity,* and have plans for several more. We have a seminar series that they promote and I deliver about four times a year, which draws people from all over the world from large firms and small. And I continue to write articles and reviews for their publications.

people who visit local gyms and spas to talk about health, equipment, and fitness. Medical device manufacturers might sponsor people who visit healthcare facilities, assisted living homes, and schools to discuss emergency procedures and preventive care. Pet food manufacturers may support people who address community groups and civic associations on proper animal nutrition, health care, and treatment of strays.

I've met quite a few former nurses, dental hygienists, physical therapists, and others who have maintained successful consulting careers exclusively subcontracting for healthcare organizations and appearing on their behalf. Despite the obvious sponsorship, these people are nonetheless regarded as authorities in their fields and are highly credible with the audiences and customers.

To explore this potential, find firms that are determined to improve, maintain, and/or solidify their public image or customer relationships and seek to do so through the provision of expertise and education. Trade associations are often key sponsors of these initiatives and seek external expertise and credibility to represent them and their industries.

Alternative Learning

I'm tempted to call this category "everything else," but it lends itself strongly these days to eCommerce and varied media. At this moment, for example, I have joint-ventured with the following:

- A firm that takes my books, turns them into courses on the web, promotes them to major organizations, and pays me a commission based on volume. They provide a portal on my own website, as well as market the programs unilaterally. I am also a part of their seminar series.
- A web human resource center, which features my columns and editorials to that profession, provides a link to my site, promotes my products, and gains visibility for me as an expert in that field.
- A firm that takes my videotapes, modifies them into learning courses, and markets them.
- An individual who, entrepreneurially, asked for permission to tape one of my workshops on proposal writing, created a two-tape product, and now sells them through his website, splitting profits with me.
- A firm that provides videoconferencing and pays me to appear at the studios of a local university for broadcast to their client base around the country. The two-hour sessions are simple to do and provide vast exposure to a diverse client base.
- Kennedy Publications, as mentioned in the case study above, which promotes seminars, books, newsletters, and other products and services to the consulting profession.
- Amazon.com, which, through its advantage program, carries my self-published products as well as my commercially published products, ordering the former directly from me, promoting them equally on its site, and sending me a check monthly for sales.
- A partner who initiated a video, audio, and print set of products based on

my work and who served as producer for the entire shebang. We split the expenses and profits 75 percent (me), 25 percent (him), and I promote them on my website, at speaking engagements, and in catalogs.

Not one of these relationships existed three years ago. And I have another dozen in the works. That's how rapidly advancing media can enable all of us to engage in alternative forms of distribution and income. However, my policy has been to allow the other party to do the marketing and promotion work, wherever possible. Last year, over half of my income came from passive sources and partnerships. Over the next year or two, I plan to increase that to over 75 percent.

To take advantage of this vast partnering market, seek out people who are successfully doing it and find out what the connections and contacts are. Put a note on your website that says, "Seeking established joint venture partners for. . . ." Don't ignore the form letters and generic e-mail that involves these issues. Some of it is actually high-potential, albeit poorly presented.

RULE 30

Whenever someone asks you to provide an article, editorial, column, or product placement, do so. In the worst case, you've wasted some time. In the best case, you've gained a new revenue source and distribution partner.

THE BLIGHT OF BROKERS

Although I once thought that this subject needn't be raised with highly successful people in the field, I've since seen evidence to the contrary. Consulting "brokers," unlike speakers' bureaus that can play a passive marketing role, are largely bunk and hustle.

There is a plethora of "brokers" springing up representing themselves as effective intermediaries between consultants and clients. Run for the exits.

Because consulting is a relationship business, the last thing we need is the proverbial "middle man" (no politically correct way to say that) inserted smack in the middle of it. Moreover, most brokers are simply people who couldn't make a living as legitimate consultants, so they are trying to earn some money on the backs of those who can.

A Recent Example: A friend asked me to respond to a broker's request for a consultant to deal with a major family-owned business. I demurred, explaining that I don't work that way. But she told me that the broker was eager to hear from me and would put me in touch with the buyer.

When I called the broker, he didn't immediately recognize me OR my friend. After a few minutes and his mumbling that "I've got sixty-five projects going on, it's hard to keep track of everything," he found the file. He told me he thought I was perfect, and he gave me the buyer's number, explaining that he'd set everything up. Now, keep in mind that the broker spoke to me for a total of six minutes and really didn't know anything about me.

The client was flabbergasted when I called. He said that he had "quite a few sets of materials from various consultants" sent by the broker, he wasn't even sure he wanted to pursue the project, and he certainly wasn't prepared to discuss what he thought was a confidential matter within the tightly held business.

"Look," I said, "I don't work this way. Give me a call if you'd ever like to discuss this, and I guarantee I won't mention this to anyone. But you ought to know that it was awfully easy to get your number and the background, and I would bet that quite a few of the people whose brochures are on your desk are telling their colleagues about this 'opportunity.'"

He was appalled and called the broker immediately. The broker sent me an e-mail saying it was all a "misunderstanding."

Brokers do three horrible things:

1. They simply line up bodies with prospects, like a dating service. There is little concern or sensitivity for the client or the consultant.
2. They often have a "favorite," whom they make look better by recommending "also-rans." (Think of my "choice of yeses": The broker is using you merely as one of his lower-end options.) You'll find that certain consultants with a high profile will get all the business by being constantly placed in the best light by the broker (the best option).

3. The broker will take some of your money if, by some miracle, a match is made. The broker deserves none of it.

The Internet is especially rife with this stuff. Stay away from it. If you can't make if on your own without middle men, you are in the wrong business. This is not partnering or joint venturing. This is ridiculous.

THE ULTIMATE RULES

Rule #26.   Make it your practice to collaborate only when the other party offers a piece of business to you that is attractive and profitable. If you follow this rule diligently, you'll never go to jail for murdering a partner.

Rule #27.   If you're being pitched a story of how successful your potential collaborators are, take a hard look at how they dress, what they drive, where they live, and where they've been. Successful people don't drive dented old cars, and even their casual clothes are impressive. Shallow? No, prudent.

Rule #28.   Ironically, higher-level collaborations are far easier to develop if you parlay your current level of success and experience into a value-added proposition for your potential partner. It's like a bank loan—much easier to secure when you don't need it as much.

Rule #29.   You don't know until you ask. Many organizations support and sponsor a myriad of activities, but don't ask external consultants to become involved on the assumption that it would be an unfair request or interpreted as a condition of maintaining the consulting assignment. You have to volunteer for this duty more often than not.

Rule #30.   Whenever someone asks you to provide an article, editorial, column, or product placement, do so. In the worst case, you've wasted some time. In the best case, you've gained a new revenue source and distribution partner.

Final Thought: There is absolutely no reason why you can't develop at least one potential joint venture client a month, meaning that you will have a dozen a year. If a third turn out to be lucrative and fulfill their potential, you can cash in on the repute and credibility that you've deservedly gained at this point in your career.

Liz Ahearn generates in excess of $1 million for The Radclyffe Group, LLC, a training and consulting firm focused on brand image. She is the CEO.

Q. What is the single key factor in your success?

A. I understand the core issues of the clients in my niche market and have learned how to effectively cultivate their pain and then offer a solution that is measurable. This is the way I gain credibility from the beginning. I ask strategic questions to identify their specific pain and then lead them to my firm as the only solution.

Q. What would you do differently if you did it over?

A. I would provide more outreach to my prospects. I would love to have the time to provide them with information that is relevant to their issues on a more consistent basis. I would like to be able to invest more money in important research for our niche market. (We already have completed four industry studies.)

Q. What is the major achievement you have yet to accomplish?

A. I would love to be awarded a million-dollar-plus project in one contract. My biggest was $555,000. Additionally, my vision for this firm is to grow at a controlled pace that ensures world-class service delivery to our clients and will maintain and enhance our current outstanding reputation in the market.

CHAPTER 7

International Business

The Peripatetic Consultant

Some consultants salivate over international business, others eschew it. The latter may want to skip this chapter (or, perhaps, read it in order to gain a new perspective and change their strategy).

I've traveled to fifty-one countries and done business in well over half of them. My wife has accompanied me to about thirty-five of them, and fewer than a dozen of them were completely unassociated with a business trip (and that figure is suspect if you consider that free air miles, gained on business trips, bought the first-class tickets that we used for the purely recreational trips). Consequently, most of my world travels have been completely or partially subsidized by client work.

Over the years, it hasn't been uncommon for me to earn over $250,000 annually solely from international business, in addition to my domestic work. Here are the reasons that I've found international work to be attractive and that I find it even more so today.

TEN REASONS WHY YOU SHOULD GET OUT OF TOWN

1. Money.   It is very lucrative. Your fees should be increased significantly for the closer work (Europe and Latin America, if you live on the East Coast) and dramatically for the farther work (Asia and the Pacific Rim, if you live on the East Coast). Clients seldom want to send you for a day or two, so they will collaborate on maximizing the amount of work you do while onsite. Finally, expense reimbursement tends to be highly advantageous, including at least business-class air fare and excellent hotels.

2. Relationships.   You solidify your relationship with the client, as you often know more about the international operation within a brief duration than do the organization's officers. Even those who do travel tend to be responsible for limited areas, and the trend is often to delegate accountability to regional, on-site executives who aren't frequently in the home office. I have had executives seek me out to test local morale, business conditions, staffing, and policy enforcement after my trips, because I had contemporary, apolitical information about key issues based not only on my project, but also on simple observation. (My favorite was the Asian office, staffed by Americans, that didn't open until well after local business hours and then immediately went into prolonged coffee-break mode. Business was so brisk, and the investment service so well-positioned, that the office staff were simply order takers and resembled a motor vehicle registry more than a sales office!)

3. Marketing.   While traveling, you have the "excuse" to visit prospects and important future contacts, even if it means taking an extra day or two at your own expense. When I travel from Rhode Island to New York, prospects don't feel a huge obligation to put time aside "while I'm in town"; when I travel to San Francisco, they almost always agree to spend an hour or so with me, because I've come from such a distance; when I'm working in London or Hong Kong, prospects and potential partners welcome me with a flexible schedule and usually offer dinner. It's an ideal time to develop:

- New business leads
- Publicity sources
- Local partners

4. Perspective. Your perspective broadens enormously. This is an increasingly global economy, and Americans are not as adept as others at appreciating and exploiting that fact. We seldom speak more than our own language (although it is becoming the world business language), are relatively ignorant of foreign history, and don't appreciate local cultures. Travel attends to those shortcomings quickly and expeditiously. Consequently, your worth to domestic clients increases significantly with the ability to provide a first-hand, personal, world view to your consulting methodology.

RULE 31

A consultant with international experience is always more valuable than one without it. Period.

5. Receptivity. Despite point four above, Americans are nearly universally well-received as consulting experts. In Australia we're known as "wise men from the East" (even the women). American management expertise is highly regarded, authorities such as Peter Drucker and executives such as Jack Welch are read and respected the world over, and the American economy and stock market have strong global impacts. With some unsurprising exceptions (France, of course), language is seldom a problem (even the Japanese are highly accommodating), and our counsel is eagerly sought. In other words, we're in the catbird's seat, and ought to take advantage of it.

6. Access. The Internet has made global marketing, publicity, visibility, and contacts available and relatively simple for even solo practitioners. If you have a website, it's easy to orient at least a part of it toward international work, or make it truly global in its overall approach. (If you don't have a website, you probably shouldn't be reading this book, but it's certainly inexpensive to establish a good one.) You can even track "hits" on your site by country of origin and consider that in your strategy for publicity, contacts, and site orientation.

About a year ago, I was contacted via e-mail by a Swiss business journal, which publishes the largest German-language business magazine in Europe. The editor explained that she had visited my website, using a word search that included "strategy," and had learned of one of my books, *Our Emperors Have No Clothes.*

She read a review of the book and then ordered it from my website. Once she read the entire work, she concluded that a similar article would be an important addition to her magazine. She explained that "European writers, particularly in Germany and Switzerland, are reluctant to be critical of any business practices for fear of offending colleagues."

The editor said that, from the style of my book, she didn't believe that I would have any trouble with that!

She requested an eight-to-twelve-page article, offered $2,500, and asked that I have it to her within a month. Her preference was for a piece on executive errors and how to prevent them.

I completed the article, based on my book, which received prominent mention in her magazine, in about forty-five minutes, and submitted it the next day. The editor suggested two minor changes that I provided, and she then translated the piece into German. My check arrived within two weeks, in U.S. funds, and it and the magazine copies she sent me a few months later were the only things that were not handled completely through the Internet.

That reprint goes to every client and prospect who does business in Germany, wants to do business in Germany, or is owned by a German parent company. (You never know until you investigate. No fewer than three of my clients at one point—Mercedes-Benz North America, Allianz Insurance, and Cologne Reinsurance—were owned by German parent organizations.)

---

7. Culture. The chance to enjoy your life with a significant other or spouse, to experience otherwise unappreciated art, architecture, scenery, cultures, food, music, and a myriad of other diverse pleasures is absolutely invaluable. *National Geographic* magazine or a documentary on the Discovery Channel might be one thing, but let me assure you that floating in a dugout canoe near Thailand's floating markets with a small alligator swimming alongside giving you the eye is quite another. Aside from the major cities such as London or Rome, places like Venice, Bangkok, Grenada (Spain), and the countryside of England are experiences that will change your life.

8. Profitability.   The business is inexpensive to develop, because there are so many American multi-nationals and so many foreign multi-nationals with significant operations in the United States. You don't have to solicit the business overseas, but merely go there to deliver it. In many cases, in fact, the business is yours for the asking if you make the right inquiries within your existing client base.

9. Collaboration.   There are many local management groups seeking collaborations with Americans to fill their own needs and those of their clients. By establishing a true collaboration with a local management institute or association, you can gain access to their members or clients and/or be sponsored by that local, credible source. Few consultants appreciate the fact that organizations such as the Hong Kong Management Association host conferences, recommend consultants, sponsor symposia, and generally make introductions as a benefit to their members.

10. Publishing.   The foreign press is quite amenable, in general, to articles, interviews, and book excerpts from Americans (and from any source outside of their own country) to improve diversity of views and education. They will often provide the translation of your material (or you may have it translated by your own expert for a very reasonable sum[1]). It is very impressive to have foreign language reprints with your name on them in your

---

1. If you need a translation quickly and inexpensively, go to the language department of a major university and offer the job on a contract basis to a faculty member expert in the language. You will get a thorough job for an inexpensive hourly rate (or you can offer to include a translation credit on the manuscript and perhaps have the job done for free).

press kit, adding a universality to the legitimacy of your approaches. My work has been translated into Italian, Portuguese, Chinese, German, and French.[2]

APPROACHING AND EXPLOITING U.S. MULTI-NATIONALS

If you have clients with overseas operations, make sure you reach out laterally to the executives responsible for various international functions. If you're involved with strategy or communications or team-building work, the chances are that some of these people are part of your project. If you're involved in a narrower project, then you might have to identify them and arrange introductions.

In either case, your approach should be similar. Develop a relationship with the key individuals. Offer them value. For example, if the foreign operation is a "poor cousin," offer to provide some equivalent help so that the data being gathered represents them equally with domestic operations. You can often begin this with phone, fax, and e-mail, so there is no immediate significant expense entailed. Generally, international managers are overjoyed to be included and will be highly cooperative, responsive, and flexible in scheduling.

Find out what kind of projects have been undertaken in the past, either by internal resources or external consultants. Have they been local and onsite, or have they been flown in from elsewhere? Is there a precedent for consultants to visit? (If so, build on it. If not, suggest that there may be reason to begin one.)

---

2. If you publish a book commercially, ask the publisher to pursue foreign rights aggressively. If the book is translated, you will have a strong impetus to solicit business, speeches, and appearances in the countries of that language, even if you personally work only in English. A local language publication or book is a tremendous advantage.

> If the client is flying internal, domestic resources to help in overseas operations, there is no added expense in sending an external consultant. In fact, you can make the case for a savings, as the internal resource can remain in place doing his or her normal job.

Keep the international executives on your contact list, whether or not you've established tentative work or submitted a proposal. You never know when the need will develop and, more often than not, the need surfaces in a panic mode when someone is needed instantly. You want your name, your prior conversations, and your credible relationship with the domestic operation constantly in mind.

Demonstrate your "internationalism." If you have had foreign articles published, distribute them to appropriate parties. If you've traveled to certain relevant areas, let it be known. If you've studied or experienced something pertinent, make it clear. For example, whenever I'm introduced to anyone from a Latin American subsidiary at a U.S. conference, I greet them and ask where they're from completely in Spanish. This immediately captures both their attention and the attention of the U.S. executives (many of whom actually have to ask what we've just said!). I know enough Spanish to make a greeting, get a meal, and use a taxi, and that's sufficient to make a fine impression. Inevitably, my Spanish colleagues compliment my accent, not because it's actually very good, but because the attempt to greet people in their own language is regarded as such a rare courtesy.

If your client is a legitimate multi-national (and not just a U.S. firm with a sales office or suite sitting in a foreign city), do your homework. Find out from the annual report what the contributions are, establish relationships with the key executives responsible, demonstrate your "internationality," and continually provide value and suggest ways you can be of help.

There were times when, following this strategy, I was doing more work

Chris Fink is the principal of Senior Associates, Inc., in Winston-Salem, NC. The company works in "go-to-market" strategies and related support by providing senior executives for hands-on roles. Revenues are in the $400,000 to $600,000 range.

Q. What is your greatest success factor?

A. A consistent revenue stream: Being able to generate a sufficient, steady revenue stream to cover the overhead while avoiding the "feast or famine" syndrome of many small shops.

Q. What would you do differently if starting over?

A. Spend more time completing the marketing infrastructure up front: Clear positioning, supporting brochures/literature, effective website, and networking arrangements (article writing, speech giving, etc.).

Q. What major accomplishment still awaits?

A. Reinventing myself ahead of the curve while managing to deliver current client assignments. This was not hard while in a large consulting organization, but as a solo "virtual shop" this is more challenging.

internationally than domestically for such true global powers as Merck and State Street Bank.

WORKING WITH FOREIGN-BASED FIRMS

It's difficult to begin working from scratch with an organization headquartered in Japan, England, South Africa, or Australia. But it's relatively easy to begin that work with their U.S. operation.

If your strategy is to work internationally, then target these firms: Siemans, or Sony, or Nokia, or Michelin, or whomever. Find the local target and hone in, using the marketing gravity that we've discussed in earlier chapters. For example:

- Can a current client provide an introduction to the subsidiary of a foreign multi-national?
- Can you speak at a conference or event that those executives tend to support? This could be anything from a trade industry conference for automakers that will draw the Korean, Japanese, Italian, German, and other manufacturers to an expatriate organization specifically geared to Japanese executives transferred to the United States (for example, there is a huge enclave in northern New Jersey in and around the town of Ft. Lee, including Japanese shops and markets).
- Can you demonstrate a competency or specialty that is attractive to these firms? My work with IBJ Whitehall, for example, a Japanese-owned institution, at one point included counsel to Japanese managers on a rotational assignment to the U.S. operation. Do you have a background in diversity, counseling, cross-cultural business, languages, or other areas that might make you immediately attractive, given the needs of these firms?
- Can you publish articles (or position papers) that you've tailored expressly to the needs of these foreign-owned businesses and circulate them to the key buyers and recommenders?
- Can you provide information and value on your website that targets the needs of these organizations?
- Can you serve on committees or task forces and take advantage of other pro bono opportunities in the community, so that you can meet these buyers on a collegial basis?
- Can you teach at a local college or extension program where these companies may be sending their managers for development, thereby gaining recognition and relationships with potential recommenders?
- Can you help the local American executive to deal more effectively with a boss or directors who are of another culture, geographically remote, and applying a different set of cultural norms? I've found this to be some of the most effective and lucrative executive coaching I've done, as the local executive usually has complete budget discretion, can't look for help of this

quite sensitive nature internally, and is often completely at sea in terms of how to deal with foreign superiors.

The answer to all of these questions is, "Yes." The only real question is whether you have the discipline to formulate that strategy and implement it. Not enough consultants are targeting foreign multi-nationals with substantial operations in the United States through a value-added, focused approach. Consultants tend to treat them as just another organization, often lulled by the fact that the local executives may be American.

RULE 33

One highly effective entry into a foreign owned U.S. operation is to help the local management team more effectively deal with their direct superiors overseas. This coaching is virtually never tenable on an internal basis.

Once you are successful with the U.S. subsidiary, begin to develop the proper rapport and contacts to extend your help to headquarters. After all, if local management needs help dealing with headquarters, it may just be that headquarters requires help dealing with local management. Foreign firms often desire local analysis that is not filtered through its own management team. And the true nature of a real multi-national (as opposed to a company that views itself as local with many overseas units) is that it utilizes local help to provide inputs to its strategy and tactics.

OVERSEAS ALLIANCES

We briefly discussed above the professional associations that exist around the world, which are usually quite receptive to American expertise and participation. Consultants without name recognition but who have solid track records and who are willing to invest some targeted resources in acquiring partnerships can be highly successful in this market. Consultants who have a higher profile—books in print, previous work in certain countries, local articles published—can enter into these collaborations fairly easily.

As in all relationships, the key is to bring value to your partner and to mitigate the adverse aspects of the collaboration. This usually means some combination of the following:

Bringing Value

- Provide speeches and/or participate in panel discussions for your host
- Have some of your articles and position papers translated into the appropriate languages
- Provide favorable fees, with the perception of a discount through the auspices of your local partner
- Offer onsite development for your partner though their collaboration in your consulting projects, and/or naming them as your local project director
- Provide rapid access and responsiveness through e-mail, fax, and phone to offset the distances involved
- Pay a commission to the sponsoring organization for speeches, consulting, product sales, and other revenue generators
- Schedule immovable, dedicated dates for trips around which your local alliance partner can firmly plan activities, marketing, sales calls, and so forth
- Provide free development work for your partner's own staff
- Participate aggressively in long-distance media interviews to publicize your alliance and your visits

Mitigating Drawbacks

- Treat your alliance partners as if they were next door—don't cancel, fail to respond, or provide inferior service because local clients and alliances receive priority
- Try to schedule your visits around other client work you may have in the locale so as to reduce your alliance partner's expenses
- If you have no other work in the area, subsidize some of your expenses through either absorbing some of the costs or using frequent flyer miles for

transportation (or combine the trip with a vacation and use some of the money you would normally use for a vacation)[3]

- Learn enough of the language to greet someone cordially, order a meal, converse with a hotel desk clerk, and take a taxi. Also, learn enough of the local culture and history so as to avoid gaffes and demonstrate your interest in the country or region
- Don't expect superstar treatment. On the other hand, do accept whatever courtesies your hosts extend; it's as poor form to reject an offer to go to dinner as it is to complain that your hotel room is too small
- Leave an American arrogance, imperious nature, colloquialisms, and jargon at your departure airport in the U.S. You can reclaim it when you return home
- Listen carefully to your partners, and ignore a great deal of the pseudo-advice and mythology that you hear in consulting circles in the United States (often from people who make a living giving advice, but who have never actually worked abroad or done much consulting). For example, people in other countries are as sensitive to Americans making cultural errors as Americans are to visitors here. We tend to create unfortunate ethnic stereotypes here much too readily (for example, the Japanese won't confront poor performance, the Germans react only to logic and never emotion)

Overseas alliances are more possible and desirable today than ever before, because the Internet provides for unprecedented communication and marketing, and the pervasive nature of the English language and American dollar are creating an ideal dynamic for U.S. consulting expertise.

If you have a staff, it may be wise to assign this strategy to an energetic marketer. If not, assign a half-day a week or whatever makes sense to developing these overseas partners. You'll find that the only reason you may be unsuccessful is that someone else got there first.

---

[3]One of the major reasons that consultants and serious potential alliance partners never consummate a deal is not because of a poor market or a poor synergy, but rather because the initial travel expenses are prohibitive, either in fact or symbolically.

You can provide absolutely superb international consulting to a U.S.-based global organization or to a foreign-based global organization, simply by carefully listening to what are often called "people on the ground"—the local staffs.

In traveling to six countries in Europe and Asia for a Boston-based company, I found the following simply by holding focus groups of mid- and lower-level management:

- Brochures provided by the home office had only the Boston address and no local contact points.

- Pictures of local currency were printed on the corporate brochures, but the practice is actually illegal in countries such as England, where the brochures were therefore useless.

- Global communications—whether by mail or e-mail—were often undermined by "Americanisms," such as "dress-down days," "chinos," and sports analogies. This was equally true in other English-speaking nations such as Australia and New Zealand.

- The home office provided no accommodation for time differences, and headquarters executives often called their overseas subordinates at 4 a.m. local time or demanded they participate in global conference calls at that time. Often, entire service functions were virtually inaccessible to overseas operations during their own business hours.

In reporting these problems to corporate executives, with factual examples and recommendations for reconciling the issues, I was seen as providing real-time and rapid resolutions to clear and chronic problems. I was also able to demonstrate that the existing avenues of communication were proving insufficient to allow for such internal correction and also needed adjustment.

It's often as simple as that. It's not exactly rocket science, but that type of assistance is highly visible, highly valuable, and greatly needed.

One Final Point: There is even less pressure for per diem billing overseas, providing even more opportunity to educate your partner and your prospects that you'll work together on a single fee, value-based approach.

RULE 34

"Cultural differences" are a chimera. If you focus on listening to your prospect, creating practical solutions, and demonstrating value in your partnership, you will be successful anywhere from Kuala Lumpur to Katmandu.

TEN WAYS TO ESTABLISH AN INTERNATIONAL PRESENCE

Even without a local alliance partner, you can accomplish a great deal to promote yourself internationally, either with a targeted approach to a specific market or with a generic approach to global business.

Here are some cost-effective, pragmatic, immediate tactics to promote yourself to an international audience of recommenders, buyers, and partners. You can begin today and, over the course of several months, develop a strong international "presence."

1. If you commercially publish, use your publisher's overseas operation to push for international translation and distribution. My books have been translated into German, Italian, and Chinese in this fashion. Not only will you gain additional income from your share of the local license, but you will have an instant claim to fame. My German publisher, Campus Verlig, actually reprinted *Managing for Peak Performance* more times than Harper-Collins did in the United States. (It helps when you're writing the book to make it as international as possible, avoiding U.S. colloquialism and including international examples to support your points. This doesn't hurt domestic sales and considerably augments international appeal.)

Alex H. Cunningham is the CEO of Profit Management Consulting. The firm exceeded $10 million in revenues in the 1997–1999 period. It specializes in profit enhancement strategies to middle-market clients.

Q. What is the major reason for your success and dramatic business level?

A. Our success is predicated on our project-oriented system not being retainer oriented. We focus on short-term projects that can have a major, measurable impact on profitability, cash flow, and net worth. Our process unbundles the firm's consulting services so that the client can purchase the assessment portion, which potentially develops several succinct individual projects without obligation to purchase any or all of our proposed project implementation. This allows our clients to select and purchase our services on a more ala carte basis.

Q. Despite the success, what would you have done differently?

A. More comprehensive market analysis, segmentation and target analysis, and the economic commitment required to obtain market share. Traditional professional service firms are slow to recognize the resource allocation necessary to generate and maintain sufficient work.

Q. What is your major unachieved goal?

A. Recognition and respect is the goal of every worthy organization. Our firm's character must begin with our common, adamant, unswerving adherence to clearly stated principles and values on which we were founded and by which we singularly intend to perpetually operate. The primary purpose of growth is to provide challenging opportunities for achievement-oriented employees. The ability to build such an organization that perpetuates itself beyond my involvement as the firm's founder and principal is my most pre-eminent goal.

2. If you self-publish, seek out foreign publishers who might be willing to publish and distribute the book. If you provide them with most of the revenues, they may underwrite the translation costs (and will do it far better locally, anyway). In exchange for sacrificing most of the revenue, you'll have a translated book to promote your consulting locally.

3. Use those Internet sites with strong overseas participation to publish articles, advertise, list your services, provide an interview, and so forth. Even better, approach those that are dedicated to local management and business issues in your targeted regions.

4. Make yourself "internationally friendly." Some toll-free numbers in the United States can't even be accessed in Canada, much less Italy. Include the U.S. country code before your phone number and fax number. Insert some position papers and/or articles of international appeal in your press kit. (Once again, these will not confuse your American audience, but will appeal significantly to your international audience.) If you do have an international partner, provide that contact information in your materials.

5. If and when possible, include international references, testimonials, and examples in your publicity material, website, and press kit.

6. Submit articles, either in hard copy or by e-mail, to international publications. Ironically, this is sometimes an easier "sell" than are domestic publications, as the editors find the inclusion of American articles of appeal to their readers, especially an "exclusive" for their publication.

7. Start doing research on the countries of your greatest priority. Develop a file on business and economic issues, so that you "hit the ground running" when you do establish a promising lead or partner. The time to educate yourself is *before* you begin developing the appropriate relationships.

8. Think about beginning on the path of least resistance: Choose the English-speaking areas that also have the greatest need for your expertise and approaches. But be creative—while the U.K. and Australia may be obvious, Hong Kong is at least equally appropriate.

9. Plan a vacation you were going to take anyway to an area of high potential, and take an extra day or two to see what you can learn and/or develop locally. I've never yet been to a country with high business prospects that doesn't also offer wonderful vacation and recreation opportunities.

10. Finally, consider offering your help to an established international consultant or firm that needs your expertise. In this way, you can establish

yourself overseas through established channels and learn what your sponsoring firm does well. Be frank about your objectives, so there is no implication that you are there to steal business or market share. Even if you haven't subcontracted in years, this can be an advantageous approach to accelerate your international entry.

Before we leave this topic, I want to re-emphasize that you can begin publicizing yourself internationally at any time, gradually, and with little or no investment. At worst, nothing happens and you have some additional fodder for your press kit. At best, you'll be preparing for an entirely new and exciting source of business.

Personally, I can't imagine any successful consultant ignoring this lucrative and high-potential market.

PROTECTING YOURSELF AS AN INTERNATIONALIST

There are some unique considerations for international work that catch many consultants by surprise. Here are some of the potential land mines and the paths around them.

Financial Considerations

Always quote all fees, prices, and expense reimbursement in U.S. dollars. This is vital as nearby as Canada, where the currency exchange is otherwise deadly. Ask your clients to remit in U.S. funds drawn on a U.S. bank. (If you receive a check in U.S. funds, but there is no corresponding U.S. bank, you will be charged for the translation of foreign currency to dollars nonetheless, and some banks charge as high as 25 percent.) I've often accepted entire payments on credit cards, which take care of all exchange issues at that day's rates (often an advantage for an overseas client, as exchange may adversely affect them by the time the actual services are delivered), and I'll gladly absorb the credit card fee of 2 to 3 percent.

If you are working with someone with whom you've never worked before, *especially a partnering organization,* insist on partial payment in advance as a sign of good faith. Ensure that local charges such as hotel rooms and meals are picked up by the client in local currency, which is best for both of you. Ideally, arrange for the balance of your payment to be delivered at the conclusion of your onsite work.[4] It's also possible to have expenses reimbursed in the same manner, as your travel expenses are known and documented by that time.

Be aware that bartered goods and services—for example, a local sponsor providing a vacation in return for your work—are usually subject to U.S. tax laws, and you ought to consult your attorney and financial advisor on the most advantageous conditions.

Safety Considerations

There are some places that are simply dangerous. The rate of street crime, kidnappings, robberies, and other mayhem in cities such as Mexico City, or Rio, or Lagos are much higher than elsewhere. That is simply a fact, and not a reflection on the worth of those nations or cultures.

Never assume your safety in a foreign country. Ask your local partner, client, or sponsor what the best travel and hotel arrangements are. In Rio, for example, it's best to travel by private car, and then only when the driver's identification is verified by the hotel. Often, the client will provide a private driver for your entire stay. Sometimes local taxis are safe; sometimes they are dangerous. There are cities in which you can walk the streets safely at 3 a.m., and others in which you can't walk far from the hotel unescorted at 6 p.m.

When you're on vacation, those sites usually take precautions to protect vital tourist dollars. But in cities and in many business venues, there is no such overall precaution provided. Some rules of thumb until you become familiar with a locale:

- Stay in large, well-known hotels in well-traveled, safe areas
- Don't walk in deserted or poorly lighted areas; exercise the same cautions you would in any large American city

---

4. There are some restrictions on currency that can be taken back into the United States. Check the regulations at the time of your engagement. Usually, checks receive a different treatment from cash.

- Don't accept rides, favors, gifts, or advice from strangers[5]
- Travel by safest means: private car, registered taxi, tour bus, etc.
- Keep your travel documents—passport, plane tickets, visa, and so forth—in a safe place at all times.
- Don't carry a lot of currency with you (use traveler's checks), nor flash expensive jewelry or accessories

---

RULE 35

Work only with U.S. dollars. Let me state that another way: Work only with U.S. dollars.

Health Considerations

This is not the problem it once was but, depending on your itinerary, check with your doctor to see whether any shots are required or need to be updated. Don't assume that medicines you're taking will be available locally in the same form or the same dosages. Make sure that medicines you do need to carry will not cause problems at customs inspections.

Carry in your briefcase a copy of any eyeglass prescriptions that might have to be filled if you lose or break your glasses or contact lenses during the trip. A small tube of Fixodent™ can usually re-cement a bridge or cap that comes loose.

Make sure that you have an emergency contact number in your wallet and briefcase, as well as basic information such as blood type and any allergies to medication.

I love sampling all local foods and have had menudo (tripe) out of earthen pots in Mexico City as one in the morning, washed down with local beer, and blowfish—toxic if not prepared exactly correctly—in Tokyo when my wife and

---

5. As an aside, I found that the famous Stanley Flea Market in Hong Kong often had higher prices than the retail stores a block from my hotel downtown.

I were the only non-Japanese within miles. But I also have the digestive system of a great white shark. Most people need to be careful about what they sample and eat, including sauces and dressings. Local tap water is still a problem in many places, and that includes salads that are washed in it.

It's best to be arch-conservative in your food politics, particularly on a first visit.

Business Considerations

Arrange for someone to have the authority to make basic business decisions in your absence if you have the staff to do so. Otherwise, arrange for someone to take care of the phones, faxes, mail, and other communications. It's wise to prepare some press kits and product mailings in advance, so that someone can simply fulfill the appropriate requests in your absence.

You can attend to e-mail daily if you take a laptop—which you should do—and you can call in at least once a day, no matter what the time differential. Using international options such as USADirect™ from AT&T, you can dial a local number in virtually any country and use your credit card to economically reach U.S. numbers. Clients are simply blown away when you return their call from Sydney or Paris, and the $10 or so is more than worth it.

Make provisions so that your business is not shut down when you travel, which isn't difficult, because most of your business is between your ears.

THE ULTIMATE RULES

Rule #31. A consultant with international experience is always more valuable than one without it. Period.

Rule #32. If the client is flying internal, domestic resources to help in overseas operations, there is no added expense in sending an external consultant. In fact, you can make the case for a savings, as the internal resource can remain in place doing his or her normal job.

Rule #33. One highly effective entry into a foreign owned U.S. operation is to help the local management team more effectively deal with their direct superiors overseas. This coaching is virtually never tenable on an internal basis.

Paul Rich is the principal of Siegel Rich, Inc., which provides services in the areas of mergers and acquisitions and strategy for firms with revenues of $25 million to $100 million. They are headquartered in New York. Paul generates over half a million dollars in revenues for the business.

Q. What is the single key factor in your success?

A. Understanding that owners and senior management of middle-market companies feel alone. It is my ability to offer affirmation and care, through an intense and intimate level of interaction, and to provide a safe place so that CEOs can talk about who they are and the processes they go through in trying to make decisions. They need someplace where they can talk about fears, hopes, failures, successes, and ambivalence. They need guidance from someone who not only has a solid understanding of how business works, but a deep feeling for the dynamics of making decisions. It is an ability to create a relationship with the CEO transcending that of an advisor to that of "Rabbi" or "Consigliore": The ability to make people feel safe and understand the needs and insecurities of powerful people.

Q. What would you do differently if you did it over?

A. I think I would spend much more time in continuing my formal education through post-graduate programs offered at the better business universities.

Q. What is the major achievement you have yet to accomplish?

A. I would like to teach on the graduate school university level to seasoned accountants, attorneys, and other consultants how to be more effective by merging their technical expertise with the understanding of the human dynamics of their clients in order to appreciate moving from the project-based client or assignment to a more holistic approach, which I believe would be more effective.

Rule #34. "Cultural differences" are a chimera. If you focus on listening to your prospect, creating practical solutions, and demonstrating value in your partnership, you will be successful anywhere from Kuala Lumpur to Katmandu.

Rule #35. Work only with U.S. dollars. Let me state that another way: Work only with U.S. dollars.

Final Thought: This is a truly global economy. If you choose to work solely in the United States, you are deliberately isolating yourself.

Managing Time

Or How to Be at the Pool by Two in the Afternoon

I don't know about you, but I don't feel very successful if I'm making a million dollars or more a year and spending 80 percent of my time on the road. Yet that's the situation I found myself in several years ago. Airline pilots and fight attendants don't even travel that much. There's a quality to the life afforded by this profession that we too often ignore.

When you're working for someone else, learning the ropes, subject to their paycheck, you tend to get on the airplanes and stay in the hotels they (or the client) specify. You're trading freedom for security to a certain extent. But when you go out on your own, subjecting yourself to the inevitable risks and rigors required to be successful, you deserve the rewards. And those rewards are not just financial: They are realizational. By "realizational" I mean that we deserve to "self-realize," meaning that we deserve to maximize our personal and family goals.

I've sometimes been accused of being mercenary, focusing on optimally raising fees and generating higher levels of revenues and profits (*Million Dollar Consulting, How to Maximize Fees, Money Talks: How to Make a Million as a Speaker*). My overriding rule here is that you can't help others unless you help yourself. You can't provide pro bono work, contribute to worthy causes, teach in the evening, mentor, coach, serve as an association leader, and invest in other concurrent activities such as these *unless you have financial security.* (It's true that many of these are also fine marketing opportunities, but they are engaged in far more comfortably and with much less stress when there is no immediate financial pressure.)

What does this have to do with managing time? Simply this: Time is your greatest asset—and your most crucial non-renewable asset. As a writer, I constantly bear in mind that the minutes the reader has invested in the current pages can't be regained; consequently, the worth must be in the higher quality future derived from those pages.

Managing time isn't about more effective client responsiveness or juggling more projects, although those are desirable by-products. Managing time is about self-realization, and the ability to capitalize fully on the fruits of your success.

 RULE 36

If you can focus on the effective management and conservation of only two things, make them time and money, in that order. The second is, after all, renewable, but the first is not. Money lost can be regained. Time is forever gone.

There are two questions I'm asked far more frequently than all the others put together. The first is, "How do you convert to value-based pricing and significantly increase fees based on value?" The second is, "How do you manage your time to accomplish so much and yet still have time for a rich personal life?"

The second question is actually more important than the first, and I've addressed the first in many places. So let's focus here on the second, and on those elements that will exponentially increase your discretionary time and allow you to be realizational.

AVOIDING SCOPE CREEP

This is by far the greatest single client-related squanderer of a consultant's time. If you're a solo practitioner, it's deadly and delimiting; if you're a small firm principal, it can quickly erode your margins and empty your own pockets; if you're a partner in a large firm, it creates tremendous pressure to maximize billable hours elsewhere to offset the losses.

"Scope creep" is the gradual enlargement of a project at the client's behest *but with the willing collaboration of the consultant.* Let's be uncomfortably clear— scope creep cannot occur unilaterally. The consultant has to agree. More horribly, scope creep is often initiated, not by the buyer, but by a client manager at a low level who, maliciously or inadvertently, sees the opportunity to get some free help. Yet, even here, the consultant agrees.

The primary causes of scope creep are twofold: First, unclear project objectives and, second, a reluctance or inability to adhere to those objectives.

Unclear Objectives

At the outset of any project, the objectives to be accomplished—the client business outcomes—should be a part of the proposal and contract, as should the measures of success and the methodology to achieve them.[1] With the exception of some retainer arrangements (wherein the client is paying for the general access to your "smarts" as needed), every client project should have these specifics signed off by the buyer.

These proposals are no mere nicety. They should be used as the template for the projects and shared with the consulting team and the client team, so that everyone is clear on the parameters of the project. (There is no need to share the full proposal with fees and terms, and the objectives, measures, and methodology can be excerpted.)

Once these objectives are used on a daily basis, they will become the accepted boundaries of the project. Clients don't usually maliciously try to take advantage of consultants, but they will certainly continue to push along the

---

1. For detailed examples and templates, see my book *How to Write a Proposal That's Accepted Every Time* (Kennedy Information, Fitzwilliam, NH, 1999).

paths of least resistance. The clear objectives, measures, and methodology will provide the backbone you need to avoid being bent backwards.

Reluctance to Adhere to Objectives

This category really represents a case of out-and-out fear. The consultant—sometimes even the partner, principal, or owner—is fearful of pushing back against a

CASE STUDY

While working with Hewlett-Packard's technical consulting arm, we determined that project profitability often suffered *by as much as two-thirds of the original estimate* due to scope creep, which HP termed "undocumented promises." Undocumented promises were informal agreements made at relatively low levels between HP consultants implementing the project and the client implementers assisting them. The latter felt that so much money was being paid to HP (although no one actually knew the project fee) that it was legitimate to ask for nearly anything, including programming assistance on unrelated projects and trouble shooting on daily operational problems. The HP consultants didn't want to jeopardize the seven-figure project, so they agreed to almost anything short of polishing the floors, though they might well have done that if pressed.

We solved the problem with several actions. First, we created clear project objectives, outcomes, and deliverables, which every implementing consultant received and discussed with project managers. Second, no request outside of those parameters could be approved short of the project manager level. Third, the relationship manager position was created at a senior HP level, so that a credible HP partner interacted with client peers, ensuring a top-level contact to discuss and resolve requests outside of the original scope.

The preferred method for dealing with such requests was established as addenda to the proposal *with a commensurately increased fee.*

With these simple procedural changes, HP was able to immediately increase project profitability and was also able to intelligently accept project enlargement that could be demonstrated as added value to the buyer for future business.

client request that may, in his or her mind, threaten the relationship. This is abject nonsense, largely because high-level buyers tend to respect people like themselves, who will resist unfair pressure and say "no" to unreasonable requests.

Once you agree to actions outside the scope of the engagement, you become an enabler, and you and the client have joined in a conspiracy to lower your margins.

The key here is to realize that you are doing the client and yourself a favor by refusing to be defocused from the real objectives of the project, and that you don't want to establish a precedent whereby the client is able to say, "But you agreed to that last time. Why not this time?" The more you fold, the harder eventually to resist. Educate your new clients correctly.

One more point: Low-level people can be much more unreasonable and demanding than high-level people, mainly because they are overburdened and have real-time operational needs. There's no need to get into a pitched battle. Simply tell them (or instruct your people to tell them religiously) that any changes have to be approved by the client buyer, so please refer the request to that person. Then you can deal with a single source who will be sensitized to the amount of increasing demands the organization's people are making. With that strategy, you develop an ally not to accept expansion, rather than an advocate for expansion.

Scope creep is an entirely consultant-controllable condition. Effectively setting objectives and sticking to them will safeguard profitability and save huge amounts of time to be invested elsewhere. Consequently, effectively directing this element of your implementation is the most important management responsibility you have. Delegate to others with the greatest trepidation.

MINIMIZING LABOR-INTENSIVE REQUIREMENTS

If you bill by the hour, you will have to demonstrate hours of work, onsite or offsite, to justify your billing. Lawyers and accountants engage in this backbreaking activity (or fictitious exercise, depending on your point of view). I find that attorneys billing eighty hours a week are simply not credible, and I feel the same about consultants billing even forty hours a week. No one is perpetually busy during the business day, consumed with client affairs.

So, rule number one is to abandon hourly billing. I doubt many people reading this book have achieved great success putting a premium on their time, as opposed to the results and value they create, so I'm not going to preach to the choir here.

However, even when you're billing based on value, a great deal of your time investment will be determined by the client's expectations of your

Anne Pauker is a human resources strategy consultant with revenues in the mid six figures. She formed her practice in 1995, based in Hazlet, NJ.

Q. What is the single key factor in your success?

A. My reputation—for anticipating and shaping trends in my field (human resource practices), simplifying complex problems, and creating innovative solutions.

Q. What would you do differently if you did it over?

A. I'm pretty happy with the way my practice has developed. However, there is a down-side to being on the "bleeding edge" all the time. Often I have a solution to a problem that does not yet appear obvious, so it takes a while before the market recognizes the issues. And larger corporate clients often look to larger, "name brand" consultants to work with. My competitive advantage has always been having a better product that's truly customized to meet my client's needs, delivered faster.

Q. What is the major achievement you have yet to accomplish?

A. When I worked for a major corporation, I was seen both internally and externally as a "thought leader" in my field. This is tougher when you are in your own firm rather than affiliated with a large consultancy, private corporation, or university. My professional goal is to move the field of human resources forward in a significant, recognizable, and meaningful way.

The Ultimate Consultant

involvement. Rule number two is to be non-specific about the degree of your methodology. In other words, it's fine to state that focus groups, interviews, and surveys will be used to collect information. But it's another to specify that there will be twelve focus groups of fifteen people each, 125 one-on-one interviews of thirty minutes each, and a sixteen-question survey sent to 1,500 people with an expected response rate of 70 percent.

The dangers are two-fold. First, the buyer is prone to say, "What if we cut the interviews in half? How will that affect the fee?" (It shouldn't, because your fee is based on outcomes, not methodologies.) The second is that you find you can move more quickly than anticipated once you receive early results, but the client is asking, "Why didn't you do all the focus groups?" or "Why are the interviews only twenty minutes?" or even "Why can't we capture the other 30 percent in the survey?" Of course, none of these quantitative differences will make a whit of difference in the qualitative client results.

The client is the expert in content, for example, knowing how to build cars, fly airplanes, or sell insurance. But you are the expert in consulting, for example, knowing how to sample a population, interpret results, and observe behavior. I don't tell Mercedes how to build better cars, and I don't expect Mercedes to tell me how to conduct better focus groups. That always seemed fair to me and, apparently, it seemed fair to them.

The final rule, number three, is achieve a relationship (and level of education) with the client so that it is understood and accepted that your help needn't be onsite, face-to-face, and immediately present. Access to your help may be by e-mail, fax, phone, and correspondence. You can attend meetings "remotely," via conference call and teleconference. Effective sampling means that you need only see a representative slice, not every slice.

RULE 37

Focus on outcomes and results, not on your methodology, tasks, and inputs. Educate the client so that the buyer understands that your contribution is in the improvement to the buyer's operation, not in your presence.

Sometimes it is important for the consultant to be present and a part of various client meetings; but often it's sufficient that key managers simply have access to the consultant and can call when help is deemed necessary. Sometimes it is important for the consultant to visit the client's customers; but often it's of even higher quality to conduct a phone interview, as it's less intrusive and easier to arrange logistically (as well as being less expensive). Sometimes it is important to provide coaching by "shadowing" an executive through meetings, office work, and customer calls. But often that coaching is just as effective by meeting periodically, discussing what's happened and why, and providing options for future behaviors. (After all, no therapist that I know of accompanies patients on their daily rounds.)

From the outset of the first discussion about a possible project, begin to educate the prospect that you will jointly focus on results, that you are always accessible in some fashion, but that your value to improving the prospect's condition is not a function of your showing up someplace. A $200,000 project that demands ten days onsite every month for six months is less productive and less profitable than a $50,000 project that you complete over the same period, appearing onsite once or twice a month. And that's not because of the irrelevant daily amount you get by dividing fee by days. It's because of the larger discretionary time it allows you to invest so much more in other projects and/or in your life.

By the way, the true "ultimate consultant" acquires the $200,000 project and completes it to the client's stupendous delight by spending only a couple of days a month onsite.

UTILIZING CLIENT RESOURCES

One of the nine categories in my proposals is titled, "Joint Accountabilities." In this section I detail what I'm accountable for (for example, sign non-disclosures, provide client "hot line," and so forth), what the client is accountable for (for example, scheduling internal focus groups, duplicating materials), and what we're jointly responsible for (for example, informing each other of unforeseen developments, honoring meeting commitments).

I try to maximize the client accountability for logistics, support, administration, and all other related details. This is not immoral, unethical, or illegal. It is smart business, and an extraordinary time-saver.

I never use PowerPoint™ or similar technology, because I find it cumbersome, prone to glitches at the worst possible moment, usually unnecessary, and often "overkill" given the message. (Other than that, it's great.) However, State Street Bank demanded its use in the course of a $330,000 project. No amount of my dissuasion, rationale, or downright pleading could change my client's mind. "We use this technology for any major meeting, and the participants expect it," was the less than convincing rationale.

Well, I faced the fact that I had to use the approach. So I told the coordinators that I would have my overhead transparencies converted to PowerPoint by my design firm, and that I would pass that cost along to the client. The client would then be responsible for placing the presentation on the computer to be used that day, and we would jointly test it an hour before the session. I further asked that a technician be present backstage for the duration of the meeting, and that I simply be given a remote control device to change the screen at the appropriate junctures.

In other words, I didn't want to touch the computer, nor be responsible for the formatting or programming. The client thought that those "requests" were reasonable (I suppose they felt they had won a victory by getting me to use the technology at all), and we were all happy. You never know how much support you can get, until you ask for it.

Actually, the presentation went quite well, and I'd do it again—under those exact circumstances.

No matter what the size of your firm, the client will almost always have greater administrative and logistical resources *and those resources are already geared toward the client's culture and environment.* Consequently, it makes eminent sense for both partners to depend as much as possible on the support systems and infrastructure already in place to serve the client. Those resources are the client's, not yours.

I arrange for the client to be responsible for issues such as these:

- Internal scheduling of meetings, focus groups, training, and so forth
- Duplication of materials

- Notification of the client's customers, when necessary
- Local travel and housing[2]
- Offsite meeting logistics and preparation
- Information sent to me via courier
- Internal personal voice mail for me, when needed
- Overseas coordination (travel, phone)
- An office to use while onsite for prolonged periods
- Access to secretarial help while onsite
- Use of client's graphics department for presentation help
- Onsite coordinator during focus groups, interviews, and so on

If you're a solo practitioner, it's essential to move as much "busy work" to the client as possible. Don't be squeamish about this—the client is already set up for "busy work," and you are not. If you're in a small firm, you can't handle too many concurrent projects if you're drowning in administrative trivia. And if you're in a large firm that can handle many of these details, at least charge the client for the privilege. However, even here, I'd suggest that the client is actually better suited and equipped to do this.

RULE 38

Establish as much of the project support function as possible within the client organization, on the quite intelligent grounds that the client is far better prepared to provide it than is an outsider. Consider this "reverse outsourcing," and get good at it. It will save enormous amounts of time and money.

---

2. I insist on taking care of my own plane travel, because I want to fly comfortably and in accordance with my schedule, not the client's nor the client's travel agent.

MANAGING CONCURRENT PROJECTS

As I was preparing to write this section, I received an e-mail from a woman in my mentoring program who specializes in corporate image and naming. She works successfully with CEOs in the middle market, and her quandary is that she is being forced to turn away business, which makes her somewhat uncomfortable.

Well, refusing business makes me near-suicidal, so I guess she's taking it rather well.

In my entire independent career, I've never once turned down a client engagement due to time demands or a full schedule. (I have turned some down because I didn't like the client, the buyer, or the intent of the project which I find, ironically, a lot more frequent than scheduling conflicts.) My nightmare is that every time I refuse otherwise legitimate, sound business, I am degrading my life style and shortchanging my retirement. Money I refuse today is never recovered, in my mind, because the business I eventually acquire to replace it is business that would normally have been in addition to what was lost.

With that philosophy, I'm not about to refuse business because "there's too much of it."[3] That's taking lemonade and turning it into lemons, and I'm pretty sure that's not the way it's supposed to happen.

Assuming you're busy by whatever definition you use, let's examine specific techniques that will allow you to continue to accept engagements that are otherwise consistent with your values and business strategy. (For the record, literally, I once worked with thirty-four clients in a single year.)

TEN TECHNIQUES TO ALWAYS SQUEEZE IN MORE BUSINESS

1. Provide a Client with Timing Options.   If a prospective client indicates that the project has to begin within a time frame that is already committed elsewhere,

---

3. Although this book is written for sophisticated consultants, I suspect that a few newcomers may have slipped in, so I'm including this note. One of the most dysfunctional behaviors of newer consultants is that they turn away business too readily, often because they already are working on as few as two projects concurrently. Especially early in one's career, this is self-destructive business strategy.

Vickie Sullivan runs Sullivan Speaker Services from Tempe, AZ. Her firm creates revenue streams for clients, using professional, public speaking as the marketing tool. Her business has grown dramatically to the mid six figures.

Q. What is the single key factor in your success?

A. The unrelenting drive to do whatever it took to exceed customer expectations. I would intersect what clients say they want with what was practical and possible in the marketplace and gave my clients much more than what they bargained for. My reputation grew quickly because my solutions were different and got results.

Q. What would you do differently if you did it over?

A. I would let go what doesn't work much faster. I had client and vendor relationships that worked great for years, but became obsolete as my business changed. Result: miserable situations that took way too much energy because I was too loyal to our shared past. Now, I understand that leaving clients and vendors when the relationship no longer works can be an act of loyalty too.

Q. What is the major achievement you have yet to accomplish?

A. I'm not satisfied with the extent that I'm using the Internet to serve clients or to promote my business. I want to have more solutions on my site, to interact more with potential clients and include more processes that can serve without my direct involvement.

don't simply say "no" or "that's a conflict." Respond with other options ("I can begin one week later, or I can start that week with a single day, but not two. Which would be better?") so that the prospect is facing the joint accountability for how to make this work and is not faced with a "go/no go" decision.

2. *Position a Full Schedule as an Asset.* Make it clear as soon as you sniff a conflict in the air that you're always quite busy because you're quite good. In other words, the prospect shouldn't expect that you're sitting by the phone with nothing to do. You are constantly engaged, and your other clients find that an asset, not a liability.

3. *Establish a Project Participation Hierarchy.* Simply stated, it can work like this: For unlimited access to my help, plus responsiveness within twenty-four hours to any communications, the project fee is $225,000; for unlimited access to my help and responsiveness within the week, the project fee is $165,000; and for limited access to my help and responsiveness that fits into my schedule, the fee is $125,000. You can play with all the numbers, but the point is that the clients who are "hungrier" for immediate help have to pay for the better meals. It's certainly better to gain three projects at varied, highly profitable fees than to have to turn two of them away.

4. *Subcontract All of the Legwork.* Assuming you have developed a network of and relationships with reliable professionals, use them regularly to deliver the aspects of the project that don't require your judgment, your relationship with key client members, and your expertise. Typically, these project aspects might include: interviewing (at lower levels), focus groups, surveys, observations of workplace behavior, summary and report writing,[4] and canvassing of the client's customers by phone. The subcontracting should never include any work whatsoever with high-level client managers, sensitive areas, or critical project turning points (for example, a facilitation of opposing views with the client).

---

4. If you haven't been successful persuading the client to provide this help, bring your own administrative person to strategy meetings and other sessions where substantial summations have to be gleaned from the easel sheets and team work. If that person is present, the job goes much faster and your involvement is that much less if you don't have to explain it all to someone later or, heaven forbid, do it yourself.

5. *Utilize the Client's Support Systems.* If you haven't already done so, shift as much of your administrative and support requirements to the client's accountability as you can. This will significantly diminish your time requirements in any one project. Because no sane client relationship should require your consulting work on an eight-hour, seven-day basis, a great deal of your lost time will come from the support side. Try to move all of that elsewhere, either to the client or to subcontractors.

6. *Consider Changing Your Work Model to Make It Less Labor Intensive.* This is a near-chronic problem among successful consultants, because the behaviors that have helped them to reach a certain level of success are not those that are easily critiqued or abandoned. Yet this is exactly what you should be doing, even if you need outside help to do so. Examine your complete client approach to ensure that you aren't doing work or providing "deliverables" that are now completely unnecessary or could be accomplished much more easily through other means. I can analyze virtually any consultant's business and delivery model and eliminate about 25 percent of his personal work, if he doesn't have an anxiety attack in the process.

7. *Develop an Alliance Partner.* Find someone who can do the work nearly as well as you can, and offer a reciprocal arrangement. When you're "fully booked," you pass additional business to her at a 25 percent or 35 percent commission paid to you. When that person is fully booked, he or she sends overflow to you with the identical arrangement. It's better to get a quarter or a third of something, rather than a lot of nothing. Moreover, this might result in "found" business for you when things are slow at your end but busy at your partner's.

8. *Provide a Discount if Your Client Can Wait.* Some projects are urgent, and the client can't be expected to quietly tolerate declining sales or increasing turnover while you wrap up other assignments. However, if the project concerns a long-term reorganization, or an increase in teamwork, you might be able to tell the client that you can provide a 10 percent courtesy discount if the client can accommodate a thirty-day delay before launching the project.

9. *Create a Gradual Start.* Structure the project so that it begins immediately, but the initial steps are not labor intensive. Begin with a two-hour organizational meeting, not twelve focus groups; start with a one-on-one scheduling ses-

The coordinator for a project at Mercedes-Benz North America had left a message for me one July day concerning the status of the project we were in the midst of designing for the auto dealer principals. Everything was on plan, but it made him comfortable to touch base once or twice a week, as this was to be the major initiative to improve customer service at the local level.

I returned the call from my cell phone, apologized for doing so, but said that it was the only way to get back to him quickly. He knew at the time that I was also working on projects for three different divisions within Merck, one for GE, and one for Atlantic Electric. The president of his division hadn't cared, but he had been somewhat concerned and had required assurances that I'd be responsive to him. He greatly appreciated my fast return of his calls, which never took longer than ninety minutes.

After we had spent ten minutes discussing the current status and what was to come over the following week, we engaged in the usual couple of minutes of small talk. Then he said to me, "Alan, I've been puzzled all through this conversation. Which client are you with right now? What is that dull roar in the background? Are you doing some manufacturing work?"

"Ron, actually I'm sitting on the beach at Cape May. My wife and I are on a four-day vacation down here. That's the Atlantic Ocean you hear."

There was a brief pause, and I thought I had lost the connection. Then I heard Ron clear his throat.

"Someday," he said, "I'm going to grow up and become you."

---

sion with your buyer, not an audit of the backroom operation; initiate a phone conversation for the coaching project, and not a week of shadowing your client. You should begin this education process at the time of the proposal formulation, so that it is no surprise to the client that you're starting slowly and prudently.

10. Mesh Joint Client Needs.   Make a trip that brings you to two clients on the same day, or on two consecutive days, and not separate days in the same week. (Most clients will change their own schedules if it means you can prorate expenses.) If you're doing customer survey work for different clients, subcontract it all at once and set up one group of people to handle all the calls. If you have to develop instructional programs—even for different topics in different industries—you can usually combine a great deal of the research, material preparation, and visual aid creation.

There are a great many reasons that consultants cite to explain why business must be refused, and most of them are weak. But the most specious of all is that "there isn't enough time." Clients are often more flexible and understanding than we give them credit for, and our own work habits are not as scrutinized as they should be. If you choose to turn away profitable, sound business because you don't need it and are just accepting selected assignments, that's a legitimate life style decision. But if you're turning down money that you need for your short- or long-term goals, then you need to rethink your approach.

One Final Thought: Your clients are probably not turning down business because they don't know how to accommodate it. Do they really need a consultant who isn't as good as they are at business efficiency?

RULE 39

If the potential business is within your competency, ethical, profitable, and otherwise desirable, then find some way to accommodate it. If you don't, that business is gone forever, and with it the learning, relationships, and referrals that would have accrued. If you don't accept it, you're not only losing short-term income, but also long-term strategic development.

THE SIMPLEST, MOST EFFECTIVE TIME MANAGEMENT TOOL EVER CREATED

I'm going to let you in on the absolutely best way to manage your time, personally and professionally, that exists. In this day of contact managers, palm-sized electronic assistants, wireless e-mail access, and leapfrogging technology, it's not hard to imagine what it is.

It's the pad and pencil.

Spend just a few pages more with me here, before you allow your skepticism to reign. I've used simple lists to keep track of what I have to accomplish for many years. I haven't evolved to electronic organizers, because they're not as effective. Simple "manual" lists are wonderful, because they:

- Can be used at bedside, on your desk, on a plane, anyplace the spirit (or the memory) strikes you
- Serve as prompts constantly in front of you at your desk or on your calendar page
- Provide the reward of accomplishment as you strike off tasks that are completed
- Can be handed to someone else, with the tasks on them delegated (warning: never do this to a spouse or significant other)

This morning, my list included completing this chapter, so when I reviewed it last night I knew that I was going to get up early to write, as is my habit. The list includes some personal and business errands, which I can combine into one car trip (and take along the dogs, who love to ride, which makes me even more of a hero to them today). I have to reorganize my product inventory of books and tapes, which have been giving me a real problem due to their unorganized growth, and about which I've been procrastinating. But I put that job on my list for today, meaning that I've got to allocate some time to attack it (and finish it, because I don't want to see it on the list again). I also have a couple of proactive things I want to do for two clients—nothing that's expected, but some value-added I thought of last night, which will be a nice surprise (and a powerful marketing impetus). This would have been lost if I hadn't written it down when I thought of it.

In fact, a great many wonderful ideas and fine initiatives are lost by consultants who assume they will "get to them," but never do. Unfortunately, these are almost always the proactive, bar-raising, innovative actions, because the reactive actions are usually forced through the need to solve a problem, respond to a complaint, or answer a client call. Some of my finest ideas and most original actions have only been fulfilled because I immediately wrote them down and made myself accountable for action *the same day or the following day.*

I keep a pad and pen at my bedside, on a table alongside where I usually watch television, on my desk, in all of my cars, and in each of my briefcases.

(I actually use different sizes and shapes of pads, depending on their location, but I won't burden you with that degree of my fanaticism!) I spend some time combining lists, because I tend to develop separate ones as I'm moving around, and I want to see all my tasks together so that I can coordinate them and set proper priorities.

RULE 40

Time is constantly flowing by. You need a mechanism to review your use of it, because every lost minute is non-renewable. A simple list will focus you on the present and on how best to invest your most valuable resource at the moment.

TIPS FOR THE TRULY TIME-CHALLENGED

If you really have time management problems, accept the fact that you have to attack them on a personal and professional level simultaneously, because looking at only one dimension is delimiting. You don't have a personal life and a professional life, you simply have a life. (You've never worked at home, or made personal calls during working hours?) You can often combine the various elements of your life:

- Vacations are easily built in around client trips
- Business errands and personal errands are usually complementary
- Reading time can be allocated between business and recreational reading, although I've found significant overlap from one to the other
- Do things when you feel like doing them. There's nothing wrong with tackling a client project in the evening *if* you also feel free to use a Tuesday morning to do some personal shopping

My Suggestions for the Truly Time-Challenged
1. Make a list for the following day that is realistic. Don't overload it with everything that remains undone. Choose a reasonable number of things that require a short-term resolution.

2. Add one thing to the daily list that is longer term; otherwise you never get to them.

3. Make sure that the list has personal as well as professional needs; otherwise one aspect will be completed at the expense of the other, and that's not the objective.

4. Include personally rewarding and pleasing things. Don't provide a reward only when the list is completed, which is the sure way to enter a rat race. Include stuff you like to do and look forward to doing. Just make sure that you also include the harder and more onerous work as well.

5. Judge your time. If there are eight items on the list, and you've only concluded one of them by lunch, then turn on the afterburners. If you're moving things from the current day's list to the next day's list, you're accomplishing exactly nothing.

6. If you complete your list early, don't go looking for more stuff. Take the rest of the day off. However, if you finish the list early every day, then you're not committed to enough items each day.

7. When you master the daily list, move on to formulate a weekly and/or monthly list for longer-term items that you want to attack in a coordinated manner. If a monthly item is still sitting there on the 27th with no work done, you know you're in trouble.

You might feel you're well beyond my simple lists, and you're firmly in charge of your life and time. I respect that, and Chapter 9 is just a couple of pages ahead. But if you find that you're not accommodating as many projects as you'd like to, that you're forced to turn away business you'd dearly love to have, and you're constantly reactive and seldom proactive, think about starting with a daily list, easily created and constantly reviewed.

I'm done now, and I'm crossing this morning's writing off my list.

THE ULTIMATE RULES

Rule #36. If you can focus on the effective management and conservation of only two things, make them time and money, in that order. The second is, after all, renewable, but the first is not. Money lost can be regained. Time is forever gone.

George Phares runs Strategic Direction Resources, which has generated 20 percent growth in revenues continuously since its founding in 1994. Last year, however, it grew by 49 percent. The company represents clients during audits, with both onsite and offsite assistance. They have retained 90 percent of their clients over the years.

Q. What is the largest factor in your success?

A. It is very difficult to isolate one single key factor, when success is contingent on so many things falling together in unison. I am often referred to as a "subject-matter expert" in the area of affirmative action program development, but I don't believe this is the key factor. Being an industry expert is of little value if no one knows you (and your practice) exist. So for me, I believe it boils down to networking. My first consulting opportunity was from a referral from another consulting firm. (I'm still working with that first client, and have landed at least six more clients as a result of that initial contact.) I am a frequent presenter for networking associations and am actively involved in many such associations, serving on committees, as an elected officer and on their boards of directors. People hear me speak, see my written contributions to association newsletters, and know me through my willingness to donate my time and energy to the success of those organizations. Bottom line: If they don't know who you are and what you do, they can't refer you to those who would benefit from your services.

Finally, I credit my tenacity and perseverance. I never envisioned failure and refuse to quit. I attend seminars, read, study, and network to maintain my expertise. I do everything I can to learn the business of consulting, and maintain a technological edge. If my practice fails, I can't help those who would benefit from my services. I owe it to my family and clients (both current and future) to remain solvent and profitable.

Q. What would you do differently if you could do it over?

A. I've learned not to chase variables. I define "chasing variables" as blindly pursuing something that may have worked one time, but may be unsuccessful ninety-nine times after that. I'm an expert in affirmative action compliance for federal contractors. I enjoy giving workshops and presentations on those subjects. However, I let myself get diverted on a couple of occasions by developing and presenting classroom training on workplace conduct, that is, harassment training. It was a severe distraction, a drain on resources, and took me away from the needs of my affirmative action clients. Just because something new works well once, make sure that it is not an anomaly, to be chased without continued success. How does one prevent chasing variables? Stay focused on success. Pay attention to what works and what doesn't work. Don't get so personally involved in an idea that you can't let go when it doesn't ultimately succeed.

Q. What is the major achievement you have yet to accomplish?

A. Publish. I want to publish. I've built a successful practice generating a good, sustained income, provided jobs for myself and others, and generated value for my clients. Now I want to share what I've learned with others.

Rule #37.   Focus on outcomes and results, not on your methodology, tasks, and inputs. Educate the client so that the buyer understands that your contribution is in the improvement to the buyer's operation, not in your presence.

Rule #38.   Establish as much of the project support function as possible within the client organization, on the quite intelligent grounds that the client is far better prepared to provide it than is an outsider. Consider this "reverse outsourcing," and get good at it. It will save enormous amounts of time and money.

Rule #39.   If the potential business is within your competency, ethical, profitable, and otherwise desirable, then find some way to accommodate it. If you don't, that business is gone forever, and with it the learning, relationships, and referrals that would have accrued. If you don't accept it, you're not only losing short-term income, but also long-term strategic development.

Rule #40.   Time is constantly flowing by. You need a mechanism to review your use of it, because every lost minute is non-renewable. A simple list will focus you on the present and on how best to invest your most valuable resource at the moment.

Final Thought: If you don't manage your time, everyone else will. The default position will be everyone else's priorities. Effective time management requires a healthy selfishness.

CHAPTER 9

Working with Family-Owned and Smaller Businesses

What to Do When You're Competing with the Mortgage Payment

Some of the most impressive consultants I've met are those who have *successfully* carved out a niche in the family-owned and small business market (which I'm going to define here as below $100 million, with the preponderance at or below $50 million).[1] You can fudge the definition in any

---

1. After all, giants such as Cargill and the Carlson companies remain family-owned, even though they are multi-billion dollar monoliths. And even huge publicly traded businesses such as Ford and Motorola are essentially controlled by the originating families through strong minority holdings and important board positions.

direction you choose, but I'm including this category in the book because I see an increasing trend toward the growth of this market segment, and it's one that consultants who have been successful elsewhere just might want to consider.

THE LARGE AND THE SMALL OF THE SMALL BUSINESS MARKET

Some of the advantages of these organizations as client include:

- There are more of them close to home, no matter where you live, so that travel is dramatically lessened, often to the point of elimination. (Do I have your attention now?)
- The owner is almost always the buyer and is easy to identify. He or she is rarely guarded by legions of minions whose sole job is to block the door. If the owner isn't the buyer, then it's always the president, who is an outsider brought in to manage the place professionally, and that person is also relatively accessible.
- You, yourself, are running a small business, so you should be able to relate to the buyer's position. (This is particularly true if you are both running a small business that is selling to predominantly larger businesses, as would be the case for any successful consultant or consulting principal.)
- The principals are frequently highly involved and visible in the surrounding community, in civic events, fund-raisers, other boards, charities, social soirees, and so forth. Consequently, networking through common friends, meeting them, and developing relationships is not terribly difficult. The odds are that, as a successful person yourself, you at least know someone whom they know, and you may well have seen the small firm owner yourself somewhere along the way.
- Results generated through consulting interventions are rapid and often dramatic. There is less heft to "absorb" change, and there is less inertia to oppose it. Your impact will be felt and known quite quickly when you are successful.
- The community talks regularly, through service clubs, common affiliations, and its own network. Your success will be rapidly disseminated

because many of the owners are old friends, not competitors, and they actively seek to help one another out.

- Access to the small business community leadership is readily gained through the local media, pro bono work, knowing neighbors and friends who work in the organizations themselves and can recommend you, membership in local service organizations (Rotary, Kiwanis, Elks, and others), university adjunct positions, and civic duty (League of Women Voters, United Way).
- There is only one real sponsor to worry about, and the owner's blessing and active support will usually be sufficient to propel most projects.

Some of the disadvantages are:

- MacLuhan's "mixed media" effect is in full swing, and the entrepreneur who built the business assumes that he or she knows how to do anything well, including consult, find talent, fix transmissions, and beat the stock market.
- Money is always a problem, ironically, not because it's in short supply, but because it is coming right out of the pocket of the person to whom you are talking. Your consulting project is competing for funds with next month's mortgage, car payments, tuition bills, a contribution to the local symphony, and a vacation to the Costa del Sol.
- The problem that the organization has is often the owner, or a relative of the owner, or a friend of the owner. Enough said about that one.
- Decisions will sometimes be influenced by non-business members behind the scenes and off the property, and you'll feel the effects but be powerless to deal with the source.
- The business feels the waves and weather changes far faster and more violently than larger organizations. Your project can be derailed or cancelled by one of your client's customers who has a downturn or a quality problem.
- Word does travel. If you have a poor experience, no matter how unavoidable or how much you were not at fault, you could be ruined in the local community for years.
- There is only one real sponsor to worry about, and the owner's blessing and active support will usually be sufficient to propel most projects. Of course, lack of that blessing and support will mean certain death.

The relationship aspect of your work is even more important in the small business market, because the enthusiastic support or apathetic lack of support of the owner or principal will usually mean success or failure, no matter what else you do.

My experience is that successful consultants in other marketplaces are often in a better position to penetrate and exploit the small business market than are those consultants who have tended to specialize only in it. The reason is that the former bring the credibility of successful work for high-recognition organizations, they have a surfeit of diverse experience dealing with difficult managers and buyers, and they can afford to test the small business waters, because their income stream originates elsewhere.

The reasons to test the waters, however, are significant. Small businesses:

- Are on the rise. More and more people, disillusioned by downsizing and layoffs and finding "security" of major organizational employment to be a chimera, have chosen to entrepreneurially start their own firms.
- Include the high-tech, bio-tech, and you-name-it-tech start-ups, which all fall into this category, and all need help in marketing, talent retention, funding, organizational change to accommodate growth, and a host of other areas.
- Are being turbo-charged through eCommerce. The Internet has made every business a global business and has opened unprecedented growth opportunities at extraordinarily low cost.
- Are receiving more and more institutional attention. SOHO "summits" (SOHO = small office/home office) are sponsored by the likes of Visa and Staples, among scores of others, and sponsorships and opportunities for consultants to approach the market on a high-visibility basis are expanding.
- Are under pressure from financiers, from banks to venture capitalists, to get their houses in order. It hasn't been unusual for my consulting relationship to be listed as an asset by small firms seeking to guarantee their funding sources that they are taking care of their internal business.

- Offer diverse compensation possibilities. You can reasonably expect to discuss traditional fee arrangements, bartering arrangements, stock options, phantom stock, and other desirable alternatives that GE or Bank of America might not be willing to offer.

In short, this is a growing and vibrant marketplace, so you ought to at least make sure it's on your radar screen.

CASE STUDY

I had been called in by the owner of a $20 million firm who was seeking consulting help and who knew the president of the state university, for whom I had wisely done some pro bono work. That single reference was good enough for the owner. He hired me during our initial meeting, even though he found my $16,000 fee for a brief analysis of why profitability wasn't growing fast enough to be "pretty steep" and my demand for full payment in advance "quite unusual." Nonetheless, we began the following week.

In short order, after a few interviews and some brief observations, I found that the owner was the problem. He undermined his own subordinates, did not share the business strategy with anyone (and barely had a coherent one even in his own head), violated his own company rules (he could smoke, but no one else could), employed his wife in a job down the hall that no one could define, and so on. It was something out of a bad novel.

After about four visits and a total of eight hours onsite, I met with him and told him that we could solve the problem of poor productivity and resultant profitability right in his office, and I gave him specific behavioral evidence of his own actions. He hit the roof and stayed there. He ranted and raved. He told me that he didn't hire me to hear that he was the problem, that he had built the firm from scratch, and that he certainly wasn't about to change anything about himself.

"That's it," he said, "this project is over. You can stop."

"Okay," I said, and got up to open the door.

"Wait a minute," he yelled. "I've already paid you the entire fee."

"What's your point?" I asked. And when he remained speechless for a few moments, I left.

COMPETING WITH THE RENT MONEY

The value proposition is more important than ever in these organizations. "Investment" isn't heard too often, but "cost" is a daily chant. Especially in those businesses unaccustomed to consultants, any "new" expense is by definition evil and should be minimized or extirpated.

Therefore, you must focus on the value end of the equation. Find out what the owner/principal has had the most trouble with in terms of growth or expansion or why the competition has consistently usurped market share. Demonstrate a powerful bottom-line return on the investment in your help.

Beware: These buyers will often feel that they are safest with a "pay for performance" arrangement and offer you a contingency on improvements, in place of a fee for your value. Don't be lulled. Despite the smaller relative size, these firms have as many or more variables as larger firms do that can influence the result of an initiative far beyond your poor power to add or detract. (For example, the loss of just one key person to illness, injury, or the competition can significantly undermine sales, service, accounting, and so forth, far more than in larger organizations with more resources.)

As appealing as it may be, resist contingency fees and demand at least a part of your payment on commencement of the project. You need money in the bank to safeguard you and emotionally hook the "heart and mind" of the owner. If you haven't been paid, it's easy to cut you loose. If you have been paid, it's tough to part with a sunk investment. If you've been paid in full, you're there for the duration.

(There is a special section later in this chapter specifically on the techniques that are important to consider in accepting equity in lieu of direct compensation. Particularly in high-tech and start-up operations, this is increasingly an option.)

 RULE 42

Emotional, personal objectives are as important as objective, business goals. In fact, they are often inextricably entwined. Acknowledge that, and work with it.

Find out what constitutes the important life goals of the owner; cater to them, not merely to the business goals. In IBM or United Airlines, the chances are that the personal goals of the vice president of marketing or director of customer service might not play a role in the project or your participation in it. But in small businesses, the personal goals of the owner and the goals of the business are no less intertwined than your own, as an entrepreneur with a small firm or solo practice.

Demonstrate how the family's legacy, the children taking over the business, the intended hospital wing named after the deceased parents, the longed-for new facility, the emotionally important acquisition of the competition, or whatever the objectives are will be met, accelerated, and ensured by your project's intended goals. Because logic makes people think and emotion makes them act, build on the latter, which is far more readily apparent and easier to discuss in the small business environment. That's why building relationships and establishing sufficient levels of trust to approach these issues are so important.

MANAGING THE OWNER'S EMOTIONS AND EXPECTATIONS

Educating the buyer is more important in small businesses than anyplace else. The owner's inclination will be, once you're hired, to use you for everything possible, from painting lines in the parking lot to refilling the vending machines in the cafeteria. After all, isn't that simply exploiting the return on this very expensive investment?

Scope creep isn't something to be on the alert for here; it's a way of life. Make your boundaries very clear. Discuss them several times, then document them, then discuss the document. I've seen small business consultants completely undone after a wonderful project was successfully completed, only to have the owner say, "Aren't we behind on the other parts of this?"

As opposed as I normally am to socializing with clients, I have to (grudgingly) concede that sharing a dinner or a social event with the owner's immediate family is always a good idea. Not only does it solidify the relationship with your buyer, but the event enables you to become more than simply a disembodied name to the owner's major advisors: his or her family members. Your name will be mentioned at the dinner table regardless of whether you're actually present (and it will range from "this consultant we hired" to "this smart advisor I've retained" to "Jane has suggested . . ." to "that $##@!!*&^ robbing consultant").

Aldonna Ambler has been a consultant for twenty-nine years. She began her firm with $276 and "an unemployed husband." She built it to a 158-person, six-office (one in Europe) operation, specializing personally in the strategic issues of rapidly growing companies. She provided testimony at over thirty Congressional hearings on economic development.

Q. What is the single key factor in your success?

A. Sometimes I think it has been my sustained focus on fast-growth companies. Not every consultant can handle the egos of the leaders of companies growing 500 percent per year. Other days, I wonder if that choice just makes me more tired trying to stay ahead of some of the brightest, most aggressive people in the world.

Sometimes, I think it has been my commitment to become a CEO and actually grow my businesses. Clients have a range of needs. Their lack of available backup keeps many solo consultants from even hearing or seeing needs beyond what they can handle. Plus, I find my first-hand experience with growing companies adds to my depth of understanding about what my CEO clients are facing and feeling.

Sometimes, I think it is my commitment to marketing over sales. We have never done any cold calling. We're big fans of consultative selling techniques. Clients come primarily from repeat busi-

The more you are a "face" and a person, the less you are an expense and an impediment to other things that could be accomplished with your fee. It doesn't hurt, either, to support the community events and charities that are important to the owner or that the owner subsidizes.

If there is a single key to managing your buyer in these environments, it is

ness and referrals. Our marketing program has about twenty elements, but association networking, published articles, and media coverage have been the most important parts. Recently, Internet presence has been important.

Q. What would you do differently if you did it over?

A. The first few years were tough. Mind you, at the time I started, there weren't that many women in the field. Perhaps it could have been easier if I had become an employee of one of the Big Eight (at the time) first before going out on my own. Maybe I could have saved some time and mistakes if I had access to their resources, learned their systems, and understood the ins and outs of pricing earlier. But, the ONLY thing I would never do again is a 50/50 partnership. I did that once several years ago. My partner was and is a very talented consultant, and we enjoyed working with one another for about five years. But where do you go when you have conflicting strategies for the future of the business? We dissolved that firm, created two new ones, and have done things very differently. I've found that it's easier to have thirty-three partners than it is to have one.

Q. What is the major achievement you have yet to accomplish?

A. I guess the answer to this question would be related to me as an author. Although I have published eighty-five articles and have a few books, I haven't done THE book yet.

constantly separate the objective and behavioral from the assumption and emotional. The simple questions to focus on are:

- What is the evidence supporting that view?
- What have you actually seen that validates that position?

- What, specifically, was said or done in your presence?
- Would you bet the company on that belief?

I've found that in the absence of the multi-layers of management in larger firms, in the absence of strict legal department rulings, and in the absence of the constraints that larger organizations impose on the impulsive tendencies of any manager or executive, there is a need to "impose order" on the action-oriented and sometime mercurial owners of these businesses. It's up to us to help them focus on the evidence and the behavior and to demonstrate the serious loss of money, business, talent, repute, and other important resources that can occur if the owner simply acts viscerally.

RULE 43

Scope creep and small "favors" are common in small business engagements. Guard against them like a junkyard dog.

As the relationship develops, an interesting dynamic can occur: The same inertia that impeded you earlier as a new and suspicious expense in the owner's life now transforms you into a trusted advisor who can do no wrong and who will be valuable in all aspects of the owner's life. It's time to be very careful. It's one thing to advise on the proper salary levels for new hires, but it's another to help select the owner's kids' colleges; it's appropriate to recommend the termination of certain non-productive employees, but suicidal to take sides in a family dispute.

When you have specialized degrees or expertise, the danger increases to the point where lead will melt. Listen, you're a Ph.D. in psychology, so the question: "How would you analyze the habits of my daughter's fiancé?" should send you rapidly to the asbestos protective suits.

Create clear boundaries early with the owner. Be willing to engage socially, but even there make it clear that your advice doesn't extend beyond the walls of the business. Never talk business to other family members in the owner's absence. And never talk about the owner at all—to anyone, under any circumstances.

SPECIAL SECTION: ACCEPTING EQUITY FOR YOUR SERVICES (OR WHY THE CRAPS TABLES SUDDENLY LOOK GOOD)

Consultants (and a raft of other professionals, including carpenters and plumbers) are increasingly considering equity participation in the place of old-fashioned cash on the barrelhead. Sometimes it's because the clients can't (or claim they can't) come up with the cash, and sometimes it's because the allure of the client's potential payoff is so great that vast riches clog the consultant's synapses.

Equity offers exist in two basic situations: In the first, the company is a start-up, usually high-tech but not always, which is so cash poor that it can only apply the precious venture capital for R&D and marketing. Anything else is superfluous, so everyone from accountants to gardeners is offered a stake. In the second case, a legitimate "going concern" offers a consultant the chance to participate in the fruits of his or her advice, usually because the client thinks the chances of reaching the goal are slim, doesn't want to pay for anything but tangible performance, or is simply cheap.

In either case, there is a strong and rare potential up-side, and a strong and frequent absolute downside. Let the equity seeker beware (caveat equitus or something).

Some Things to Consider

Before you jump to accept an equity position, you should make sure that you possess the basic information about the client AND about yourself. In any given instance, equity can make sense for you and not a partner or vice versa. In other words, this is like driving a Ferrari: It seems like a great idea and you know you'll look good, but not everyone can handle it and there are some places you just can't take it.

You have more of a chance hitting a roulette number during an evening at the tables than you do hitting the big time with an equity start-up. Even in established organizations, where you're taking equity on increased sales or growing market share, there are hazards.

You'll have to get a reading on the likelihood of key talent staying the course. That means that you'll also have to be absolutely confident about management's ability to lead and to retain key people. Look at the culture. Is it one of relatively low turnover (no turnover is not good, because it fails to clear deadwood), fun, challenge, and collaboration? Are people talking about the excitement of the enterprise or about the potential for jumping ship?

Is the initiative capitalized sufficiently? Are resources and knowledge readily available and shared? Are people running full speed to gain momentum or to flee a fire? Ask yourself whether the operation in which you are considering taking an equity position is one that you would enjoy working in and/or managing. Ask yourself whether you would invest $50,000 or $150,000 of discretionary funds in this opportunity, because that's precisely what you're doing.

Do you like these people and do you trust them?

Your deal about equity must be clear-cut and as unambiguous as possible. The chief executive officer and the chief financial officer of the client should sign off on the agreement, which itself should be created by your attorney. If the client insists on his or her own attorneys, then agree only with the provision that your attorney will then review their work. Sometimes seemingly trivial matters, such as the state in which legal disputes will be adjudicated, can make a huge difference later (some jurisdictions have laws that could make your position untenable and your contract worthless under certain conditions).

Use as much "cement" as possible to seal the deal. For example, if there is a board of directors, have the agreement approved by the board and read into the minutes. If key personnel change—especially likely in start-up companies—then have the new officer acknowledge and sign off on the old agreement, even though technically it is binding without that signature.

Evaluate the opportunity not in terms of an individual investment but in terms of your overall cash flow and financial picture. Can you support yourself and your business adequately without the equity position paying off? If not, then you're taking a huge gamble. If so, then you're taking a prudent risk. Determine whether you can simply let this run its course, albeit with you contributing as a consultant, or whether you'd be up during the night and distracted during the day trying to worry this venture over the finish line.

There is no sense getting sick over a piece of business. You have to be careful that, even if the equity position pays off, it doesn't totally undermine all of your other marketing and delivery efforts, which may suffer by comparison.

Some Things to Do

There are some very specific things you can do to protect yourself in equity relationships. They don't always work, just like fire protection doesn't always work, but at least it's better than simply depending on the sprinkler system.

The absolute toughest factor in taking equity is that it can color your judgment and blunt your effectiveness as a consultant, ironically causing you to become detrimental to your own interests. For example, you might come upon a manager whom you know is toxic and ought to be fired. But will you recommend firing him or her, even though it's essential for long-term success, if the position won't be filled for months and you desperately need a body in it to make this year's plan? How much of the future do you sacrifice to guarantee your short-term equity stake?

The answer, of course, is that you have to do what's in the best long-term interests of the client—and not the best short-term financial interests of the consultant. Understand this and evaluate the potential for conflicts at the outset. If you anticipate them, either don't take the job or refer all such decisions to a consultant or insider who doesn't have the conflict. Then abide by their decisions.

You may do everything humanly possible within your accountabilities, and the contribution should have led to success. But the unanticipated resignation of three top salespeople, the competition's breathtaking new technology, or the government's unexpected regulatory interference might send a torpedo into your best efforts. Try to clarify what you can and cannot control. You won't be able to collect if the goals aren't met, no matter what your contribution (because there will be no equity to share), so if you find this downside potential high, don't get in the water.

You may also find that there are managers or highly influential contributors who are rewarded, directly or indirectly, for the exact opposite of what you are trying to accomplish (for example, a marketing vice president who wants to incorporate sales into his unit and would love to see the expansion in Europe fail so that he can make a case for the integration). If those turf battles are present, you're going to get killed in the crossfire.

Throughout the project, act as you always should—as an independent, objective, and decisive advisor. Don't allow yourself to be persuaded by short-term scares, and never enter into discussions that might indicate your judgment is suspect (or can be "bought"). Make some tough calls early, if possible, to show that your only objective is to improve the client's condition for the long term.

Alan Fortier has seldom ever had to market aggressively. He has built a near-million-dollar practice. His solo practice, based in New Jersey, helps senior management of manufacturing companies embark on high-profit strategies to achieve dramatic growth. All of his business has been through referrals. When I met him, he didn't even have a press kit or brochure.

Q. What is the major reason for your success?

A. I am driven to hit a home run on any assignment I undertake. This isn't a plan. It's in my personality. I have learned to choose my races carefully. But once I go, my motivation and commitment are significant. I want to exceed expectations, even if it requires non-budgeted time and expense. Carefully ID what the manager really has on his or her mind and address it in ways that go beyond what they'd ever see from their direct people re: strategic thinking, solution elegance, and experience. A second reason for success has been time and experience, which have refined my facilitation, strategic thinking, and executive counseling skills, each of which adds value on every assignment (sixteen years at this).

Q. What would you do differently?

If you're working with a start-up, confront management often and early. These entrepreneurs are the chronically narrow. They can see their technology and its implications, but can rarely see the market, the buyer, or the elusive profit goals (known as spending less than you take in). If you're working with a large organization in a specific initiative (for example, the sales force and its business growth), then make sure you become very familiar with every key player. Never simply accept someone's word about someone else's performance or morale. See it for yourself.

A. (a) Stronger commitment to understanding software tools and the Internet earlier on. (b) Devote a little more time to relationships with my high-level contacts (and those that are going places) when I don't have active projects with them. I have never taken the time to develop a comfortable, time-effective formula for this. I would then be even more selective about the types of business I would try to develop. (c) Develop more expertise in, and more work in, M&A: It has potential for very high value added and fees. (d) Perhaps make a greater effort to bring in and train a full-time associate, leading to a slightly different organization model. (e) Take a much more active role in one of the chemical industry trade groups and perhaps in a consultant/peer group.

Q. What is your greatest unachieved goal?

A. I want to achieve an industry-wide reputation as the premier advisor for strategy regeneration. This is my reputation within many of my client organizations, but I have never addressed how to promote myself beyond word of mouth. Also, I would like to establish non-time-related sources of income. While this is an important goal, I don't have a plan, or even good ideas for this one. On another day this might be more important than the above goal.

If someone at IBM wants to offer you IBM stock in return for your consulting efforts, that's far different from someone at silverware.com wanting you to take equity in their new electric fork. Equity in a blue-chip company is like investing in the best market stocks and funds: If you hold on without panic, the market ultimately rewards you. But do you want to invest in either a high-tech start-up or to take your chances with factors you can never completely control with a more mature organization? It depends on your tolerance for risk, your eye for opportunity, and your consulting expertise. And on luck.

Don't be afraid to take equity, but don't do it in lieu of cash you need to support your loved ones and your business.

TEN WAYS TO AVOID THE PERILS OF CONSULTING WITH SMALLER BUSINESSES

In the small business/family business environment, some standard practices that have worked for you elsewhere may not be applicable or well-received. Focus groups and interviews, for example, are often seen as dangerous and threatening, because somehow "the boss will find out" who said what to whom. I've actually had people taking part in one-on-one interviews ask if the session were being secretly recorded. On another occasion, people claimed that mailed survey forms had coding marks identifying the recipients, which could be seen if the forms were held under a strong light.

Here are some steps that may ease the process, no matter what area of consulting you're involved with, and that may also speed things along and keep relationships intact.

1. Never Accept a "Secret" to Be Told to You with a Guarantee of Confidentiality. In small firms, these secrets may involve highly sensitive issues that you are ethically obligated to tell the client. There may be computer theft, or people stealing cash, or quality defects overlooked in order to meet production goals. Inform the employee that you can't keep anything confidential that affects the well-being of your client or the organization as a whole, and that you are the sole judge of that impact. You're better off being honest and missing a piece of gossip than having your integrity compromised. You'll serve your client far better and be more highly regarded by the troops if they know where you stand.

2. Find the Informal Leaders and Try to Establish Relationships with Them. These people may or may not be obvious. Sometimes they are union leaders or key front-line supervisors. Sometimes they are the senior people who "knew the boss when it was just a dozen of us in rented space." On occasion, they are other family members working their way up through the business. There may even be what I call an "untouchable," meaning someone with such

I once accepted an assignment on retainer from a man who owned a community bank. My job included helping in the attraction, hiring, and retention of talent for positions such as head teller or chief loan officer. In assessing people and their possible role in the bank, I usually used as part of my evaluation a validated psychometric test instrument, which provided an analysis of behavioral patterns. The client and I believed that people could be trained in the bank's content areas, but that certain behaviors were either present or not, and the organization didn't have the resources to risk positions on people who were innately unsuited to the demands of various positions.

Our partnership had worked well for about a year, and the owner loved the testing process. I hadn't appreciated how much until he came to me and asked if I would test him and his fiancé so that they could work on areas of compatibility and lack of compatibility prior to the marriage.

If I had really been a smart consultant I would have run away as fast as I could, but instead, believing I could do anything under any conditions, I agreed.

Needless to say, they were like opposite ends of a pencil. One wrote and the other erased. One was neat, the other disorganized. One was big picture, one was micro-manager. As I read them the results after hours in his office, the room grew continuously chillier.

There was good news and bad news. The couple agreed to ignore the feedback and focus on their love for each other, which resulted in a happy marriage not long after. My retainer wasn't renewed, but the owner appointed me to the board. I think he figured that I could do less harm helping to set the organization's strategy than I could fooling around testing whomever he told me to. He was right.

unique and singular experience that even the owner can't touch him or her. This may be a high-tech expert, the top salesperson, the general counsel, or other person with singular responsibilities.

3. Get Your Money in Advance, or as Much of It as You Possibly Can. This is an implementation advantage, not just a financial advantage. In this market, a mercurial owner will fire you and invite you to sue, rather than adhere to a contract, unlike DuPont or Ford, which just might be advised to honor their commitments no matter how bad the news delivered by the consultant. If you're going to be honest with the buyer, then you have to arrange for your own independence. Ironically, the larger the project fee and the more you have at risk that hasn't been paid, the more pressure you have to compromise your findings and tone down your language, further putting the project at risk. It's a vicious cycle. Try to collect a minimum of 50 percent at commencement and the rest not long after, while you're still in the fact-finding stage and before you have to deliver unpopular or personal news in your recommendations.

4. Don't Rely Overly on What You're Told. Instead, place greater credence in what you see. People tend to self-select their participation in these environments, and you're much more likely to hear from those who have a personal agenda (positive or negative). Unlike larger organizations, there isn't a huge sampling with the safety of numbers, nor will focus groups tend to be honest and self-sanctioning. Determine whether what you see in the environment backs up what you are told. If you're led to believe that morale is high, but people work in a tomb-like silence, something is amiss. If you're told that the "team" is highly participative, but no one asks questions in meetings, then you've got more work to do.

5. Talk to Your Client's Customers. More than anyone, they will have some pithy and accurate feedback on your client's performance in terms of service, responsiveness, quality, dependability, and so forth. Try to make those contacts a condition of your project. If you can't obtain it, there is nothing unethical about contacting them independently and not revealing your connection with the client, but just asking some innocent questions: "What's been your experience with Acme's quality of phone support?"

Your ultimate job is to improve your client's condition. You don't do that by protecting your client, or by protecting yourself through flattering interpretations of unflattering situations. Protect yourself contractually and financially, but be honest and forthright or don't accept small business contracts.

6. Shop the Client Yourself. Call the client's service line, try to return a product, enter one of the retail stores as a tough customer, make an unusual request. If you may be recognized, enlist the help of a friend or business colleague. (My wife loves these roles.) Test whether your client's genuine belief in what is happening with customers, products, and services is matched by reality as you perceive it. Points five and six combined can be essential in overcoming prejudice and bias about the business and focusing on objective facts (and avoiding blame, which is covered below).

7. Focus on Cause, Not on Blame. Personalities, reputations, and sensitivities are always heightened in smaller businesses. Everyone knows everyone else. Some people are good friends, some people are related. In poorly run organizations, there will already be a tendency to place blame and escape accountability for problems. Stay above the fray, point out the symptom and its cause, and suggest remedies. When you are faced with poor performance or lack of competence, suggest training or transfer. If people perceive they will get "whacked" for poor performance, more problems will be swept under the rug and your investigation will become tougher and tougher. Never make it personal.

8. Don't Assume the Owner Can Change Things Easily. Just as in a larger organization where the department head is a real tough authoritarian, it doesn't mean that fear will readily change behavior (nor that great affection will change behavior if that change is personally threatening). You will still need the commitment—not merely compliance—of those doing the work. Don't burn your bridges by assuming that you and the owner can force changes. All you can force is movement, and that will be temporary, unless you gain the enthusiastic support of the implementers.

9. Tread Carefully on Tradition, but Do Tread on It. There will be a strong mythology about the company's origins and a strong hagiography about the founders. (This exists even in huge organizations, as can be seen by the reverence for the garage in which Dave Hewlett and Bill Packard founded their company.) Sentiment is nice, but it can hold back progress. (Hewlett-Packard no longer operates out of a garage.) Demonstrate that it is the intent (exploration, innovation, service quality, and so forth) that must be carried forward for growth, but not the actual design (the old building, the poor operating systems, the limited inventory). "Historical inertia" can be an unseen force against change, and it has to be confronted.

10. Provide for a Clear Disengagement. This isn't about scope creep so much as effectively transferring the accountability for change to the client. It's too easy for the owner to assume that change is happening merely because you're still present and still being paid. Small business issues are tough, but not terribly complex. Make sure you have a clear ending point with specific accountabilities established for further work. It often helps to offer to return in six months for a complimentary day to audit the progress.

RULE 45

Small businesses have less provision to atone for error in areas such as hiring, retention of key customers, "failure work," and forecasting. Keep the projects simple and focused, and never assume that "if this doesn't work, we can always try something else." That "something else" may be bankruptcy.

Family owned and small businesses constitute a growing business segment, one that can be highly lucrative and fulfilling for consultants prepared for the unique demands. You can bring some of your large company and "big city" practices to this market. You just can't bring a large company and "big city" attitude.

THE ULTIMATE RULES

Rule #41.   The relationship aspect of your work is even more important in the small business market, because the enthusiastic support or apathetic lack of support of the owner or principal will usually mean success or failure no matter what else you do.

Rule #42.   Emotional, personal objectives are as important as objective, business goals. In fact, they are often inextricably entwined. Acknowledge that, and work with it.

Rule #43.   Scope creep and small "favors" are common in small business engagements. Guard against them like a junkyard dog.

Rule #44.   Your ultimate job is to improve your client's condition. You don't do that by protecting your client or by protecting yourself through flattering interpretations of unflattering situations. Protect yourself contractually and financially, but be honest and forthright or don't accept small business contracts.

Rule #45.   Small businesses have less provision to atone for error in areas such as hiring, retention of key customers, "failure work," and forecasting. Keep the projects simple and focused, and never assume that "if this doesn't work, we can always try something else." That "something else" may be bankruptcy.

Final Thought: There are some close similarities between small businesses and smaller business units of large companies that operate semi-independently. You might have more experience in this area—or more call for these skills—than you think.

Marcia Ruben is the principal of Ruben Consulting Group, begun in May of 1998, which has grown from $20,000 in billing quickly to the low six figures. She specializes in organizational change and leadership.

Q. What is the single key factor in your success?

A. The biggest factor in my success is my ability to develop good, trusting working relationships with my clients and to be perceived as flexible and versatile. I bring a variety of skills and experience to the table, so I am called on to do a variety of things, from acting as a project lead to creating change and communication plans to doing leadership development and to facilitating meetings. I care about my clients and what is important to them, and I competently complete deliverables on time.

Q. What would you do differently if you did it over?

A. Before I went out on my own, I did a fair amount of networking, but was quite busy with the consulting I was doing for the firm I worked for. I had worked to line up some work before I left my job, but only with one company. After I had resigned, that contract fell through, so I basically had to start from scratch. I spent the first few months trying to line up subcontracting work, thinking that this would be a quicker way to get started. This did not turn out to be the case. I would do two things differently. One, I would do more networking before I started so that I had more eggs in my basket. Secondly, I would put more emphasis in marketing directly to possible clients, rather than to subcontracting. Finally, I would make a greater effort to get speaking engagements and do more pro bono work.

Q. What is the major achievement you have yet to accomplish?

A. One of my goals was to establish myself as a speaker and writer as a way to market myself and my business. I love to speak and to write, but have done only a little of both. Part of this is due to time—I am fully booked. The second major achievement I have yet to accomplish is to integrate talented and trusted colleagues into my practice, that is, to find a project we can work on together and leverage our collective talents. I have networked quite a bit with people I know and some new ones. As yet, I have not found a way to position projects for more than myself. I certainly did this when I was part of a larger firm, so I know how to do it. The opportunity either has not arisen, or I have not created it.

Q. What key factor created the propulsion that moved you from $20,000 to over ten times those revenues in such a short period of time?

A. As I mentioned earlier, when a contract I was counting on fell through, I started from scratch. I spent nine months very focused on marketing efforts. I created my marketing materials, networked, became active in IMC [Institute of Management Consultants], made calls, and followed up. I was certified in a leadership assessment process. Marketing was a full-time job, when I was not working on the few small projects I had. I stayed in touch with people I had worked with at clients and tried to find ways to give them information or ideas or something that they would value. When, after nine months, I obtained my first large contract, which represented 50 to 60 percent of my time, I spent the remaining 40 percent of my time in continued marketing efforts. These included meeting people in other divisions of the company or other companies, writing an article with a colleague, going to conferences, and making calls. I let people know of additional services I offered. Soon, I got other contracts. In addition, three of the clients who hired me at the first company moved to other companies and brought me in. So I think that focused marketing, developing solid client relationships, and doing good work helped propel me in my business.

Avoiding the Success Trap

Creating New Approaches and Taking Prudent Risks

We all encounter the "success trap" at one time or another. Sometimes it's a temporary setback, and sometimes it's a cul-de-sac with no escape. The success trap occurs when we think we're continuing to prosper and grow but are, in reality, coasting on past strength and occupying a plateau that eventually erodes into decline.

The success trap is particularly pernicious, because it strikes consultants who have endured the risks inherent in the business; survived through adverse economic times; and accommodated the competitive, technological, and sociological changes that have transpired during their growth years. However, once successful, these consultants have focused on what they have done well, rather than on *what they are capable of doing well.* They tend, ironically, to stop taking the same prudent risks that helped them climb to their present plateau.

SIGNS OF THE SUCCESS TRAP

As you can see in Figure 10.1, the success trap plateau appears when the consultant does not take proactive and aggressive steps to create positive change. Because there is a plethora of change in the marketplace and there are always burgeoning prospects, the lack of positive change is almost always the fault of an advertently or inadvertently conservative consultant.

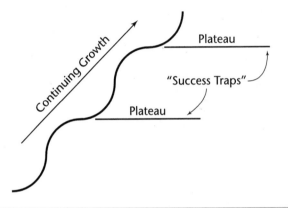

Figure 10.1. The Success Trap

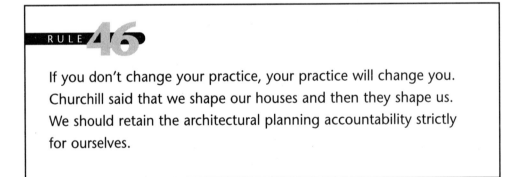

RULE **46**

If you don't change your practice, your practice will change you. Churchill said that we shape our houses and then they shape us. We should retain the architectural planning accountability strictly for ourselves.

Ten Signs That You May Be in a Success Trap
1. Your revenues have slowed considerably from your historical average, and you tend to assign it to your decision to "take a more selective approach" or "turn away business you're not happy with."

2. Your revenues derive overwhelmingly from the same historical sources, both in terms of type of work and of actual client organizations.
3. Your acquisition of new clients is rare and constitutes less than 15 percent of your current business.
4. You rarely jettison any business, no matter how uninteresting, how small the margin, or how low priced.
5. Your marketing materials, website, and public "presence" have increasingly narrowed to the point that you may be considered a specialist, content expert, or "one trick pony."
6. Your practice is entirely regional, you seldom travel, and you pride yourself on being able to make a living "without getting on any airplanes."
7. Your last published article or interview is at least two years old.
8. You have few alliances, affiliations, mentorships, or collaborators, and you don't personally know any of the "movers and shakers" of the profession who do appear in the media.
9. Your office equipment, electronic aids, website, and/or business property are not new, state-of-the-art, or even in very good shape.
10. You have not failed at anything you've tried professionally in several years.

The success trap is pernicious, because you suddenly find yourself drifting through it. If half of the above list applies to you, you've probably entered the plateau. If more than half apply, you've been blithely moseying across it. If all apply, you're on the decline, and that pace is accelerating.

Why do consultants enter the success trap plateau? Often for the best or reasons. They want a deserved "slower pace," they don't need to reach out for business due to their current reputation and client base, or they simply follow the path of least resistance. The problem is that of entropy: You cannot coast along a plateau. Eventually friction will overcome inertia and you will slow; if you come to a decline, the descent will be rapid because you're not prepared for it and the brakes may be worn.

USING NEW TECHNOLOGIES

You probably haven't had much difficulty adapting to a cell phone or a computer. There's no reason not to adopt other technologies or advances to further your business at key junctures. There is no practice that I've ever seen that is impervious to the advantages of new approaches and fresh thinking.

For example, executive and management coaching is growing in import, and it has become particularly appropriate for a variety of web applications. Follow-up with past clients has always been a major marketing thrust, and e-mail has provided an additional, superb opportunity to do so.

There is nothing inherently contradictory about seeking to cut back on travel and continuing to grow your business. Substituting phone and electronic coaching and marketing for onsite visits is just one example. In fact, your publishing, coaching, mentoring, and client follow-up *globally* is now easier than it once was locally, thanks to electronic support.

Any suggestions about utilizing emerging technologies will, by definition, be outmoded by the time you read this! However, here are some historical examples to give you the idea. These require very little capital investment, are relatively easy to master and implement, and have been highly effective as components of an already successful business. In other words, the hardest part is *volition*.

Teleconferencing. This can be used for national meetings as well as for quick client updates. You should have an outstanding speaker phone in your office, so that you can take notes or consult your files. Even better is a lightweight headset that has superb sound quality and a "mute" button. These can be purchased with wireless options for maximum roving.

Videoconferencing. These are increasingly useful for seminars, workshops, report delivery, and even focus groups. The technology improves every day. I've presented to buyers in Montana simply by stopping by their New York office and sitting in front of a camera. You can usually establish a relationship with a local university or training center that has the equipment and is all too happy to rent the facility when not in use.

Interactive Internet Conferencing. This is an extension of the "chat room" concept; you engage in a question-and-answer session with a client "live" over the web. Sometimes an intermediary can serve as a host who screens questions and places them in a coherent sequence. This is an effective global approach, providing that everyone can accommodate the various time zones.

A consultant I'll call Larry created a productive marketing consultancy in the San Francisco Bay area. He assisted mid-sized firms ($50 to $150 million) to expand their scope. He was a one-man show, little overhead and rapid response, and clients loved him for the "quick hits"—he was able to frame the marketing weaknesses, design a new program, help implement the elements, and disengage—all within about four to six months.

Word spread in the community, and Larry didn't even have to visit Los Angeles, San Diego, and Phoenix, as he had when he started out. He never even created a marketing package, didn't have a press kit, and never considered moving up-market or down. In fact, Larry simply cashed the checks and enjoyed himself over the course of eight years and was generating revenues up to $500,000 annually.

Eventually, Larry's successful clients grew to the size where they had to move to firms with significant national resources. The mid-market he was comfortable with became more sophisticated and moved strongly toward eCommerce, not an area that Larry ever bothered to become involved with. And he wasn't comfortable with the predominantly family-owned ventures of smaller firms.

When Larry finally realized the decline, he had no presence or repute in other cities; he had no pipeline of prospects; he was not media savvy and hadn't published in many years; and he no longer "remembered" how (or had the energy) to beat the bushes as he had as a younger man.

Last year, Larry generated $175,000 in revenues and was busily engaged in trying to determine how best to cut back his life style.

Compelling Websites. By offering products for sale, free articles and techniques, the opportunity for third parties to meet, links to other relevant sites, and so on, you can create a dynamic international marketing site that requires a small investment of time each month to update and monitor. Hire a web designer to do the heavy lifting—their prices continue to plummet and it's a great investment to minimize your own time involvement in the administration.

Cell Phones and Laptops.   Increasing light devices with long-lived batteries make this dynamic duo extraordinarily flexible. I have to laugh at the consultants who brag that "I don't take any work on vacations, and don't even buy a newspaper." The problem, of course, is that they take precious few vacations. I take a lot of vacations and don't mind taking an hour a day to take care of business, satisfy clients, and respond to prospects. I don't mind because I'm doing it from the beach, the ski chalet, or the boat. Don't fall into the trap of "business or vacation, you can't do both." Of course you can, and very reasonably so, if you use the proper tools.

Our business is about communications. You cannot expect to continue to improve your business if you refuse to adapt and adjust to new forms of proactive and passive communications.

RULE 47

Once you've attained a certain level of success, you have value in areas that you once struggled with or took for granted: intellectual property, name recognition, and cachet. These are legitimate sources of wealth.

CREATING PROPRIETARY MODELS AND TECHNIQUES

Although there is nothing new under the sun, there are certainly unique approaches and methodologies that you've created and perfected over the years. These are potential sources of income, which can offset or improve on your more traditional consulting revenues.

Your approaches to strategy development, time management, merger and acquisition work, executive search, executive coaching, or any other area of individual and organizational performance are appropriate for a wide variety of alternative applications. If you possess trademarks, service marks, registration, copyrights, patents, and other protections, your position is that much stronger. If you do not, then you should pursue those avenues for any of your work that qualifies.[1] Although you can accomplish trademark searches on the web, it's a better idea to invest in a good attorney who specializes in the area. The relatively small additional investment is well worth the safety of doing things right in a very critical (and litigious) area.

Among the options available to create revenue from your existing methodologies and approaches are:

- Self-published books, manuals, workbooks, checklists, and other materials that can be sold on the Internet, by third parties, through normal distribution channels,[2] and other means. For example, a seven-dollar booklet of fifty pages on the subject of diversity can be sold by the thousands to organizations that choose to use it as the basis of one of their internal workshops.

- Newsletters, whether print or electronic. Use your "brand" as its title; charge a subscription fee if the objective is revenue growth or circulate it for free if the objective is marketing exposure; and encourage others to cite it. One mention in a trade publication or a popular website and your newsletter will grow by hundreds of readers per week.

- Offer to mentor others. My mentoring program is extremely successful and is marketed only by word of mouth, website, and an insert in my products. Use your expertise as a coach—either to business clients or to others in your profession—but work remotely, via phone, fax, e-mail, and correspondence. You can provide various levels of participation, certification, and continuing access to you.

---

1. It's a good idea to sit down with an appropriate legal specialist once every two years to review your entire work output to determine which are most appropriate for legal protection.

2. Place an ISBN (International Standard Book Number) on your printed and recorded work, for example, and you will have no problem listing it for sale on such high-profile distributors as Amazon.com.

John Bennet is a consultant, trainer, and author who has been in business only three years and has passed the half-million-dollar mark. He helps organizations exploit change to excel and has published a book on that topic.

Q. What is the single key factor in your success?

A. Drive and desire. No question about it. I have a strong work ethic and desire to be successful. This has enabled me to keep going, keep pushing, keep trying new things, etc.

Q. What would you do differently if you did it over?

A. Not much. The only thing that might be done differently is to spend more energy on marketing through relationship management and self-promotion. Most of my work has come through referrals. I have found that paid advertising does not pay for itself. I wish I had taken more time to make cold calls and work my network. Because this is not something I am completely comfortable doing (self-promotion), maybe I should have hired some-

• Reach out to new media. Place your work on CD, cassette, video, and other forms to be developed. You will tend to reach entirely new audiences that purchase and learn in a variety of manners. Consider approaches that may not have been appropriate in your more traditional venues. For example, I had amassed a significant number of stories in my travels that I could never tell to my traditional corporate audiences during my keynote speeches. The stories were all true, but slightly controversial, bizarre, or totally out of a business context. One day my future collaborator, hearing one of them, suggested that we create a video called "Stories I Could Never Tell" with a proper disclaimer for potential purchasers. It has become a terrific product, often among those business people who wouldn't want me to tell them live from the stage.

one to make calls. Oh well, at this point I am motivated to promote my book. I believe this will allow me to promote myself through it.

Q. What is the major achievement you have yet to accomplish?

A. I would like to create better balance in my work and personal life. It is difficult in the early phase of my speaking, training, and consulting practice to say "no" to work. When the client base needs to grow, you continue to experiment with your niche (product and market), and you are uncertain about the next paycheck, maintaining balance is difficult. I hope to get to a point where I have a balance in the type of work I do (between speaking, training, and consulting), the amount of work I do (I would like to work about one hundred days per year), and reduce the travel time (so that more days are spent in real productive time). With this accomplished, I will have more time for hobbies, home, relationship, and so forth. When you like what you are doing and have a strong desire to succeed, it is easy to work ALL the time.

- If you have a sufficiently unique and protected technology, you can license it, franchise it, or "lease it" to others. Since my "formula" for sharing revenues has always been one-third each for business acquisition, methodology, and delivery,[3] you can acquire a third or more of other people's revenues by making your trademark methodologies available to them. I know consultants who have provided their approaches to time management, strategy formulation, sales acceleration, and business valuation to others for a one-time fee, annual license, situational piece of the

---

3. See *Million Dollar Consulting* for details.

action, and other consideration. These assets are enhanced if your approach has a general market brand attached, whether by a trade name, your own name, or other identifier. As a rule of thumb, if your technology or methodology in and of itself, by repute, enables others to secure business, the more valuable your asset. Thus, it's always a good idea to create an identifier and protection early, in order to cash it on it later. Everyone knows that H&R Block are the tax people.

While you're on the "upswing" and ahead of the plateau, think about which of your approaches, your repute, your "status," can be used for passive income via licensing, franchising, mentoring, coaching, or other sharing.

THE CONSULTANT AS ENTREPRENEUR

We seem to begin in this business as entrepreneurs and then evolve to business people of a more conservative and stereotypical sort. But perhaps we need to revive and revivify that entrepreneurial edge consistently as we ensure that we are continually climbing, even if by means other than those we used at the beginning of the journey.

Here are some ideas and actual examples of adjuncts, alternatives, and additions to a successful consulting career. These may replace some exiting work or serve to turbocharge what we want to continue doing.

Part-Time Executive

There is a precedent of retired executives who emerge for a temporary period to serve a firm needing their content help in finance, marketing, or operations. Why not agree to serve for a limited period as a firm's vice president of sales or chief financial officer until a full-time replacement is found? There is no need to make a forty-hour, five-day commitment, so you could continue to provide consulting help to other clients if you so chose. This alternative is downright dangerous early in a career, when it actually puts you into corporate work and takes you out of the marketplace, but later in your career you can certainly manage it, especially since you're in a position to name your own terms. It's often ironic how approaches from our early career that seemed deadly or untenable become valuable and pragmatic later on. Yet we don't often make use of our success to revisit these alternatives.

Don't assume that an approach that didn't make sense when you started out will never make sense. The acquisition of money, fame, experience, and confidence can turn an unimaginable alternative into a practical tactic.

Part-Time Professor

There are few things as rewarding as teaching and, unlike professional speaking, you don't have to worry about a critical audience demanding its money back.

Most colleges, universities, professional schools, junior colleges, and related institutions embrace adjunct faculty members for a variety of excellent reasons:

- They bring a real-world, real-time, external perspective
- They are not politically involved and don't seek tenure or the department chair position
- They are inexpensive resources, with either no pay or minimum pay[4]
- They teach in less desirable time frames—often in the evening or on weekends—when their schedules permit and full-time faculty is least interested in participating
- In evening classes, they identify well with the audience, which is usually holding down jobs in companies not unlike the clients of the consultant
- The school is aided in broadening and diversifying its elective offerings
- With the right repute and promotion, the consultant often serves as a "draw" to a course or program of study
- The consultant can often become involved in committees and task forces where his or her expertise is desperately needed (and otherwise unaffordable)

---

4. In most schools with a unionized faculty, you will receive at least the minimum pay scale, which can go toward some hobby or charity.

This kind of visibility results in local media attention, word of mouth in the students' organizations (I've been contacted by scores of people who say their colleagues were in my courses), and increased cachet on your biographical sketch. "Adjunct professor" has a nice sound and instant credibility.

Intermediary

Once you've established years of client work and contacts, and assuming you've maintained your database and key relationships well, you're in a position to serve as a matchmaker. There are vibrant business opportunities today for those who can bring capital, alliances, expertise, contacts, and other synergies to the right need at the right time.

There is nothing wrong with taking a piece of the action, so long as it remains win/win/win. Your ability to speed the acquisition of funding, accelerate growth, obtain subcontractors, and other key assets is worth a great deal.

This is almost always non-travel, non-overhead business. I once represented a $2 million dollar training firm that had outgrown the plans of the founders, who were basically researchers, to larger firms interested in making an acquisition. My role was to target the prospective buyers, help the sellers create the best possible sales package, and bring the parties together where there was mutual interest. For that, I received a fee plus a percentage of the sale price. This is nothing that I advertise or promote, but people approach me from time to time and, instead of reflexively responding "I don't do that work," I began to think about why I ought to do that work. Now I do, when the conditions are right.

The R&D Factory

Many consultants have spent years perfecting various techniques about their craft. These may be in sales, strategy, search, technology, response centers, and so on. They can be technical or non-technical, tactical or strategic, individually oriented or team-based. The point is that many of us have become "experts" in certain aspects of business, learning, execution, finance, and so on.

There are organizations seeking to remain leading edge and state of the art that cannot afford a resident group of experts (or choose not to create such a group because it quickly becomes incestuous with no external frames of reference). I've seen consultants establish relationships with everyone from bank training departments, to catalog customer response centers, to specialized training firms with the agreement to provide continued expertise in these areas. Sometimes the consultant is expected to deliver periodic updates and advances to current methodologies, and sometimes he or she is expected to review and critique the client's own developments.

In either case, these relationships constitute the potential for long-term contracts with little onsite work and a focus basically on the consultant's "smarts." They are an ideal alternative to becoming the resident expert and long-time advisor at a stage in your career when your repute supports such profitable arrangements.

RULE 49

As your repute and credentials grow, stop viewing yourself as a *provider* of expertise and methodology and begin viewing yourself as a *resource* of wide-ranging potential. One of the potholes in the success trap is that we continue to see ourselves as we were when we began, rather than as we are today. The more we've learned and experienced, the more our mere involvement becomes valuable in and of itself.

Retainers as a Strategy

In line with hiring us to have access to our smarts, I'd be remiss if I didn't specifically mention the power of retainer arrangements. Retainers *are not* the guarantee of so much time per month in return for a set billing fee. They are a means of obtaining access to you as a resource—without specific objectives, projects, or time guarantees—in return for a fixed, single fee.

In other words, a client may hire you for $15,000 per month, with a guarantee of a minimum of three months and the option to renew at the beginning of the third month for another three. In return, you are available by phone, fax, letter, e-mail, teleconference, and in person, subject to mutually convenient scheduling (all travel expenses are paid by the client). You will provide assistance on anything that you and the client agree is within your competency. You agree to

Several times a week I've been contacted by either firms interested in finding subcontractors in a tight labor market or by solo practitioners seeking to augment their practice through subcontracting assignments. I was caught between the willingness to help everyone out and the difficulty of taking the time to decide who was a good match, avoiding omitting anyone qualified, and taking the time to correspond with everyone.

Last year I began a subcontractor registry. For a modest fee, those interested in subcontracting list their specialties, geographical preferences, fee ranges, and other qualifications. When I'm approached, I obtain the criteria from the firm requiring assistance and provide the candidates based on those specifications.

The process is objective, of service to both parties, and profitable. In addition, it draws still more attention to my firm's overall services.

There are a lot of inventive and fulfilling ways to enhance our businesses, especially on terms that are quite pleasing at this point in our careers. Ironically, they are often right under our noses and require little or no investment, technology change, or promotion.

---

be reasonably available and to respond with top priority, and the client agrees not to abuse the privilege and to provide as much advance notice as possible.

I've helped many consultants arrange such retainers for six- and twelve-month periods, and my experience is that one can manage several of these at any one time. They are most sought when the consultant is recognized to have provided excellent help in the past and has a "name" that is appealing. Consequently, they are very effective with long-time clients for whom you have provided assistance on a wide range of projects over the years.

Clients often don't know you're willing to work in this manner, or they interpret retainers in varying ways because they are used incorrectly by others. Introduce this possibility as an issue whenever:

- You're engaged in several projects at once for the same organization
- A client expresses a need for your help but can't identify specific projects or issues

- A client is trying to set priorities about which projects you should work on from a longer list
- A client seeks to gain some priority on your time, responsiveness, and assistance
- A client insists on a non-compete clause for some period
- A client is expressing misgivings about the growing investment required to involve you over the course of time

Retainer arrangements are lucrative, fulfilling, and non-taxing. Astoundingly, the people who have the most trouble with them are often the consultants themselves, who seem to fret if the client isn't using them regularly and worry if the client says, "I haven't had need for you this week (or month) and I'm wondering if the retainer is worth it?"

One piece of good advice can be worth an entire retainer. I've often said that my ideal annual work would be to help a single client for twenty minutes for a fee of $5 million. My wife says that if I can work for twenty minutes, I can work for forty minutes.

THINGS TO COME

What's coming down the pike that may enhance consultants' abilities to gain new business from new sources? Or, for that matter, what may be in store to make a consultant's successful years even more leveraged and varied?

The ultimate consultant has to stay ahead of the curve, so here are some considerations for you to evaluate, given the nature of your particular practice.

Licensing and Certifications

The debate has waxed and waned about certifications, licensing, and credentials. The largest consulting organizations have been either against it or apathetic, with only the small Society of Professional Management Consultants actively agitating for state licensure. At the moment, a manicurist, dog groomer, and palm reader all must have certain competencies certified by the state, which is far more rigorous than any consulting requirements anywhere.

Consulting is so fragmented and diverse that licensing is unlikely in our lifetimes. In the medical field, whether a physician is an internist, psychiatrist,

Gene Pepper works with owners of businesses that need marketing and sales help, financial planning assistance, and someone who can offer sound and objective advice. His annual revenues are in the low to mid six figures.

Q. What has been your key to success?

A. There are two: First, many years ago I learned to network very effectively. I was taught by a master who showed me how to give referrals before I expected any. So when I meet someone I ask questions about not only what they do, but how they work, who their best clients are, and who they would like to be introduced to—not so much by name but by business or industry group. Everyone I meet for the first time always gets a "nice to meet you" letter on personalized letterhead—not company letterhead. I never enclose a business card with these notes. Networking counts for at least 75 percent of my business. Second, I have always asked lots of questions. My prospects or clients oftentimes will tell me that I am the best listener they have ever met. I find that not only will people open up if they are talking about themselves, but they take normal, natural barriers down. People get to trust me very quickly because I am sincere with the questions and rarely does anyone feel they are being "set

plastic surgeon, or obstetrician, one must master common medical practices and procedures before going on to a specialty, and even the specialty is board certified as the highest degree of accomplishment. There is no body of knowledge or set of methodologies that apply to consulting. Even if one were to make the case that, say, problem solving or conflict resolution were essential, the measurement of mastery is subjective at best.

up." And I never try to close someone on the first visit. I need time to digest what I have learned and decide whether I want the assignment.

Q. What would you do differently the second time around?

A. (a) Become a master speaker. Take all the coaching I could and speak as often as possible in the beginning. (b) Enter the consulting business much earlier than I did. Maybe work for a bigger firm to obtain more structure and basics, then move on individually. (c) Take more financial training. A good deal of my practice is assisting companies with financial problems. It is not unusual for me to encounter an owner of a good-sized business who has no clue as to where his or her company is. I am no longer surprised when I meet a company bookkeeper who is incompetent.

Q. What is your major unachieved accomplishment?

A. I would like to work for a major company that has vision and money (not so much for my pocket, but to implement the changes that need to be made as a result of my work). All of my client companies have sales volume less than $15 million. My assignments tend to run eight to fifteen months. I would like longer relationships, but that has not happened.

Consequently, it is highly unlikely that a consulting standard certification or governmental licensing will evolve. That means that our individual credibility and sanctioning will rely on our ability to convince our prospects of our professionalism, ethics, and acumen. Self-sustaining credibility will be critical, including references, publishing, public image, professionalism of materials, and so on. (And if some form of licensing ever does develop, it is highly likely that those who have these high profiles will more readily gain the certification. As an example, the Institute of Management Consultants today waives several of its requirements to qualify for its Certified Management Consultant designation if the applicant provides evidence of such professionalism and history.)

Professional Credentialing

There is a strong trend toward situational credentials in the United States and, to a lesser extent, around the world. Various professionals apply for and are credentialed as "Certified Meeting Planners," "Certified Speaking Professionals," "Certified Management Consultants," and so on, ad nauseum. I've seen people list four and five sets of otherwise unfathomable initials after their names, which tends to make them look more desperate than dignified. (Another practice is the placing of a master's degree designation after one's name, as in "June Jones, MA." I once thought that an inordinate amount of people were from Massachusetts.)

The problem with these privately bestowed honorifics is that they are not recognized by the public at large. And that is the test. Everyone knows what an MBA or a Ph.D. represents, including the rigor and study that went into the acquisition of the degree. Without that public recognition—and the potential buyers' sensitivity—the artificial honorifics are meaningless. Most professional organizations don't understand this, and they use the "degrees" they award primarily as methods of internal professional association recognition and elitism.

There have been some exceptions. Canadian consultants have done a fairly effective job of educating potential buyers about the credibility of their Certified Management Consultant designation, showing that it can be done. However, it is not likely that anything equivalent to CPA, for example, is going to emerge as an indicator of achievement for the consulting profession.

Taxing of Services

This is a distinct threat. Many venues are considering or have begun to tax professional services despite the origin of the provider or the site of the delivery.

At this writing, professional speaking fees in North Carolina are subject to a state tax in excess of 4 percent unless the provider can certify that such services are for educational purposes. (Subsequent to the passage of that law, it's stunning how much of the speaking in that state took on an educational tone, moving a topic such as "Why to Vacation in the Bahamas" to "Instruction in How to Choose Career Stress Reduction Alternatives During Downtime.") California has tough laws about taxing services. Most of the states require (although enforcement is vague and often impossible) taxes to be collected on products sold to their residents, even through mail order and the Internet, and those consultants selling products have experienced the need on occasion to withhold sales tax, at least in their home states.

The innovative consultant will have thought through these implications with legal and financial experts and developed a strategy. For example, the policy may be as simple as passing the tax on to the client or purchaser, but there will still be issues of collection, reporting, and payment in what could be a bewildering array of venues. Consultants will probably have to be prepared for this eventuality and take pains to ensure that the result is not lower margins.

Globalization

American consulting expertise will be increasingly welcomed abroad (just one of the results of residing in the economically dominant power in the world), and non-American consultants will increasing find work outside of their native countries. Consulting is a process, and the commonality of searching for higher quality, better performance, and superior service will propel the consulting profession around the globe, particularly among emerging and rebuilding economies. (If you doubt this, think about the quality movement's international appeal after enjoying the original receptivity of Japanese industry.)

RULE 50

The future is what you make it. Strategically, invest some time and resources in determining how best you can exploit the trends. After all, isn't that what you'd advise your clients to do?

If international travel is appealing—perhaps in conjunction with vacations—the globalization evolution is a wonderful opportunity. If travel isn't desirable but development of new markets and revenue sources is, the Internet provides excellent access and delivery potential, particularly for some of the options we've discussed earlier in the book, such as coaching, product sales, and publishing.

In any case, even for those consultants who choose to confine themselves to U.S. work, it will be imperative to understand global markets, competition, and distribution alternatives. Every potential U.S. client, even in the small business and "Mom and Pop" markets, will be involved in some way in the global market.

Technology Advance

You needn't be a futurist to see a world in which one phone number can track us down no matter where we are (already crudely being done), computers allow for thriving twenty-four-hour commerce in service as well as products, coaching and mentoring are provided electronically, vast data can be recalled to hand-held devices, and physical presence becomes less of an issue than access to wisdom on demand.

I'm not advocating the disappearance of business travel or the "paperless" office, which are simplistic projections we've all heard for two decades. But the fact is that our work will be both more challenging and easier. Easier in the sense that the wear and tear of travel can be reduced, even if not eliminated, and more challenging in that clients (especially global customers) will reasonably require knowledge-on-demand and access to our "smarts" in a variety of channels.

The consultant who ignores—or even fails to exploit—technological advances, especially in communications, will be relegated to the sidelines. After all, we deal in information, which must be communicated in some form. Ultimate consultants will make the investment in technology and their own learning so that prospects and clients can access their help on an "as needed" basis, utilizing what is today the primitive "fax on demand" but what tomorrow will be computer-provided analysis and response to business issues. We won't need twenty-four-hour consultants who never sleep, but we will need twenty-four-hour electronic access with knowledge that is never obsolete.

This is a better time than ever—at least in my memory of over a quarter century in the profession—to be a consultant, and I suspect the future will shine even brighter given the overall increasing prosperity of the world. *Now* is the time for successful consultants to consider and make decisions about their future success, future leisure, and future life. It's a splendid opportunity, and one that is ignored at one's own peril.

This is the perfect juncture to turn to life balance, the subject of our final chapter.

THE ULTIMATE RULES

Rule #46. If you don't change your practice, your practice will change you. Churchill said that we shape our houses and then they shape us. We should retain the architectural planning accountability strictly for ourselves.

Rule #47. Once you're attained a certain level of success, you have value in areas that you once struggled with or took for granted: intellectual property, name recognition, and cachet. These are legitimate sources of wealth.

Rule #48. Don't assume that an approach that didn't make sense when you started out will never make sense. The acquisition of money, fame, experience, and confidence can turn an unimaginable alternative into a practical tactic.

Rule #49. As your repute and credentials grow, stop viewing yourself as a *provider* of expertise and methodology, and begin viewing yourself as a *resource* of wide-ranging potential. One of the potholes in the success trap is that we continue to see ourselves as we were when we began, rather than as we are today. The more we've learned and experienced, the more our mere involvement becomes valuable in and of itself.

Rule #50. The future is what you make it. Strategically, invest some time and resources in determining how you can best exploit the trends. After all, isn't that what you'd advise your clients to do?

Final Thought: There may be nothing new under the sun in consulting, but innovative and creative ways to apply what we know to evolving societies, economies, and technologies will be the key to leading-edge consulting.

Esystems, Inc., is an information technology service provider based in New York City. They help clients gain a competitive edge through the intelligent application of technology. The president is Glenwood (Woody) Elam, and their revenues have grown from under $200,000 to almost seven figures within five years.

Q. What is the single greatest factor in your success?

A. The single contributing factor to my success is my belief and faith in Jesus Christ. Christ directs, sustains, motivates, encourages, protects, and directs me.

Q. What would you do differently if you could do it all over?

A. If I had anything to do over again, I would have developed a well-thought-out marketing plan. When first starting we did not have a well-developed marketing plan. Fortunately, we do now.

Q. What is your greatest unachieved goal?

A. The major achievement I would like to accomplish is to build gross sales to at least $1 million and build my personal net worth to at least $1 million.

Life Balance

The Ultimate Outlook

The consulting profession is a means to an end. No one ever died pleading for one more consulting assignment or client presentation.

About a decade ago I discovered that I did not have a personal life and a professional life, but that I had *a life*. That conceptual breakthrough, at least for me, was a landmark event. Suddenly, time was freed up, flexibility was enhanced, and the synergies of my life made me stronger is all aspects of my endeavors.

The more holistically we view our lives, the better consultants we will be, because we are enriching our business acumen with our other experiences and values. The more we focus solely on consulting—become workaholics and totally immerse ourselves in our discipline and methodologies—the poorer we are as consultants. We become people who know more and more about less and less, and we eventually drill down so narrowly that no one notices our impact.

Throughout this chapter I'll be offering you some ideas about life balance and techniques to achieve it. We sacrifice other aspects

231

of our lives early in our careers because we have to create momentum and visibility. The problem is that such single-minded drive often becomes our business model, even after we have created a viable practice, name recognition, and marketing "gravity." We enter the "success trap" of our personal existence, assuming that the behaviors that initiated our success must be those that will perpetuate it.

Nothing could be farther from the truth.

Whether you are a solo practitioner, principal of a small firm, or partner in a large firm (or aspiring to any of these roles), it's time to work smart and not hard.

RULE **51**

"Work" is not the evil side of your life, and "personal" is not the good side of your life. Your life is what you make it, and all components of it ultimately reinforce and enrich the others *if you allow them to do so.*

WORKING LESS AND LIVING MORE

We plan our work, it seems, but not our lives. Our jobs get in the way of our careers, and our careers get in the way of our lives. Just as you employ consulting methodologies, you must employ techniques that provide for life balance. This applies whether you are married or not, young or old, have children or do not, live in an extended family or an empty nest. Life balance leads to better consulting, and better consulting provides the rewards that enhance life balance.

Here, then, are some techniques to consider to enhance your life, work, and relationships.[1] Of the fifty, how many are you already engaged in, and how many more can you add?

---

1. These are taken from my work in creating workshops, coaching, and materials to enhance life balance. For a free subscription to my monthly, electronic newsletter called "Balancing Act," send an e-mail to: join-balancingact@summitconsulting.com. Or visit my website and simply click on the button for the subscription: *http://www.summitconsulting.com.*

Fifty Techniques to Enhance Life Balance

1. Decompartmentalize.   One of the worst mistakes I've ever made was to "compartmentalize" my life. It dawned on me a few years ago that I don't have a "personal life" and a "business life," but simply A LIFE. Consequently, I do things when they feel right, which might include writing an article or taking care of client work on a Saturday morning and sitting at the pool on a Tuesday afternoon.

2. Set Priorities Well.   Time is the great equalizer, since we all have the same amount of it available. When we say that we don't have the time to help a spouse, watch our children perform, fix things around the house, or improve ourselves, we really mean that we don't consider it a priority. We actually do have the time.

3. Weed Out Useless Reading.   When you receive reading material that you may or may not want to review, place it in an obvious pile where you'll see it every day. Whatever you haven't read after two weeks, simply throw out. It's not urgent and you don't need it.

4. Savor the Immediate Moment.   People often make the mistake of allotting time for various aspects of their life each week, thinking that the technique provides balance (for example, two hours a day with the pets, an hour every other day exercising, a weekend day with a significant other). But this meting out of hours only provides quantity, not quality. The real test is in the intensity, fulfillment, and enjoyment of the time, not the mere expenditure of it.

5. Understand Your Anger.   Most anger is actually self-directed anger that is transferred to others in order to achieve self-preservation. If you're angry a lot of the time, don't assume you've met a rash of incompetent people on the phone, at work, among customers, and in social settings. Find out why you're really angry with yourself.

6. Utilize Stress Productively.   A certain amount of stress—eustress—is healthy because it keeps the adrenaline flowing and provides for a sense of urgency. We've all heard others (and/or ourselves) say, "I work best under pressure and approaching deadlines." Don't try to eliminate stress, but do try to manage it so that it creates energy but stops short of anxiety and paralysis.

7. *Exploit Strengths.* Most people I've worked with place an inordinate emphasis on correcting weakness and do very little about building on strength. No one excels by correcting weaknesses (which simply serve to maintain the status quo a little more easily). Find out what your real strengths are (many people are totally unaware of some of them) and make plans to exploit them in work and at play.

8. *Capture Ideas Immediately.* Always have a book and a pad and pen next to your bed, even when traveling. If you can't sleep, read the book. If you suddenly have a bright idea, write it down. I find that many people lose their best ideas because they don't capture them quickly after thinking of them.

9. *Value Variety.* Balance in life and work is not about equal distribution. It is about variety, diversity, and establishing the correct priorities for yourself. I don't care if I never manage people again, because it's an activity that I loathed. But I get skittish if I don't have a book to read at any given moment when I have the urge to do so.

10. *Follow Your Passions.* The "success trap" occurs when you are rewarded and lauded for something that you're good at but actually dislike. This is how jobs get in the way of careers and how necessary evils come to impede our lives. Let your internal gyroscope tell you what's right for you, not external influences.

11. *Leave the Comfort Zone.* Every year (Is that too much to ask?) set a goal to do something you've never done before. Smoke a cigar. Sky dive. Buy a $500 bottle of wine. Go to a spa. Attend the opera (I don't blame you if you avoid Wagner, though). You get the idea. After a few years, you've added immeasurably to your life.

12. *Add Music.* Put a stereo unit or boom box or something that can produce music in your work area. Cue up the music that you can't get enough of, no matter what your taste. Arrange things so that you can simply hit a button—or better still, a remote—to start your music. Turn it on whenever you're working on something that is enhanced (or merely not interfered with) by background music. I try to regularly go through all my Sinatra, Billy Joel, and Bobby Caldwell. (Hold your critique; I'm a romantic at heart.)

From the time I first began traveling for business, my wife and I agreed on some ground rules that would make it, at first, less intolerable and, later, quite attractive.

We agreed that I would call at least once every day, not matter where I was in the world or how frenzied the client activity. I do that to this day. We agreed that travel would be a normal part of our children's growth experience and, indeed, they were flying transcontinental with us even before they were in school.

When my wife and I chose extended vacations, even during the school term, we sometimes took the children, even when it meant a heated argument with a narrow-minded teacher who had to be reminded that we were making the decisions about our children and not her.

When we could afford it, we began to schedule *business around vacations,* meaning that the vacation time went on the calendar early and was sacrosanct. Clients would simply have to choose other dates or I would have to pass on the business.

To this day, when others ask my wife, "How can you have lived with a man for over thirty years who has traveled so much, and how could you raise the children that way?" she has a stock answer: "How could you not?" In almost every instance, we're the ones with the longest lived, most successful marriage and, not coincidentally, the richest life style.

---

13. *Learn Constantly.* Find a book on the basics of something in which you're deficient—art, music, theater, architecture, whatever—and then create an experience to match your new learning. Go to a museum or exhibit, attend a symphony or opera, visit the theater, go on a walking tour. I learned something about architecture in Barcelona, of all places, using this technique.

14. *Surprise Others.* Surprise someone who means a lot to you. Forget about significant, recognized occasions. Buy a gift, write a note, send some flowers, provide a compliment—completely out of the blue. Has anyone ever done that for you? If so, how did it feel? If not, how would it feel?

15. *Explore the Unknown Roads.* Pull off your beaten track and drive up a road that you've never traveled before. See what's up there.

16. *Vent.* Don't be afraid to vent. Stress is either internalized (making you ill) or externalized (making someone else ill). My wife tells me I'm a carrier. Nevertheless, if you're upset with service, quality, responsiveness, or results, speak now or slightly later, but don't forever hold your peace. It's unhealthy. Let it out, and then let it alone and move on. Nothing makes me crazier than people who go around informing me, "What I should have said was. . . ."

17. *Compete.* Find a competitive activity and throw yourself into it. Hear me out before you send me nasty e-mails. If you want to be physically active, chose tennis or racquetball or something like it; if not, try chess, or Monopoly or some other board game. Healthy and cordial competition gets the juices flowing, exorcises hostility, and provides the opportunity for some passion. Life's not about winning, per se, but about joyously entering the fray and engaging with our best effort, win or lose.

18. *Use Your Own Model.* Do not be lulled by these "models" that have you plot out the various components of your life on some wheel-and-spoke system and then ask how much attention you're paying to each. The implication is that you should "balance" your time commitment quantitatively, which is nonsense. (You heard it here.) The point is really to balance your interests *qualitatively*. A lot of useless time with the kids doesn't measure up to an hour spent at their recital or soccer game, and spending hours speechlessly sitting next to your significant other doesn't hold a candle to the two seconds it takes to say, "I love you." (I see a lot of people having breakfast with their families at restaurants, with husband and wife both hidden behind the morning paper while the kids play with the silverware. Quality, anyone?)

19. *Be Selfish.* Decide on something selfish you're going to spend a few hours a week on. Make that time inviolate (you may shift the schedule but not the commitment). Whether it's a hobby, volunteer work, fixing up the abode, or sitting on a rock contemplating the universe, make it your sacrosanct time. It's not what you concentrate on, but the quality and passion of your concentration that counts.

Dean Fowler runs a mid six figure practice in family business management, including intergenerational conflict resolution and succession.
He is a solo practitioner located in Elm Grove, WI.

Q. What is the main reason for your success?

A. Specializing in a focused niche market, namely family business,
with a unique and differentiated specialty.

Q. If you could start over, what would you do differently?

A. Start using project billing rather than hourly billing earlier in my
career to focus on the value-added benefit of my services to the
client, rather than on the hours I spend and my hourly fee structure.

Q. What is your greatest unaccomplished goal?

A. I have developed an Internet-based assessment for families in business that I plan to begin marketing world-wide. This will be
accompanied by a book on family business I will publish during
2000. My major achievement will be to see these endeavors as
successfully implemented on a global basis.

---

20. Remove "Necessary Evils." Sit down and list six things that you hate
doing, or that get on your nerves, or that generally make you crazy. Eliminate
three of them. (This includes relatives.) Stop suffering the "necessary evils."
Take control of the stuff sapping your energy. Here's a silly but effective example. I know a terribly bright and rather charming guy who was driven to distraction by the staples that his dry cleaner utilized to attach the identification
tags to his clothing. He'd struggle with these in the early morning while trying
to catch a plane or keep an appointment. He went to the cleaner and said, "Find
another way or you'll lose my business!" The cleaner now painstakingly puts
his tags in with easily removed safety pins (and affords him a wide berth when

he enters the store). He's ecstatic at having removed one of the thorns in the side of his life. So am I.

21. *Charm When You Must.* Be very polite to the people in service jobs who often verge on the invisible: airline counter clerks, receptionists, wait staff, and so on. I find that "pre-emptive politeness" accomplishes two objectives: It provides better service even if they're having a bad day, and it eliminates the stress involved in having to deal with someone treating you rudely because they're having a bad day.

22. *Say No.* If you have a hard time saying "no," provide options. "No, I can't meet with you today because I have to leave at noon, but I can meet with you tomorrow or the next day, talk on the phone this afternoon, or respond by e-mail before this evening. Which is best for you?" This defuses a confrontation over "no" and turns it into an examination of which "yes" is best.

23. *Exploit Airplanes.* Don't look on a long airplane trip as an ordeal, but look at it as an opportunity. I write articles, read the "tough" books, watch a movie I missed, make some calls, listen to music I might not otherwise (even Country and Western, to my shock), and think about my goals. Those of you who talk to other passengers have even more options at your command. I usually finish a flight with a great sense of accomplishment.

24. *Let It Go.* Arguments with a loved one are not threats to the relationship, nor are they tests of fidelity or commitment. They are merely temporary disagreements, which grow worse only if we attach too much import to them. Holding a grudge against a loved one over a trivial matter is like refusing to use your legs because you bumped your knee.

25. *Ask Provocative Questions.* Don't ask your kids IF they liked or disliked a movie, a dinner, a vacation, or any other experience. Ask them WHY they liked or disliked it. This helps you understand their reasoning, biases, and premises, and occasionally teaches you something that you missed the first time around. (Doesn't hurt with an adult, either!)

26. *Treat Yourself.* You're going to write me nasty letters about this, but if you want to buy a special gift for a loved one, buy yourself something as well. It gets you in the mood, provides a bit of a reward, and makes it more of a joint venture.

27. *Look Around in Awareness.* Recently, we took a three-day mini-vacation in Boston (one hour from our home) and walked the Freedom Trail. I know people in New York who have never been to the Statue of Liberty or the Empire State Building. Don't miss what's in the backyard. (We went to Paul Revere's home, and I discovered he was different from what I had imagined or been taught forty years ago.)

28. *Communicate Assertively.* If you want people to listen to you in a group setting, no matter how informal, simply practice this technique: Speak loudly and firmly, use a recent example, and look people in the eye. For example, "I thought that *Sixth Sense* was a good movie with a surprise ending" is better posed as, "*Sixth Sense* reminded me of Hitchcock at his best, and the ending created a silence in our theater that lasted while people walked out."

29. *Create Traditions.* Create a time of the week—we like Sunday afternoons—when you get in the car and drive for at least an hour to have dinner or just to take in the scenery and explore a new place. It's a great tradition to share, even if you have few other interests in common.

30. *Avoid Acting on Platitudes.* Don't get caught in the war of the bromides. "Don't sweat the small stuff" is offset by "For want of a nail . . ." and "Haste makes waste" creates a conflict with "Time waits for no one." For every aphorism, there is an equal and opposite aphorism, which is Alan's Fourth Law of Thermodynamics. Live your life according to what's right, not what someone has memorialized (and trivialized).

31. *Learn from the Learned.* Read "Acres of Diamonds," a transcription of a speech presented frequently by Russell H. Conwell at the beginning of the 20th Century. I now suggest the sixty-page book to you (I obtained mine in hardcover from amazon.com for about $8). Despite some dated references and what may seem like the glaringly obvious opening stories, Conwell makes some remarkably timeless points about life balance and society (for example, making money through honest work is a key to helping others, success is about understanding the other person's needs, and women have never received due credit for some of the great inventions in our history). Spend an hour with a glass of brandy reading a Civil War veteran's view of contemporary life.

32. *Ignore Trifles*.   Don't waste your time telling spammers to remove you from their e-mail lists, or junk faxers to remove you, or overbearing catalog companies to stop mailing ponderous tomes. They won't do it, or they'll stop only temporarily, or they'll be happy that they have your accurate address and increase their onslaught. Simply throw the stuff out or delete it and get on with your life.

33. *Harness Your Emotions*.   If you want to communicate with your loved ones, never generalize a specific. In other words, don't tell your children that they have no respect when they abruptly interrupt you. Simply point out that they shouldn't interrupt without saying "excuse me" (unless the house is on fire). Once you say to a spouse, "There you go again with the same old . . ." (fill in the blank), you might as well go to a movie by yourself, because rational conversation is over.

34. *Appreciate Your Status*.   One of the greatest lines I ever heard was spoken by actor Dudley Moore playing the title role of "Arthur" when he drunkenly says to his long-suffering valet (Sir John Gielgood, no less), "Don't you wish you were me? I know I do." Hey, shouldn't we all?

RULE **52**

No matter what your material wealth or resources, are you leading the kind of life that is admired by others, or do people say regarding your life, "It's not worth it." Ensure that your work is multiplied exponentially into the richness of your life.

---

35. *Luxuriate in Pleasure Reading*.   The bromide is that we should read slowly for business and professional purposes and speed read for recreation. I don't think so. Most professional stuff I can race through, but I love to savor a well-written book I'm reading for pleasure. We've got that one all reversed.

36. *Share Your Good Fortune.* Around the holidays, I've sometimes gone to the town welfare people to ask which families really need help desperately. I then leave an anonymous gift in their mailbox with what I estimate is enough money to take them through a month or so. It assures me that the help goes directly and completely to those who need it the most. I call (from a public phone, now that caller I.D. is so prevalent) to make sure that they know it's there.

37. *Emphasize Special Occasions.* It may be imprudent to treat every day as if it may be the last, but it's not difficult to treat each holiday family gathering as if it's the last. Special occasions should be joyous and forgiving. I've seen too many despondent people who say, "If I had only known it would be our last holiday/anniversary/birthday together."

38. *Speak Out.* Tell someone flat out when he or she is confusing you, is wrong, or acts obnoxious. I received a call recently from a woman who wanted my free help to set up a self-aggrandizing position, which she was totally unsuited for. I told her so. She got angry. Better her than me.

39. *Achieve Life Landmark Events.* Before you die, visit the following: Hong Kong, Rome, London, and Paris. See a great play on Broadway from tenth row, center. Share a corner table in a fabulous restaurant. Write a short story. Take a cruise and get the best stateroom you can afford. Give your kids a completely unexpected gift. Learn to dance well (I'm still working on that one). Make the winning bid in an auction. Get into the ocean and let a wave wallop you. Sing with exultation, if only in your own shower.

40. *Rise and Shine.* If you can arise at 6:30 in the morning and feel rested, I guarantee that you will increase your productivity by at least 50 percent. You'll get to all those things you never thought you had time to do. Gain an hour a day and you've "created" another two weeks for yourself.

41. *Love Animals.* Make a contribution to an animal shelter, pound, or animal rescue league. There are dedicated, unselfish, sacrificing people trying to do humane work, and even a $10 donation goes a long way toward food and boarding. Do the right thing.

42. *Bestow Time.* Tell your spouse, partner, significant other, and/or lover (political correctness is exhausting, isn't it?) that you've set aside an entire day just for him or her. Provide for the most sybaritic, educational, or fantastic day. (If you make this offer with a reciprocal date in mind, it sort of loses the effect, you know?)

43. *Explore Your Own Past.* Trace your family tree as specifically as possible while the elders are still with you, as a gift to the young. You really can't appreciate where you are unless and until you know where you've been.

44. *Defuse Your Own Anger.* The next time you're REALLY ANGRY, remember that virtually all such rage is actually self-anger being transferred elsewhere. Take the time to find out why you're so unhappy with yourself. Then work on the sources of that anger so that you can eliminate it, and you won't have to expend the energy constantly controlling it (or incur the costs for losing it).

45. *Let Loose on Occasion.* Attend a sports event in person and root like a crazy person. Don't worry about winning; just have a wild time. When I was an undergraduate, our "fight song" was "Nobody ever dies for dear old Rutgers."

46. *Ask Your Kids.* If you have kids, next time you need advice about something, ask them for their advice, and see what happens. You'll establish a great respect for their opinions, and you might just learn something.

47. *Revel in the Absurd.* Joseph Heller died a few years ago, but *Catch 22* remains one of the great anti-war books of all time. If you've never read it, now is a good time.

48. *Listen to Your Maturity.* Listen very closely to the words of our modern troubadour, Billy Joel, on "Shades of Grey," a song on his "River of Dreams" CD. Tom Stoppard wrote once that "Age is such a high price to pay for maturity." "Shades of Grey" is a lyric reminder of the sagacity of simply living long enough.

49. Indulge.   Get an hour-long massage, and make it a weekly treat.

50. Go with Your Gut.   If your head tells you one thing and your gut tells you another, go with your gut. Analytic and cerebral processes can objectively tell you a great deal, but emotion, not logic, is at the root of effective action. If you don't feel it, don't do it.

RULE 53

If you are not doing anything new each week, each month, each year, then you are not living, but merely existing. We are not here to stick our toes in the water. We are here to make waves.

Tack those fifty techniques to a wall in your office or den. How many are you doing, how many are you considering, how many are you accomplishing?

Read through all the varied comments in "From the Trenches" throughout this book, and pay attention to my third question: What is your greatest unaccomplished goal? Over 90 percent of all the respondents, from varied firms, diverse practices around the world, stated that their greatest unaccomplished goals were business related. This is not because they've accomplished all of their life goals, but because they are not thinking in a balanced fashion, despite their business success. This was an eye-opener for me, and it should be for you.

THE FUTURE OF THE BUSINESS

One of the great advantages of this profession is that you can continue in it for as long as you feel capable and find it exciting. There is no mandatory retirement policy, and age usually imparts an additional air of wisdom and *eminence grise*. However, another advantage is that the profession affords us the wealth to stop working and pursue an avocation, family time, part-time advisory status, and other options.

Astron Solutions provides compensation and human resource consulting in the mid-sized market. They are headquartered in New York, with four offices elsewhere, and generate revenue in the mid six figures. Jennifer Frost is the principal. The firm is only a little more than a year old.

Q. What is the single greatest factor in your success?

A. The single key factor in our success has been the simplicity of our consulting processes. We approach our consulting assignments with the attitude that we are partners with our clients. We may be the experts in our field, but they are the experts in their organization and its culture. We take a down-to-earth, plain-speaking approach. Part of this approach is our pricing. We use flat pricing for all our engagements. There are no hidden fees, no travel expenses, and no administrative costs added on. Our costs are considerably lower than our major competitors. So far, the response has been great. Our clients enjoy the freeing effect that this approach has on the engagement.

If you choose to leave the practice you've developed, and you are the principal, there are options:

- Simply close the doors
- Pass it on to others
- Sell the business

Although there are variations on those themes—for example, keep the name alive and work part-time only for those who seek you out under certain conditions—these are the three main choices available. As your success increases, it's never too early to begin thinking about how you might prepare for each. You don't have to choose which one you'll actually implement, and you may instead

Q. Would you do anything differently if you had the chance?

A. If we were to do it again, I would implement better infrastructures to control the time spent on projects and associated costs. I would also have hired support staff sooner.

Q. What is your greatest unaccomplished achievement?

A. We have two major achievements yet to accomplish. Both tie to our relative newness in this firm. First is stable financial reserves. Although we're making progress on this front, it will take a little while before they are steady. Second is the establishment of a national presence in the HR consulting world. I want potential clients who don't personally know us to think of Astron when they consider some of our competitors (for example, Watson Wyatt, Hay Group, Towers Perrin) for an RFP (request for proposal). We want to be a predominant player in the industry and revolutionize HR consulting. The market is out there. It will only take us time.

decide to simply stay in business, but the preparation will allow you to establish certain actions that you may need to capitalize on later.

In other words, it doesn't hurt to plan for a given contingency, even if you later decide not to use it. That's far, far better than abruptly deciding to retire formally with no plan in place at all for the disposition of the business, which could cause severe tax consequences and disappoint or cause hardship for quite a few clients, vendors, employees, family members, and others.[2]

---

2. All of the following assumes intelligent planning with your financial advisor and attorney.

Simply Close the Doors

There is usually little equity in a solo practice, and closing the doors is an advisable course (in fact, there often aren't even doors to close). This option applies to the individual practice and the smaller partnerships, where the worth is really vested in the principal(s) and the client goodwill, name recognition, assets, and other usual value of a firm don't extend beyond that. If the principal doesn't want to sign a contract with another firm to continue working when that firm buys his or her practice, then there is little inherent value in such a purchase.

If, for whatever reasons, you choose to simply "close the doors," give yourself a year to implement the move, assuming your practice at the time is healthy and active. (Some people have had the doors closed for years and don't know it, but this book isn't written for them.) During that year:

- Formalize your subcontractor, alliance, and colleague contacts for possible takeover of both your clients and future leads, and organize them around capabilities and availability. You may or may not request a referral fee from them, but I would advise against it, because you want your clients treated well and, presumably, you don't need those fees at this point.

RULE **54**

The business is only the business, it's not your life. There usually comes a time when it's right to let go. If you prepare for it, you and the business will be taken care of best.

- Alert your clients that your current project is your last for them, but that you have a list of high-quality referrals that they can interview for future business or the continuation of current business. (Normally, I recommend personally fulfilling any existing contracts or commitments, hence the year's notice, which should more than enable you to do that.)
- Establish a means to refer future leads that arrive due to the marketing gravity you've established. That gravitational "pull" will probably contin-

ue for quite some time, so be prepared to respond to inquiries with a form letter or e-mail, and pass the lead to the network you've established. (Someone may pay you for the rights to all your leads, which is a legitimate deal.)

- Do not buy any new equipment or upgrades, and plan to dispose of equipment, furniture, facilities, and so forth that are solely used for the business and are of no personal use. My suggestion is to donate the stuff to a charity and take a business deduction in the final year. Selling it is often a hassle, and you don't need the relatively small amount of money it will generate. In fact, the tax write-off is probably a better fiscal move.
- Wind down your marketing gravity. Change or eliminate your website. End your product sales (unless they represent a "retirement income" stream). Cancel your listings and ads. Examine your entire marketing effort and determine which should be abandoned and when. For example, a year in advance is the proper time to end listings and other print promotions.
- Alert your vendors, many of whom may rely on your business, so that they can prepare themselves to replace it over the course of the year. That's simply professional courtesy. Also alert the appropriate trade associations which may have been relying on you for input, participation, articles, leadership, and so forth.
- Investigate the possible sale of copyrights, patents, trademarks, and other intellectual property that it makes no sense to retain but which may represent significant benefit to others. Those sales can usually be made without the purchase of the firm itself.

Pass It On to Others

You may have children, other family members, or associates who are active in the business and to whom you may decide to turn over the business. If that's the case, remember that your name and repute will still be attached to the work that's performed, and you shouldn't really walk out the doors as if the cord has been severed. Here are some suggestions:

- Involve the people who will take over well in advance in the financial, business relationship, legal, implementation, and marketing aspects of the business. Most of what you do by intuition and on autopilot they will have to learn, internalize, and practice. The greatest failure of these transitions is that the founder walks out with the institutional memory and all the "brains."

- Involve them with your key buyers. Help them to establish their own relationships with the buyers who will be key in continuing the business. Don't expect them to become you. Your relationships are unique. Ensure that every important person has strong relationships established with all the current buyers and potential buyers.
- Transfer the marketing gravity to them. They should be writing the articles, doing the interviews, speaking at events, teaching at the university, and so on. This is why you need a year to set things in motion properly. You have to assertively take yourself out of a limelight you've spend years intensifying and move others into it.
- Agree on a transition period, and then get out. Your presence will influence everything that happens, but the new owners will need access to you for a while for continuity. The best formula: Transition for a year with you calling the shots; advise for three months, with you available as needed for consultation; cold turkey. Trust me, if you don't disappear, your ghost won't even have a chance.

Sell the Business

There are consultants and attorneys who specialize in the sale of small practices. Often, this is arranged as a leveraged buyout to younger associates in the firm (a practice that is increasingly common and effective in the medical, veterinary, and dental fields). Sometimes, a larger company seeking "instant" heft initiates purchases of many smaller consulting firms in an attempt to create a competitive, multi-dimensional major player. (This strategy has, thus far, been notably ineffective for the buyer, although the people selling have seemed to enjoy it!)

There must be a business to sell, meaning that there are:

- Existing clients generating important revenues
- Prospects in the pipeline at various stages of discussion
- Proposals outstanding
- Rainmakers on the staff
- Infrastructure and support resources in place
- Implementers on the staff or on regular subcontracting
- Name recognition and repute

A good friend of mine left the corporate world and went to work for a small consulting firm. He rapidly built its business and expanded its horizons through innovation, hard work, and superb client relationships. He eventually bought out the firm from the owner, who happily retired, with his name still on the door.

My friend continued to run the business well, although he had to work hard as the sole rainmaker to support a large staff and buy out others who had small pieces of the business. Eventually, through tough decisions, a grueling work ethic, and excellent quality, he succeeded in creating a leaner, effective organization. But it had plateaued, and his choices were to work even harder, find additional rainmakers, or sell a firm that had experienced no real growth for years and generated about $2 million in revenues.

He sold the firm to a "big five" auditing/consulting operation, but with the provision that he become a partner in the purchaser's consulting business, which he agreed to do at the age of fifty-five. He went through new employee orientation, immersed himself in the new business, and began visiting clients and prospects, rainmaking for a new boss.

Less than a year into this work, my friend had a stroke that almost killed him. After some very close calls and painstaking rehabilitation, he's pretty much back to his old self, retired on disability from his new firm. What's he doing now? Working off and on with small firms on special projects.

If it were I, that's not the story I'd write to end my formal career or conclude my practice.

- Extensive marketing gravity in place
- A history of profits and track record of success[3]

---

3. For valuation purposes, buyers like to see substantial cash generated in excess of operating expenses, staff salaries, and business reinvestment requirements. If the principal is taking $3 million a year for personal salary and bonus, that's $3 million that the new owner will have in cash IF the revenue generating it would still be available after the principal departs.

During your pre-sale final year (and even earlier), take pains to maximize profits *and* top-line (revenue) growth. The increase in both will be an important sale feature. An operation that is flat on both the top line and bottom line resembles one that is stuck and desperate to be purchased by new blood. Do everything possible to demonstrate continuing growth right through the sale. (Valuators will look at a formula involving sales, profits, or both.)

Ensure that you have unquestioned rainmakers on board, so that the purchaser can see that existing revenue streams won't depart with your baggage and personal effects. Demonstrate a support staff that can take care of day-to-day affairs perfectly well by themselves with little guidance from you.

Finally, consider carefully the inevitable request that you sign a contract to continue to run the business for a period of time. Even if it's "only" for a year, the only worse thing than sweating blood for your own equity is sweating blood for someone else's equity. I've seen far too many consultants finally arrive at a legitimate and financially rewarding point of departure, only to be made miserable, sick, and even impoverished by an agreement to "stay on for awhile."

I can't emphasize this enough: When you want to leave, leave. Don't hang around at the high school dance.

RULE 55

End your formal career and begin your new life with the same zest and pleasure that you began it and nurtured it. There are beginnings, middles, and endings, and every successful play is powerful in all three dimensions. The same applies to our professions and businesses.

ULTIMATE REWARDS

The end or reduction in your consulting career is merely the trigger for the next stage of your life. Don't forget, in this wonderful profession we may well be talking about a point in your late forties to late fifties, if you so choose. You're young enough to begin whatever it is you dream of doing next.

In reality, very few people arrive on Maslow's "self-actualization" level, but here you are. Now is the time to engage in the community work, charity fund raising, hobby, family support, professional contribution, and civic involvement that you've always wanted to or have actually dabbled in. I've know a great many "retired" consultants who are busier than ever, but on those areas of their lives that they next want to develop.

The ultimate reward of having succeeded in this profession is the ability to engage in life at a new level, with the financial security and sophisticated experience in place that consulting has afforded you. I've maintained all along that consulting is merely a means to other ends for us, and whether you disengage entirely or "keep your hand in," it would be a shame not to enjoy fully and learn from those other dimensions of life.

I couldn't have designed a better profession for my talents and life goals, although I never planned to enter it and didn't really understand it until I was inadvertently dragged into it. I don't know what may be around the next corner, but I do know that I'm willing to turn that corner to see what may be awaiting me.

Begin to make plans today for your life tomorrow. This is a great profession, but it's an even greater life. Godspeed on your journey. I'll probably see you along the way.

THE ULTIMATE RULES

Rule #51.   "Work" is not the evil side of your life, and "personal" is not the good side of your life. Your life is what you make it, and all components of it ultimately reinforce and enrich the others *if you allow them to do so.*

Rule #52.   No matter what your material wealth or resources, are you leading the kind of life that is admired by others, or do people say regarding your life, "It's not worth it." Ensure that your work is multiplied exponentially into the richness of your life.

Rule #53.   If you are not doing anything new each week, each month, each year, then you are not living, but merely existing. We are not here to stick our toes in the water. We are here to make waves.

Rule #54.   The business is only the business; it's not your life. There usually comes a time when it's right to let go. If you prepare for it, you and the business will be taken care of best.

Steve Loftus works for Frostbyte Computer Consultants in Australia, where he has been managing director for the past seven years. His personal accounts generate more than a third of a million in U.S. dollars.

Q. What is the single key factor in your success?

A. Understanding farming. Frostbyte's success thus far is undoubtedly due to having understood one simple principle of life: Sowing and reaping. Everything we have done is built on that principle. We have consistently sought to sow "good seed" into the companies that we work for. We have endeavored to put their business first, before our own, and have tried to find ways of making them more successful. In turn, as they have prospered, we have prospered with them. We have built enduring relationships with individuals who are now at other companies, and this has enabled us to have influence that exceeds what might be expected (given our size and general profile). If you asked me what was the second most important factor, I would name another principle: Giving and receiving. Whilst every business has to make money, we have not focused on money itself, but rather on the relationships with people we work for. Our approach is always to treat business as

Rule #55. End your formal career and begin your new life with the same zest and pleasure that you began it and nurtured it. There are beginnings, middles, and endings, and every successful play is powerful in all three dimensions. The same applies to our professions and businesses.

Final Thought: Walk not in the footsteps of men of old. Seek what they sought.
—Matsuo Basho

"giving and receiving," not as "buying and selling," which is far less conducive to good relationship building. Finally, as an example of what I mean by the above, during the first five years of Frostbyte's existence, we worked without any contracts, simply doing deals on a handshake and then backing that up with our personal integrity. This has been crucial to the building of our current relationships.

Q. What would you do differently if you did it over?

A. I think I would be more "bold" in terms of growth. When I look back today at how we agonized over whether we should or shouldn't hire our first two staff members, it seems rather silly. Yes, it was a growing process that was necessary, but if I had to do it all again I would worry less about the implications of growth.

Q. What is the major achievement you have yet to accomplish?

A. I've set a personal goal to live off 10 percent of my income and to give away the other 90 percent. In this I was inspired by hearing about people such as Colonel Sanders of KFC fame. This will obviously require me to be earning substantial income from my business.

Questions to Ask for Objectives, Measures, and Value

1. What questions develop outcome-based business objectives?

   - How would conditions ideally improve as a result of this project?

   - Ideally, what would you like to accomplish?

   - What would be the difference in the organization if we were successful?

   - How would the customer be better served?

   - How would your boss recognize the improvement?

   - How would employees notice the difference?

   - What precise aspects are most troubling to you? (What keeps you up at night?)

   - If you had to set priorities now, what three things must be accomplished?

   - What is the impact you seek on return on investment/ equity/sales/assets?

   - What is the impact you seek on shareholder value?

   - What is the market share/profitability/productivity improvement expected?

   - How will you be evaluated in terms of the results of this project?

2. What questions establish measures of success?

- How will you know we've accomplished this objective?

- Who will be accountable for determining progress, and how will they do so?

- What information would we need from customers, and in what form?

- What information would we need from vendors, and in what form?

- What information would we need from employees, and in what form?

- How will your boss know we've accomplished this objective?

- How will the environment/culture/structure be improved?

- What will be the impact on ROI/ROE/ROA/ROS?

- How will we determine attrition/retention/morale improvement/safety?

- How frequently do we need to assess progress, and how?

- What is *acceptable* improvement, and what is *ideal* improvement?

- How would you be able to prove it to others?

3. What questions establish value with the buyer?

- What if you did nothing? What would be the impact?

- What if this project failed?

- What does this mean to you, personally?

- What is the difference for the organization/customers/employees?

- How will this affect performance?

- How will this affect image/morale/safety/repute?

- What would be the effect on productivity/profitability/market share?

- What is this now costing you annually?

- What is the impact on ROI/ROA/ROE/ROS?

Components of a Sample Book Treatment

A professional treatment or proposal, for an acquisitions editor or an agent, should have at least the following elements:

1. Theme of the book and why it's needed at this time. (Keep in mind that a book won't see the bookshelves until about a year after the idea is accepted, so think ahead.)

2. Table of contents.

3. Full introduction, as it would appear in the book.

4. One full chapter (needn't be Chapter 1, and can be the one you're currently most comfortable with).

5. One or two paragraphs describing all other chapters.

6. A competitive analysis of other books on the topic, how they are similar, and why yours will stand out in the crowd. (Never say that there is no competition or you won't be taken seriously.)

7. A description of the primary, secondary, and tertiary audiences and what benefits each will derive.

8. Your credentials and particular expertise, and why you are the one to write the book.

9. Any uniqueness in the test, for example, interviews, self-assessment tests, graphs, and so forth.

10. Any unique marketing you provide, for example, you speak to twenty thousand people a year, you have a newsletter with ten thousand paid subscribers, you are the president of a major profession association, and so on.

Submit this treatment, which may run from thirty to sixty pages, with a cover letter to the agent or acquisitions editor by name. If you can establish a relationship with this person beforehand, no different from an economic buyer, all the better for your chances.

Sources for Media and Advertising "Experts"

Directory of Membership and News Sources
National Press Club of Washington

529 14th Street, NW, Washington, DC 20045
202/662–7500

Circulated to editors, assignment editors, reporters, producers, talk show hosts, and related media people.

Radio and TV Interview Reporter
Bradley Communications

135 East Plumstead Avenue, Lansdowne, PA 19050
610/259–1070

An advertising source for radio and television talk shows, published twice a month. They will help you format and design your ad.

The Yearbook of Experts, Authorities and Spokespersons
Broadcast Interview Source

2233 Wisconsin Avenue, NW, Washington, DC 20007
202/333–4904

Similar to the National Press Club book above, but more aggressively marketed; also has a website, options for press releases, and other items.

Index

A

"The Accelerator" newsletter, 80
"Acres of Diamonds" (Conwell), 239
Action Plan Marketing, 87
Adams, D. M., 57
Adjunct professor positions, 69–70
Advertising: for marketing, 63–64; sources for experts on, 259. *See also* Marketing
Ahearn, L., 139
Airplane travel, 238
Alan's Fourth Law of Thermodynamics, 239
Alliances: overseas, 70–73; time management using, 176. *See also* Joint ventures
Amazon.com, 102, 135, 215
Ambler, A., 192–193
American Council of Life Insurance, 130
American Institute of Architects, 94
American Management Association, 129
Andersen Accounting, 25, 26
Anger, 233, 242
Animals, 241–242
Arthur (film), 240
Assertive communication, 239
ASTD (American Society for Training and Development), 64
Astron Solutions, 244
Atkins, T., 105
Atlantic Electric, 177
Audio passive income, 104–110
Author website, 96, 232n.1
Awareness, 239

B

"Balancing Act" newsletter, 232n.1
Bennet, J., 216–217
Bestowing time, 242
Betterley, R., 57
Betterley Risk Consultants, Inc., 57
Blanchard, K., 95
Books in Print, 102
Brands: art of contrarianism and, 84–86; broadcasting, 82–83; capitalizing on your, 86–90; common elements of, 78; connected to future client needs, 84; consistency of, 81–82; obtaining celebrity status, 91–93; process for determining your, 79–81; simplicity, perception, and support of, 83–84; ten ways to promote celebrity status, 93–96; testing and protecting your, 90–91; ultimate rules of, 97
Brokers, 136–138
Business. *See* Consulting business
Buyer relationships: as conceptual agreement factor, 29–30; developing, 8–10; establishing your value in, 5–6, 15, 40; importance continuing, 37; with individual who control budgets, 4–7; international business and, 142; rules for establishing, 3–10; with small or solo consulting firms, 15–16, 18; as springboard to other potential clients, 18–21; ten techniques for building high-level, 10–15; ultimate rules for, 21, 23. *See also* Clients

Buyers: finding information about, 10; finding key, 4; knowing your, 14–15; reaching key, 6–7; strategic profiling from perspective of, 38f; targeting key, 7–8. *See also* Clients

C

Calgon case study, 17

Campus Verlig, 154

Capturing ideas, 234

Case studies: on ASTD listing, 64; on balancing life, 235; on benefits of smaller firms, 17; on brand name, 89, 94; on using client resources, 171; on disposing of consulting business, 249; on establishing brand, 80; on international business, 144, 153; on joint venture with Coldwell Banker, 127; on joint ventures, 122; on newsletter passive income, 110; on passive income, 103; on using role plays, 9; on scope creep, 166; on subcontractor registry, 222; on the success trap, 213; on time management benefits, 177; on value of subcontracting work, 42; on value-added fees, 31, 34, 36; on working with small businesses, 189, 201

Case Western Reserve University (Cleveland), 70, 128

Catch 22 (Heller), 242

Celebrity status brands: described, 91–93; ten ways to promote, 93–96

Cell phones, 214

Certification issues, 223–226

Certified Management Consultant (Canada), 226

C.H.A.L.L.E.N.G.E.S., Inc., 22

Children, 242

Chrysler, 93

Churchill, W., 210

Clarity Advantage, 74

Classroom teaching, 69–70

Client budgets: establishing value proposition for, 5–6, 15, 34–38; providing option over the, 39

Client needs: brands connected to future, 84; time management by meshing joint, 177–178; value-added based on, 35, 37

Client objectives: emotional and personal, 190–191; QGTRIHF to establish, 39; scope creep and not adhering to, 166–167; scope

creep and unclear, 165–166; value increase and broadening, 39

Client outcomes: collaborating with buyer for, 33–34; costs vs., 28f; value proposition in terms of, 6; value-based fees in context of, 27–28

Client referrals: establishing arrangements for, 43–44; marketing through, 68–69

Client sponsorship: as consultant, 130, 132; as featured speaker, 130

Clients: advantages of value-based fees to, 26–28; establishing buyer relationships with, 3–23; family-owned/smaller business, 185–207; Fortune 1000, 1–15, 21, 23; jettisoning bottom 15 percent of, 44; quid pro quo when reducing fees to, 40–41; retainer arrangement with, 221–223; shared business values with, 29; small firm or solo practice, 15–16, 18; springboarding to other potential, 18–21; utilizing resources of, 170–172, 176. *See also* Consulting business

Co-opting predictable objections, 11

Coldwell Banker, 127

Collaboration. *See* Joint ventures

Cologne Life Reinsurance, 130, 133

Comfort zone, 234

Commercial publishing: by foreign presses, 145–146, 154; foreign translation of, 146n.2; as marketing tool, 56–58, 59; passive income through, 101–102; placing ISBN on your, 215

Communicating assertively, 239

Communication Management, 125

Competition, 236

Concurrent project management, 173

Confessions of a Consultant (working title of *Million Dollar Consulting*), 59

Constant learning, 235

Consultant entrepreneur activities: as expert resource, 221; intermediary, 220; part-time executive as, 218; part-time professor as, 219–220; in the R&D factory, 220–221; retainer strategy as, 221–223

Consultants: advantages of small or solo practice, 15–16, 18; avoiding the success trap, 209–229; collaboration/joint ventures with, 119–139; establishing full range of services, 39–40; establishing relationships with major buyers, 3–10; establishing value package, 18*f*; maintaining life balance, 231–253; pursuit of entrepreneur activities by, 218–223; running role plays for, 9; shared business values with clients, 29; value-based fees of, 25–49; when to subcontract services, 40

The Consultant's Craft bi-monthly (Weiss), 110, 134

Consultant's News, 110, 126, 134

Consulting business: "close the door" option of, 246–247; entrepreneur options of, 218–223; future trends of, 223–229; international, 141–162; passing it on to others, 247–248; selling your, 248–250; subcontracting, 37–38, 42, 121–122, 175, 222; ten techniques for squeezing in more, 173–178; ultimate rewards of, 250–251; walking away from client, 41, 46. *See also* Clients; Value-added (value proposition)

Consulting fees: accepting equity as, 195–200; avoiding trap of "conditional," 45; considerations when reducing, 38, 40–41; established for each separate client, 43–44; establishing payment terms for, 44; establishing value-based, 25–33; incentives for one-time, full payments of, 44; for phased approach to project, 44; pro bono work vs. lowering value-based, 41; providing discount for project delay, 176; raising value-based, 42–43; retainer strategy for, 221–223; stating and explaining, 46; thirty-eight ways to increase your, 33–35, 37–46; ultimate rules on, 47

Consulting Magazine, 126

Consulting trends: globalization as, 227–228; licensing/certifications, 223–226; professional credentialing, 226; taxing of services, 226–227; technological advancements as, 228–229

Contrarianism, 84–86

Conwell, R. H., 239

Cooper, M., 134

Cooper, W., 134

Creating traditions, 239

Cultural differences, 154

Cunningham, A. H., 155

D

Data Analysis & Results, Inc., 116

Davidson, J., 95

Demcompartmentalize, 233

Disney, 133

"Do You Need a Coach?" (Morris), 113n.8

Drevenstedt Group, 86–87

Drucker, P., 143

E

Elam, G., 230

Electronic newsletters, 66–68

Emory's Goizueta Business School, 131

Emotions: anger, 233, 242; harnessing your, 240; managing small business owner's, 191–195

Equity participation: protecting yourself in, 197–201; things to consider in, 195–196

Esystems, Inc., 230

"Expert vacuum," 60

Exploiting strengths, 234

Exploring family tree, 242

Exploring unknown roads, 236

F

Family-owned/smaller businesses: accepting equity for services to, 195–200; advantages of working with, 186–189; challenges of working with, 185–186; disadvantages of, 187; founder mythology/traditions of, 204; growing business opportunities with, 188–189; less provision for errors by, 204; managing emotions/expectations of owners of, 191–195; scope creep in projects for, 194; ten ways to avoid perils of consulting with, 200, 202–205; ultimate rules for, 205; value proposition and, 190–191

Fees. *See* Consulting fees; Value-based fees

Fink, C., 148

Fitzgerald, C., 12–13

Following passions, 234

Fortier, A., 198–199

Fortune 1000 clients: establishing relationships with, 3–10; landing first, 1–2; ten techniques for building high-level relationships with, 10–15; three principles of acquiring, 2–3; ultimate rules for acquiring, 21, 23. *See also* Clients

Founder mythology/traditions, 204

Fowler, D., 237

Friedman, N., 78

Frost, J., 244
Frostbyte Computer Consultants, 252

G

Gad Consulting Services, 35
Gad, S. C., 35
General Electric, 177
Gerson Goodson Performance Management, 5
Gerson, R., 5
Gielgood, Sir J., 240
Globalization of services, 227–228
Go with your gut, 243
Gravitational field theory, 53–54, 55*f*, 77
Grove, S., 48–49

H

Hammer, M., 95
Harnessing emotions, 240
Harper-Collins, 154
Heller, J., 242
Herman, J., 57
Hewlett, D., 204
Hewlett-Packard, 9, 31, 166, 204
High-level buyer relationship techniques, 10–15
The Highland Group, 109
Holton, C., 62
The Holton Consulting Group, Inc., 62
*How to Market Professional Services: From
    Anonymity to Celebrity* (Weiss), 134
*How to Write a Proposal That's Accepted Every
    Time* (Weiss), 134, 165n.1
HRMagazine, 63
Human resources (HR), 28

I

Iaccoca, L., 93
IBM, 91, 191, 199
Ignoring trifles, 240
IMC (Institute of Management Consultants), 207
IMS (Institute of Management Studies), 69, 129
Indulge yourself, 243
The Innovation Formula (Weiss), 102
Innovation vs. problem solving, 45, 46*f*
Institute of Management Consultants (IMC),
    207
Institute of Management Studies (IMS), 69, 129
Interactive Internet conferencing, 212
International business: business considera-

tions of, 160; cultural differences and, 154;
establishing presence in, 154, 156–157;
financial considerations of, 157–158;
health consideration of, 159–160; language
translation services for, 145n.1; overseas
alliances and, 150–154; personal benefits
of, 141; professional benefits of, 142–146;
safety considerations of, 158–159; ultimate
rules for, 160, 162; working with foreign-
based firms, 148–150; working with U.S.
multi-nationals during, 146–148
Internet: electronic newsletters on, 66–68; getting information on buyers from, 10; interactive conferencing on, 212; promoting
brand name through, 96; promoting
newsletter on, 111; warning about brokers
advertising on, 138. *See also* Websites
ISBN number, 102, 215
ISSN number, 111

J

Jernudd, J., 92
Joel, B., 242
"Joint Accountabilities," 170
Joint ventures: additional opportunities for,
    135–136; with client companies, 129–136;
    international business, 145; with larger
    consulting firms, 126; with larger entities,
    125; with other celebrities, 95; with private
    and/or non-profit educational organiza-
    tions, 129; requirements for forming,
    120–124; ten criteria to test peer-level, 114;
    ultimate rules on, 138; with universities/
    colleges, 127–128; warnings about brokers
    vs., 136–138; WDWC disease and,
    119–120, 123, 124. *See also* Alliances

K

Kennedy Information, 109, 110
Kennedy, J., 134
Kennedy Publications, 126n.2, 134, 135
Kepner-Tregoe, Inc., 32
Kwaiser, J., 22

L

Language translation services, 145n.1
Laptops, 214
Learning from the learned, 239–240

and, 165–167; of concurrent projects, 173; minimizing labor-intensive requirements as, 167–170; pad/pencil tools of, 178–179; quality of life and, 163–164; ten techniques for squeezing in more business, 173–178; tips for the truly time-challenged, 180–181; ultimate rules for, 181, 184; utilizing client resources as, 170–172, 176

Times Mirror Group, 89

Trade association leadership, 69

Traditions: business, 204; creating your own, 239

Training & Developing magazine, 63

"Training News," 84

Treating yourself, 238–239

Tregoe, B., 32

Trifles, 240

U

United Airlines, 191

U.S. multi-nationals, 146–148

Useless reading, 233

Utilizing stress, 233

V

"Value package," 18*f*

Value-added (value proposition): based on client wants/needs, 35, 37; basing fees on, 34; broadening objectives to increasing, 39; buyer-consultant collaboration addition to, 37; developing continuing relationship and, 37; disregarding time as basis of, 34–35; establishing your, 5–6, 15, 40; family-owned/small businesses and, 190–191; fee reduction with decrease in, 38; focus on innovation vs. problem solving, 45, 46*f*; ideas/practices which provide, 45–46; introducing new client, 43; to overseas alliances, 151; subjective and objective measures of, 43

Value-based fees: added premium for single

qualitative source, 37–38; concept of, 26–28; conceptual agreement to, 30–31; implementation and results of, 32–33; never offering options to reduce, 37; proposal acceptance of, 31–32; raising, 42–43; rational self-interest approach to, 31; reducing, 38, 40–41; relationship factor in securing, 29; sequence of events in securing, 28, 30*f*; shared values requirement for, 29; traditional approach vs., 25–26; ultimate rules on, 47

Valuing variety, 234

Venting, 236

Video passive income, 104–110

Videoconferencing, 212

W

The Wall Street Journal, 10

WDWC (Why Don't We Collaborate), 119–120, 123, 124

Weatherhead School of Management, 128

Webb, J., 32

Websites: author's, 96, 232n.1; designing a compelling, 213; as marketing tool, 66–68. *See also* Internet

Weiss, A., 93

Welch, J., 143

What's Working in Consulting, 110, 126n.2

"White papers," 58, 60

"Why Quality Control Circles Don't Work" (Weiss), 84

Word of mouth, 68–69

Write the Perfect Book Proposal: 10 Proposals That Sold and Why (Herman and Adams), 57

Y

Young Presidents' Association, 129

Z

Zenger-Miller, 89